COWS AND COLUMNS

Gene Simon's "Think about It"

The Best of a New Mexico Ranching Journalist through Twenty-Seven Years

selected and edited by Larry Godfrey

Cows and Columns: Gene Simon's "Think about It," The Best of a New Mexico Ranching Journalist through Twenty-Seven Years

Published by Wheatmark®
610 East Delano Street, Suite 104
Tucson, Arizona 85705 U.S.A.
www.wheatmark.com

International Standard Book Number: 978-1-60494-104-3
Library of Congress Control Number: 2008923590

This book is dedicated to all those Americans whose love of country is so genuine they never cease striving to advance its cherished ideals, making it better for everyone.

To Russell —
    The big league doctor who used to tool around Natrona Heights on a bicycle with Jeff —
    May your blessings multiply —
                    Uncle Gene
                    6-29-08

A note on the newspapers that the columns appeared in:

When Gene Simon retired from 30 years of newspapering in 1977 to begin a second career cattle ranching in Southwestern New Mexico, the employee-owned newspapers he headed included the *Valley News Dispatch*, a 44,000 circulation daily serving 42 municipalities in a 4-county area with its publishing and printing centered in Tarentum, a town of scarcely 10,000 located 25 miles NE of Pittsburgh on the Allegheny River. Other newspapers were the semi-weekly *Butler County News-Record* and *North Hills News Record* and the weekly *Sharpsburg Herald*. Total circulation of the four employee-owned newspapers was 96,000. *USA Today* was also printed there for a tri-state area of Pennsylvania, Ohio and West Virginia.

The "Think about It" column was published 1977-2004 on a weekly basis without interruption. It originated in the *Valley News Dispatch*, and from Dec. 1982—when it began a 22-year weekly run in the Deming, (N.M.) *Headlight*, has always been in multiple publications. These included the *Carlsbad Current-Argus*, *Silver City Sun-News*, Silver City's *El Reportero* and *Enterprise* (oldest weekly in New Mexico). Arizona newspapers were the *Apache Sentinel*, *Mobile Messenger*, *Superior Sun*, *Maryvale Star*, and *South Mountain Star*, all weeklies in the Phoenix area that briefly carried earlier columns. Thus the columns in the book could have been repeated in a varying number of newspapers for different lengths of time.

(Does this suggest that the only certainty is the certainty of the constancy of change?)

Contents

Part V: Defense of Human Rights

Part VI: The Folly of War—The Wisdom of Peace

Part VII: Moral and Judicious Use of the Environment

Part VIII: A Rancher and the Ranch

Editor's Introduction

In his "time to 'hang it up'" announcement of February 8, 2004, terminating 27 years of creating a weekly column of commentary, rancher Gene Simon acknowledged, "You don't 'get gooder' as you get older, and all things eventually end." For the many western Pennsylvanians and southwestern New Mexicans who had grown accustomed to Gene's weekly take on the latest of human follies—sometimes of human nobility—the announcement seemed impossible, a violation of the natural order. Yet those of us who know Gene well had grown concerned that he was stretching his 88-year-old self too thin, even for him. And so he finally acknowledged in that farewell column:

> Along with worsening extended drought situation that has this working cattle ranch in crisis mode, as our 4-mile stretch of the Rio Mimbres went dry along with two key wells, it began to surface that resulting pressures were adversely affecting family, overall health, and also the "Think about It" column. This was confirmed by both my wife for 62 years and a good friend who tells it like it is. They helped me understand what my gut had begun to tell me last summer (when the rainy season wasn't) that the column's quality "wasn't getting gooder" midst building pressures.

Characteristically quipping about what obviously hurt, Gene responded to his granddaughter's "That's the best news I've ever heard," with "Golly, better find out if she's a Republican!"

Also in that farewell column Gene provided an overview of those 27 years of writing (not a single deadline missed!) which, in this editorial task of selecting and summarizing, helps in the struggle to distill that unique Simonesque quality of thinking and writing, of living and recording the meaningful, good life: twenty-seven years of creating the column involved a stimulating, educational and multi-rewarding exposure for the column's writer: A genuine learning experience in so many ways since day 1, writing the column has been enriched by friendships with a fascinating variety of exceptional and truly wonderful human beings that are a privilege to know. This also applies to some exceptionally fine newspaper professionals. Along with that it has been a window to the ample collection of complex and often unpredictable people that are out there, confirming the vast variety and contradictions of human nature.

In short, creating the column which so delighted and enlightened us served Gene as a vehicle to develop and deepen his humanism: "I fervently hope [in] the column's objectives…I have been provocative, informative, factual and, yes, controversial about significant issues affecting our lives that have enlightened and stimulated readers to do better for themselves, their families and for our country."

Those who read this book will agree that Gene's columns amply fulfilled his objectives, including arousal of controversy: at one point following a column developing his opposition to the post-September 11 Bush W. policy of bombing Afghanistan, demands for the Carlsbad *Current-Argus* to drop the column became so strident that the newspaper's editor felt the need to write a defense: "Columnist Gene Simon has sure drawn the wrath of a good share of our letter writers…We're getting at least two letters a week criticizing his columns…My job is to allow a diversity of views to appear on the page. And like it or not, people are reading Gene Simon. The number of letters about his column is proof of that." (Actually, the paper had run a "double-truck," two facing pages, to accommodate the deluge of letters responding to Gene's column.) Despite Editor David Giuliani's understanding and defense of democratic discourse, the Bush/Cheney administration's propaganda practice of lies, partial truths, and slurs on the patriotism and loyalty of its critics was clearly tracking better in the Carlsbad area than in Luna County's Deming and Grant County's Silver City, where the same columns so objectionable to some Carlsbad readers drew the usual applause.

Despite, then, the generally wide and enthusiastic appreciation for the column, its very longevity and that of its author, dictated an end to the weekly "Think about It" that had begun in a western Pennsylvania newspaper in May, 1977. For 22 of the 27 years the column ran in the Deming *Headlight* and for fewer years in the Silver City *Sun-News* and Carlsbad *Current-Argus*. Also included in those early years was inclusion in the Silver City *Enterprise* (oldest weekly in New Mexico) and the aggressive *El Reportero*. Through the 27-year span, the column saw publication in 11 newspapers in three states.

So who is this rancher-journalist who, with his wife Elisabeth (Libby), and the beauty and hospitality of their Rancho del Rio became such an institution in southern New Mexico?

Though we in the Southwest came to know Gene only when he and Elisabeth chose to relocate here in the early 1970's, he was born March 15, 1916, in Burlington, Iowa, where he received his early schooling. Beginning a temporary move east, with the death of his father when he was 12, he graduated from high school in Berea, Ohio, with its class of 1934. The year intervening between high school and college he joined the Civilian Conservation Corps, Gene's unit working at the Columbus-Belmont Memorial State Park on the banks of the Mississippi River in western Kentucky. First serving as education officer, he ultimately achieved the rank of Senior Foreman of the 200-member camp.

Having learned and served in the CCC, he next attended Ohio's Baldwin-Wallace College as a scholarship student, awarded a *cum laude* B.A. in political science in 1939. Not insignificantly, considering his later journalistic career, Gene worked these college years as a "coagulator" (news gatherer) preparing Sunday columns of college news for the Cleveland *Plain-Dealer* and covering college sports for the Berea *News*. Another scholarship took him to the University of Pennsylvania, from which he was awarded its M.A. in public administration in 1940. Pennsylvania State University then took on the promising, young scholar through the 1940-41 school year as a teaching fellow in political science (teaching "Government and Politics in Modern Society"), as he also earned credits toward the Ph.D.

As for so many of his generation, World War II interrupted Gene's formal education. Through 3½ years of the war, he served as Recognition Officer aboard a combat aircraft carrier, the *USS Belleau Wood*, in the western Pacific. Involved in every Pacific battle from Tarawa up to surrender ceremonies in Tokyo Bay, except for a brief timeout recovering from a kamikaze hit, that duty collected 13 combat stars, the Presidential Unit Citation, and the Philippine Liberation ribbon.

Gene's States-side return following the war confronted him with decision time in a big way: his career ambitions had always balanced between diplomacy, university teaching or newspaper work. Penn State offered him an assistant professorship and opportunity to continue work toward his Ph.D. Instead he accepted a full scholarship to Tufts University's Fletcher School of Law and Diplomacy, a Harvard affiliate. Before he could move

into his living-quarters assignment at Fletcher, however, fate and his father-in-law intervened. Charles Howe made an offer which determined
the future. And so Gene became a newspaper man and ultimately a rancher
rather than a university professor or a diplomat.

In Tarentum, Pennsylvania, Howe had founded the *Valley Daily News*
in 1904. His only son having died in childhood, he wished to share the
family business with his son-in-law. Gene's special needs and sensibilities
stipulated that before joining Howe and the *Valley Daily News*, he would
learn the newspaper business through a year of work with the *Patriot and
Evening News* of Harrisburg, Pennsylvania, and that no one but the paper's
general manager would know of this arrangement. For $25 a week, then,
Gene worked his way through the editorial, circulation, and advertising
departments. In 1947, with a $2,000 bonus check from his Harrisburg
learning-job, he joined his father-in-law's paper as circulation manager
and assistant to the publisher. In the two years before Howe's death, Gene
increased the paper's circulation from 9,000 to 15,000. Gene was then
elected president and general manger of the employee-owned publishing
and printing company.

This youthful achievement was followed by years of success for Gene's
journalistic efforts, despite a $200,000 fire destroying the back part of the
building in which the business functioned. Gradually acquiring two more
area papers and starting a new one, Gene helped boost circulation of the
expanded *Valley News Dispatch* to 44,000, with combined circulation of the
four newspapers 98,000 when sold to Gannett in 1976.

In the early 1960's Gene and his paper went after the mafia, which
controlled Westmorland County. A contact with Attorney General Robert F. Kennedy brought in 57 federal agents, as the newspaper accelerated
its exposure and attacks. While dodging death threats on himself and his
family, Gene saw the campaign through to federal arrests which brought
national attention and awards to the newspaper, including the *Christian
Science Monitor's* "Challenge to Morality" series and the U.S. Justice Department Meritorious Public Service Award.

Another prestigious morale builder was winning a Pulitzer Prize for
Spot Photography, recognition for *Valley News Dispatch* photographer and
Kent State undergraduate John Filo's photo of the Kent State shootings, a
photo literally flashed 'round the world. Filo's photo had been transmitted
to the Associated Press from the *Valley News Dispatch*.

A series of international experiences through these Pennsylvania newspapering years stand as clear influence on the sophistication, clarity, and
intelligence of the columns we were to see years later. From his newspaper

position in Pennsylvania he became newspaper representative of the US Society of Editors and Commentators, sending journalistic study groups worldwide. In this capacity, Gene had opportunity to interview Egyptian leader Jamal Abdel Nasser ("Boy, did I like that guy."); Fidel Castro two weeks after he had seized power in Cuba ("Castro was not then the man he is now—of course, neither am I!"); the Shah of Iran ("I wrote that this guy is not long for this world."); and Indian Prime Minister Jawaharlal Nehru ("one of the most impressive interviews I ever had.").

A fantastic attempt to get behind the Iron Curtain in 1953 unexpectedly bore fruit shortly after Josef Stalin's death. Despite *Time* magazine's characteristic dismissal of the groundbreaking trip of ten American journalists as "The Rover Boys in Moscow," Gene reported the trip for the New York *Herald-Tribune* News Syndicate and Associated Press, and sold photos from behind the Iron Curtain to *Life* magazine.

In 1969 Gene was diagnosed with Addison's disease, in part a result of over-motivation and over-work. About the same time his company had acquired some papers in the Phoenix area and later a 67,000-acre ranch, mostly in the Gila Primitive Area of southwest New Mexico. These and other factors eventually pushed toward a sale of the employee-owned newspapers and printing enterprise to Gannett, thus ending 28 years as publisher and CEO of the four western Pennsylvania newspapers and a printing company. Not wanting to be a corporate media conglomerate publisher, Gene was able to arrange acquisition of the Ponderosa Highlands Ranch in lieu of a minority interest share of his company's selling price. Thus at age 62 he launched a second career cattle ranching, now in its 34th year.

After operating the Ponderosa Ranch during the 1970's, because of three "too muches—size, debt and age"—Gene began a series of transactions that eventually resulted in his present ranch that peaked at 7,600 acres straddling the Mimbres River. Rancho del Rio has since been reduced after substantial acreage was transferred to New Mexico State Parks and its adjacent City of Rocks. Acreage to protect a valuable Indian site was also conveyed to The Archaeological Conservancy.

Unable to "get newspapering out of his blood," Gene readily accepted the invitation from his former Pennsylvania newspaper to write a weekly column that launched May, 1977. Soon after "Think about It" began in New Mexico, and its wit and wisdom continued for many subsequent years. Again, bowing, finally, to the weight and the argument of "attempting too much," Gene ended the column in February, 2004, pressured by multiple drought years and ranching demands. Today Gene and Elisabeth continue their full and satisfying life actively cattle-ranching on the four-mile river-bottom stretch of the Rancho del Rio, where the Mimbres courses along the Grant/Luna County line. While they continue their loving, skilled nurturing of critters, ranging from cattle and horses to dogs, from turkeys to African guineas, and India peacocks to royal white king pigeons, the Simons are best known in our region as passionate friends to humanity, both the individual local denizens and the species at large.

In selecting a representation of Gene's columns over 27 years, I have wished to emphasize characteristics which have forged in me an admiration for the thinking and writing of Gene Simon as profound as is my love for him and Elisabeth as friends. I would first note the liberal humanist perspective from which he views the human experience, especially the distinctive, almost 300-year struggle in which we Americans are yet involved to achieve a society of equality and brotherhood for all. To highlight that perspective I have eschewed the academically obvious, dreary, chronological organization, opting instead to build upon some distinct elements of Gene's commitments: dedication to the role of reason through a vigorous independent press and democratic discourse; to egalitarian democracy; to equity in economic opportunity; to defense of individual and human rights; to opposing war and championing peace; and to a moral and judicious use of the environment. To sections illustrating these grand—yet very real—commitments, I have added a section allowing voice to Gene the rancher, the thoughtful, ordinary man living close to the land and its creatures and deriving wisdom and understanding from both.

Commitment to this organizational scheme obviously leaves me liable to considerable overlap, for responding to and writing of a particular event—the Bush bombing of Afghanistan, for example—Simon is inevitably drawing on, exposing, more than one of these commitments. Still, this organizational scheme avoids the possible tedium of simple chronological order and enables a focus on elements of Simon's humanism. Finally, as editor, I have, of course, reproduced the columns verbatim, with no revision, except for correcting minor obvious copy errors.

Gene's columns are notable for clarity of thought and argument, for good reason's reliance on ample evidence. His thinking is markedly cosmopolitan, resulting from his ties to and reading of sources outside the United States and its often parochial perspective: this patriot, speaking out of a profound love for our land and our system at its ideal best, insists that we see ourselves clearly as we really are, with all our failures and inadequacies, not just as we rhetorically wish ourselves to be. He insists that we see ourselves as others see us, for only from these expanded perspectives can we become that to which our founding ideals have pledged us. Gene's perspective and his writing are always marked by wit and humor, often self-deprecating. Gene's humanity, this record of his thought, is thus the close touch of the crusty old rancher rather than the Brooks Brothers aloofness of the Washington pundit. Therein lies the real attraction—might I venture *greatness*—of this rancher-journalist.

I wish to thank my wife, Elvira Godfrey, for the cover art, also for her role as "editor of the editor." Midway through the manuscript, as we were midway through a presidential election campaign, she observed, "Why waste our time? We have our presidential candidate in Gene: he covers all the bases!" And, indeed, he does.

—Larry Godfrey
Silver City, New Mexico
February 9, 2008

[Valuable journalistic attention to Gene Simon can be found in Bill Pippin, "Gene Simon," New Mexico magazine (June, 2002), and David A. Fryxell, "Making Water Run Uphill," Desert Exposure (December, 2005). Fryxell's excellent piece has been especially useful to me.]

Preface

What follows is by no means a conventional preface, termed so primarily because it pre-faces *what follows. Selection of the two columns constituting the preface was largely dictated by their special status. The first column uniquely illustrates Simon's always central purpose, his attempt to provoke serious thought, including provision of heavy food for thought, a corollary of his deep commitment to vigorous, open discourse as imperative to the vitality of a functioning democracy. Here we view Simon as the journalist-intellectual, setting current events in their proper context of historical and philosophical perspective. How important that perspective now appears in this last sorry year of George W. Bush's second term. The second column is unique as an instance of Simon's post-weekly-column writing, actually produced four years following the farewell column of "Think about It." Simon published this opinion as a contribution to the ongoing controversy, electrically active in ranching New Mexico, concerning the reintroduction of the Mexican gray wolf. Amidst the task of selecting from 27 years of columns, I found myself, in reading this opinion piece printed a couple of months before Simon's 92ⁿᵈ birthday, again marveling at his intellectual acumen, courage to enter the fray and journalistic skill. What better way, then, to introduce the book!*

May 11, 2003

Among the objectives of the weekly "Think about It" column since day 1 is providing information that causes people to think about crucial issues affecting our lives.

Other objectives the column has always striven to achieve include making it informative, factual, enlightening, timely and controversial, which experience has shown stimulates reader interest. Through it all, the underlying guideline is to do all this without fear or favor and no sacred cows. This was always the way we ran our employee-owned newspapers in western Pennsylvania between 1947 and 1977, and it paid off, too, in respect, satisfaction and success.

As an aside, "Think about It" will be 26 years old on May 27, during which time there has never been a missed week writing those soon-to-be 1,352 columns. During this more than two-and-a-half-decade run, the column has been published in a dozen newspapers in eight counties of three states. And all of this has happened since "retirement"—from 30 years of newspapering, of which 28 were publishing.

There's always been more information ready for a column than space allows, so here's what goes-to-bat this time around:

History repeatedly has proven the wisdoms of the past can often be right on target today in their significance and connection to current events affecting our lives.

John Quincy Adams is an excellent example. A youth at the time of our American Revolution, he was the sixth president of the United States (1825-29) and combined brilliant statesmanship with skillful diplomacy— which gets things done right. As secretary of state for eight years prior to his presidency, he ranks among the ablest occupants of that office and played a masterful role in formulating long-standing American foreign policy. Before that Adams was an 8-term member of the House of Representatives and minister to Russia and Great Britain.

President Adams, in an 1821 Fourth of July speech, addressed the question: "What has America done for the benefit of mankind?" He said: "She has abstained from interference in the conduct of others. Wherever the standard of freedom and independence has been or shall be unfurled, her benedictions and prayers will be. But she goes not abroad in search of monsters to destroy. Otherwise the fundamental maxims of her policy would change insensibly from liberty to force. The frontlet upon her brow would no longer beam with the ineffable splendor of Freedom and Independence; but in its stead would soon by substituted an Imperial Diadem, flashing in false tarnished luster the murky radiance of dominion and power. She might become the dictatress of the world... but would no longer be the ruler of her own spirit."

President John F. Kennedy summed it up more simply: "Our arms will never be used to strike the first blow in any attack. It is our national tradition."

President Dwight D. Eisenhower, a genuine big league general unlike the crop parading their wares in the likes of Grenada, Panama, Somalia and an already crippled Iraq, bluntly scoffed at concepts of so-called preventative war and preemptive strikes. He considered these idiotic, indicating that he wouldn't even discuss them with any person advocating such actions.

Benjamin Franklin, a major Founding Father, said, "There never was a good war nor a bad peace."

The bottom line. Because of realities in Iraq—no weapons of mass destruction used nor found but massive destruction caused by the Bush invasion, with tens of thousands of Iraqis killed or maimed and the country in ruins—sanity says the war was a loser with its monthly cost of $6 to $9 billion and occupation costs of $4 billion a month (Congressional Budget Office estimates of costs to be paid by taxpayers).

Because of these truths, the principles that have formed the basis of a responsible foreign policy have been drastically altered and our reputation in the world community damaged probably beyond repair—by a government that apparently can't recognize that taking the bully pulpit doesn't mean becoming the bully. Thus basic principles that have been good for America for more than two centuries are now being torn apart, as we seek dominion rather than genuine liberty for all. America was once respected for the strength of its principles, rather than being feared, hated and fought, without support of much of the international community. A lust for power and cheap oil should not become part of its controlling principles.

George II's war arguments were numerous and frequently changed. He made us believe an attack was imminent, but never shared the reason with our allies, the United Nations, or the American people. He pushed the never-proven line that Saddam and al-Qaida were linked, but never put any actual reasons on the table, as his government brilliantly whipped up fear and distractions.

Meanwhile, there's been a dramatic decline of 2 million jobs during Bush's watch, with a 25 percent increase in those unemployed more than six months. And the jobs promised when Bush got his 2001 tax cut for the rich proved to be phony.

A lot of us know that psychiatrists look for signs of illness when someone continues to do the same thing over and over again expecting different results.

Think about it.

January 11, 2008

Contemplating the mishmash of so-called wolf recovery in the Gila National Forest and Wilderness of SW New Mexico and adjacent Blue

Range of Arizona, you will again be impacted with Man's monumental ability to "mess it up."

Any random list documenting this reality is almost endless, and along the way there's been a welter of bum dope, distortions, ignorance, irrational actions and what could aptly be called "BS" (which real ranchers know about). The very complex and vitally important issue of wolf recovery is sorely in need of a high degree of intelligence based on unemotional proven facts and realities—with the courage, political and otherwise, to do the right thing regardless. (Should I cynically say, "Don't hold your breath"?)

But look at the scatter of what we've been getting...

—Commissioners of a county not really affected, not involved in the wolf issue, with Luna's urgent needs justifying almost continual sessions, letting themselves get suckered into unnecessary controversial wild animal ordinances after some kowtowing to "beef pressure." (That action wasn't impressive to this rather major Luna County taxpayer for 29 years.)

—Wolves being eliminated after stepping over a line because they don't know about political boundaries.

—Supposedly Real West rugged individualists apparently pressing panic buttons and almost shaking in their boots because there might be a wolf around the next bend in the trail. Or to quote, "He was not afraid of me, at all. This animal wasn't afraid of anything." And county officials being "terrified."

—Wolves shot and trapped because they acted like wolves, despite being habituated to humans by excessive handling. And getting a taste for beef, because of the time-honored ranch habit of dragging a dead animal out somewhere to let nature take its course. (I've done it, too.)

—Presenting themselves as good law-abiding Americans, those who sneak around poaching wolves, with another confirmed 25 shot and more "disappeared," while the government is overdue in decisively improving its poor, only-two-cases-resolved record.

—The irrational incongruity of Catron County going off the deep end passing 21 ordinances attempting to supersede federal authority over federal land, while it gets more government assistance and money per capita than about any other anywhere, as it rants about government tyranny and interference, isn't a hallmark for resolving problems.

It's way past time for more of the "old users" of our public land to be upfront about the bigger struggle for control of the American people's public land rather than blurring the issue with the Mexican gray wolf reintroduction controversy as a false front dodge.

U.S. Fish and Wildlife needs the guts to use biological protocol rather than caving into political pressures and is overdue having innovative solutions allowing wolves to survive in the wild rather than its current focus on wolf control and the shooting and trapping that caused the extinction problem, which was barely staved off in 1976 by listing under the Endangered Species Act signed by President Nixon.

The deplorable reality of so many supposedly intelligent and informed people unable to comprehend that in Nature everything is connected with something else or dependent on it. The web of life and its survival is like a chain, with the life-and-death question being how many links can be lost before the chain is gone forever.

A moot question is whether some ranchers are making a good thing out of in effect collecting bounties for cattle kills. A Catron County ranch has already reaped well over $15,000, tops for any other ranch, and Defenders of Wildlife might get tired of voluntary forking over the $98,000 paid ranchers for losses since 1998.

Wolf baiting is the tricky question now confronting that Catron ranch, and it raises another obvious one that needs to be on the table. As experienced cattlemen have questioned, why would any ranch be foolishly branding a cow about to calve, and near a wolf den? And would any well-run ranch have a cow old enough to have a calf that wasn't branded when she was a calf?

The crying laments about dire consequences for the nation's beef needs if public land grazing is reduced are a dud. Not even a shrinking 3% of the beef Americans eat comes from cattle grazing public lands. A strong case can be made that vast areas of public lands are unable to sustain a healthy and successful ranching operation. This underlines that much of the so-called wolf problem would be avoided if cattle weren't where they were not meant to be.

As a New Mexico cow-calf rancher for 34 years in three locations (105 section Forest Service 808-head permit, mostly in Gila primitive area during the 1970's, then three sections at Lone Mountain, west of Grant County Airport, along with 7600 acres straddling Rio Mimbres and Grant-Luna line), my wife and I have learned much from numerous ranch study tours sponsored by Western Livestock Journal to dozens of ranches in every state of the Mountain West, and also in Canada and Mexico.

Here are some of the eye-openers: A third-generation rancher on the east slope of the Rockies in Alberta, in the heart of wolf country that provided those for stocking Yellowstone, told us that "Wolves don't bother us." After a lot of eyebrows raised, this highly successful rancher told about often seeing a small herd of elk in a vale with a few wolves watching from a nearby knoll. One wolf then charges the elk so the wolves can learn if any are old or crippled. As the rancher said, "This is Nature doing its job," and such survival of the fittest culling has substantially improved quality of their elk herd, with benefits to the ranch, including much less fence repair and providing more grass and vegetation.

Couple these realities and beneficial wolf-elk balance with this quote by savvy New Mexico Game Commissioner, "Dutch" Salmon: "In fact, the number of elk has increased since the wolves were introduced." So, when any Catron extremist says "wolves have run the elk out of this county," you'll know what word to use.

Before reintroduction of wolves in Yellowstone, the coyote population had exploded and aspen and willows were about destroyed by elk. Wolves like to travel the stream bank, which has spooked the elk, and the aspen and willows have returned because of a needed balance between predator and prey. (A peer-reviewed study of Mexican gray wolf scat documented their diet was 73% elk.)

Fourth generation Colorado rancher Reeves Brown is highly respected by all who know him. The reason he doesn't permit coyote hunting or trapping on his very successful ranch is because "they're doing too good a job keeping the rodent population down." This jibes with my policy of banning all coyote hunting or trapping on any of my three ranches where we've never had a coyote problem in 34 years raising cattle. How could I be that lucky for so long when other ranches hiring expensive aerial shooting and professional trappers are reporting all kinds of coyote kills? Maybe there's a lesson here and one might be "don't create a vacuum that attracts more varmints." Let Nature balance it out.

Two brothers operating a large ranch on the rolling plains east of the Rocky Mountains foothills in Alberta, Canada, (where Sitting Bull holed up after knocking off Custer) were having big trouble with gophers destroying vast grasslands. They stopped all coyote hunting and trapping and the grass was coming back when we were at their ranch.

These real world examples and many others out there verify not all ranchers are the "gotta kill all the varmints" variety. We're really not all that dumb, and it sorta bugs me that so many "outsiders" have that opinion. Most of us aren't extremists either, wearing the mantra of "Don't confuse me with facts because I've already got my mind made up."

PART I

The Rule of Reason

CHAPTER 1

Start with the Premises

As any professor of logic, as any debate coach, as any good thinker who wishes to persuade, knows, evidence, empirical data, must precede any valid conclusion. Simon enjoys telling a story of Linn Lightner, publisher of the Harrisburg Patriot *and* Evening News *where Simon cut his journalist's teeth: "If you see rain outside," Lightner would insist, "and you wish to report it, get a sample and prove H²O before you write any story." In the first column presented here, that of May 14, 1979, Simon wishes to persuade readers to vote. Rather than whipping reluctant citizens with rhetoric, then, he combs history for evidences of history-shaping close votes. The second column reproduced here relates the incredible stamina and courage of "Granny D," also, Simon's summary makes clear, an exemplary citizen as she insists on the persuasion of clear thinking, of "the open market of political ideas."*

May 14, 1979

So tomorrow's election day! What are you going to do about it?

Because it's "only" a primary election, you may be one of those who think it's not important. If so, you're among those who in effect are willing to wait until the supposedly more important general election in November so you can make your "selection" between two already predetermined candidates, the selection which you left to others.

How about that? Does that prospect make you feel good? Maybe you ought to reconsider "sitting this one out." Maybe you ought to vote.

You may think your vote among thousands and even millions in local, state, and national elections, cannot make much difference. But it does. That one vote could swing your entire ward or municipality into your candidate's column. And that's just where elections are won and lost.

The tremendous power of a single vote has frequently been demonstrated throughout our history. In fact, the course of nations has been changed because one important vote was cast, or not cast. Here are some examples:

Some of you will remember back in 1948 when most of the people in the country went to bed certain their next president would be Tom Dewey, as national polls had predicted. In fact, many Republican voters were so confident of the outcome they didn't bother to vote. But the polls were wrong. Harry Truman was re-elected. If Dewey had gained just one additional vote per precinct in only two states—Ohio and California—he would have added their combined 50 electoral votes and deprived Truman of the majority needed to win.

Andrew Johnson, who became our 17th president following the death of Abraham Lincoln, was impeached in March, 1868, after being accused of abusing his executive powers. After a lengthy trial before the Senate, which in such cases sits as judge and jury, a vote was taken and by the narrow margin of one vote Johnson was found "not guilty." That vote saved a president.

This one about set the world on fire. A new revolutionary party held a hurried meeting in a beer hall in Munich on November 8, 1923. It felt the time was ripe to make a decisive move for power in Germany. By a majority of one vote, they chose their leader. His name was Adolph Hitler. The rest is history.

And because of one vote we acquired the best bargain in our country's history. On October 18, 1867, the territory known as Russian America became American-owned Alaska. Secretary of State William Seward negotiated the "dirt cheap" purchase price of $7,200,000 for this extremely rich northern land twice the size of Texas. Short-sighted Congressmen (we had 'em then, too) jeered at "Seward's Folly," but a reluctant Senate was persuaded to ratify the Alaska Purchase. It did so by one vote.

Fate and one vote made France a republic rather than a monarchy. In the 1870's, after being humiliatingly defeated by Germany in the Franco-Prussian War, France deposed her autocratic Emperor, Napoleon The Third (nephew of Napoleon Bonaparte). The 706 French deputies met to decide the future of France, monarchy or republic. While the voting was in progress, one of the pro-monarchy deputies became violently sick and had to be taken home before he could vote. That uncast ballot avoided a deadlock and the Republic won by just one vote with the victorious margin of 353 to 352.

And did you know that but for one vote you might be speaking German now? The bitter aftermath of the American Revolution was so strong that consideration was given to cutting off all cultural ties with England

and to stop speaking English. Because of so many Germans in the colonies, a bill was drawn up to make German the official language of the newly independent country. It came to a tie vote in Congress. The deadlock was finally broken by a vote against the bill... cast by the son of a German immigrant, to keep English the official language of the United States!

July 1, 2001

Many of you may remember when the courageous and incomparable Granny D passed through the Lordsburg-Columbus-Deming-Las Cruces area in the spring of 2000 on her marathon walk to our nation's capitol to advance an ideal, the dire need for campaign finance reform to correct a rotten system.

Granny D is Doris Haddock, a 90-year-old grandmother from New Hampshire. She left Pasadena, Calif. on New Year's Day, 2000, and literally walked across America to Washington, D.C. We were privileged to have Granny D as guest in our home when she was in this area. No one have I respected more than this indomitable lady of character and courage. In a class by herself, she represents the best of America.

Doris Haddock was featured speaker at a voter rights conference in Tallahassee, Fla., this past June 17. Here are excerpts from her very meaningful speech, necessarily abbreviated because of space limitations...

After citing the difficulty of comprehending the mass horrors perpetrated upon peoples of the world during the 90 years of the past century she has lived, when more than a hundred million people perished from wars, massacres and atrocities, she said:

"In America, we are more blessed. We have come to expect that our neighbors will not be rounded up en masse and shot. We have come to expect that we will not ourselves be dragged from bed and sent away or slain by agents of our government... While we may distrust an election or a party, we have—most of us—not lost faith in the good intentions of our democracy.

"We understand that it is the absolute power of institutions that allows atrocities, for power is the opposite of sensitivity and accommodation. Power is a monster... that we keep in check but never really kill. In America, our dear Constitution is the amulet we wear to preserve ourselves from its teeth.

"Our Constitution gives us our democratic republic, which has as its intention the fragmentation of power, keeping the exercise of power as close as possible to the human scale, and letting power accumulate only where absolutely necessary for the common good of the people. Yet the parchment document of the Constitution is not enough—we also require supportive institutions and sacred processes. We need five things:

1. "We need a fair and accurate voting system that we can trust beyond the shadow of a doubt.
2. "We need a free press that takes as a sacred trust its duty to inform the citizenry on the great and small issues of the day, regardless of popular appeal and regardless of profitability of providing that coverage.
3. "We need worthy candidates who represent our interests and values, and who are free from entangling financial obligations to special friends.
4. "We must be an unhurried society, with each of us given the time and resources to be active citizens, not mere mice on corporate treadmills.
5. "We must be an educated people, forever students of the vital issues before us and also of the history, art and literature that shape our human sensibilities and our civic and cultural values so that, as a self-governing people, we produce citizens. Our immigrants must be made into citizens as well.

"In many of these five areas we are now in trouble. The stakes are very high, for the monster of power is never far from the door. It comes in quickly."

Doris Haddock then cited a congressman roughed up for peacefully protesting, a building full of people making political puppets summarily arrested and taken away, people walking calmly on a street near a political convention being arrested and brutalized for two weeks.

She herself was arrested for calmly reciting the Bill of Rights in the U.S. Capitol, and she cried when police tried to pull from her finger a wedding ring that had not been removed in 60 years. She asked what country you would think you were in if these things happened to you. What's your reaction to a man in the White House who lost the popular vote, and who won the electoral vote because of one member of the Supreme Court who is now promised the Chief Justiceship?

Continuing, Granny D emphasized that "raw power can strike swiftly, discrediting proper law enforcement and setting up new ones run by political cronies with prisons and police of their own to suppress and arrest those who dare protest. It is nothing for raw power to thumb its nose at the interests of world peace and the world's environment for the sake of corporate expansion and political power. Raw power can mistake the flowering of political ideas and dissent in democracy's garden as a dangerous tangle of plots and disloyalties. It can happen quickly. It can happen in America. (This reminds that it was Marie Antoinette who said: "It can't happen here"—on the night before the French Revolution.)

"It is up to a new generation of American patriots to preserve our dreams of individual freedom, to preserve our greatest open market, our open market of political ideas and leadership opportunities. Nothing is more important than this work, as the history of the previous century shows us so clearly, written as it was in the blood of one hundred million people. To those who died for democracy, we owe a sacred trust. For those who died for lack of democracy, we owe our efforts to make a better world, worthy of their memory."

CHAPTER 2

Ad Hominem Static

Simon's seemingly paradoxical double identity as rancher and journalist is rendered even more fascinating by two characteristics prominent in many of his columns—on the one hand a sort of folksy rural chattiness reminiscent of the home-owned newspapers of our early 20th-century past, on the other hand the clarity and disciplined thinking of the well-educated intellectual; both are evident in this column of December 30, 2001, first reproduced below. The column of June 3, 2001, also underscores Simon's aversion to wearing the blinders bridle of ad hominem *thought. Attacking another lapse of lazy thinkers, Simon's August 8, 1994, column attempts to jolt his readers "outside the box."*

December 30, 2001

Virtually everyone realizes there is probably no one in the world who doesn't have problems. Everyone has them to some extent, and these can pile up rapidly, too, because that's the way it is in life.

Yet when we think about what many are facing in other parts of the world such as Afghanistan, a largely destroyed country where millions of human beings are facing starvation and death, especially children and the aged as most vulnerable, our troubles here lessen by comparison.

Perhaps most hopelessly deplorable are those areas in the world where too many people are locked into horrendous situations that seem to defy solutions or any way out. By stark contrast, despite growing reality of hunger in America, the widening gap between rich and poor, and 44-plus million U.S. citizens without health care coverage in the world's richest nation, most of us Americans comparatively are a fortunate and blessed people.

It was a wise man who said that if your troubles were hanging on a clothesline with all the troubles of the world, you'd take yours back mighty fast. The usual pattern of problems reminds me of my mother's wisdom that recognized what happens to you being not nearly as important as what you do with what happens to you. That's where the men get separated from the boys, the sheep from the goats.

That wisdom of taking your own troubles back came from a man for whom I had much affection and a deep respect. He was my father-in-law, who started a daily newspaper in 1904, on a shoestring in a virtual woodshed, and in a town where they said it couldn't be done. He made it an employee-owned company that grew and prospered because of the hard work of dedicated people who went the second mile. A key aspect of why this unusual publishing venture succeeded was its operation on a without-fear-or favor basis with no sacred cows.

This was the way I operated my newspapers (a daily, 2 semi-weeklies, a weekly) with 98,000 combined circulation when we sold our also employee-owned company in 1976 to Gannett, the nation's largest newspaper chain that also publishes *USA Today*, which we printed for its tri-state area of Pa., Ohio, W. Va.

Our western Pennsylvania newspapers were noted for their policy of being politically independent and shunning all labels. This reflected my belief no party has a corner on virtue or the opposite. As I would tell our editors and reporters at election time: "No one running for office is as good as their friends say nor as bad as their enemies maintain." Perhaps this is why I've never voted a straight ticket in my life. But when I changed my registration from Republican to Democrat, I learned there were Democrats in New Mexico that would think some of my Pennsylvania Republican friends were communists... like Gov. Bill Scranton, Republican senators "Big Red" Jim Duff and Dick Schweicker, all personal friends.

The ridiculousness of tying labels on people is so flawed it strikes out in contrast to the superior criteria of merit and truth. Why can't more Americans drop the label blinders and apply the accuracy of truth in their judgments? And why do some presumed patriots want to kill the messenger when they don't like the message?

This reminds of the scary reality that some who think they are great patriots being so ready to stifle dissent and sabotage the cherished liberties and freedoms of our Bill of Rights and Constitution we are supposed to be fighting to preserve. Could one apply a Biblical thought to such people: "Father forgive them, they know not what they do"?

A letter writer in Carlsbad criticized my writing because I am "no longer in the publishing business." This conveys an unawareness of how it used to be compared to today. We always had a fulltime investigative reporter, almost a rarity in today's bottom-line dominated media. These were a key part in a long-running fight with the Mafia that dominated one of the four counties in our circulation area. A result of this was being featured in the "Challenge to Morality" series published by the national newspaper *Christian Science Monitor*.

Then our small daily was awarded the coveted Pulitzer Prize for a picture taken at Kent State University during the Vietnam era when the Ohio National Guard was shooting student protesters. The picture showed a girl kneeling over a fallen friend as she cried, "He's dead!" This picture was published in newspapers and magazines all over the world.

Repeats of such experiences are not frequent in today's mostly profit-demanding media governed by the tyranny of the bottom line.

Maybe this isn't a disconnected afterthought for some perspective: Yes, President Bush does continue to have very high approval ratings, but so did his father as president during the Gulf War with 93 percent approval, in the same year he couldn't get re-elected president even running against a little known kid governor of a state such as Arkansas.

Think about it.

June 3, 2001

The Sen. James Jeffords earthquake that struck the Republican Party and Washington last week—with a shattering that should not have been unexpected, jarred open memories of a personal experience from which I can empathize with the Vermont senator.

Some 20 years ago I went through a similar soul-searching experience; it was not a cakewalk, and the decision was not made quickly when I changed my voter registration from Republican to Democrat. Arizona Sen. Barry Goldwater, a conservative GOP icon, somewhat moved me in that direction when he said that religious right extremists could ruin the Republican Party if they got control. They already have in more than 30 states.

But it was excesses and sleaze of the Reagan administration, its unconcern for the little guy, dominance of the military-industrial complex President Eisenhower warned us about, and borrow-and-spend policies pushing red ink through the ceiling that triggered the change. And a man getting elected president on a promise to eliminate the deficit and balance the budget and then doing the opposite is what clinched it.

But before that I was a registered Republican for 43 voting years. Most all Iowans were Republicans when I was born in 1916, and my parents and relatives were all life-long GOPers. Understandably, my first political foray was pulling a little wagon around Burlington with a "Hoover for

President" sign. And I vividly remember the Burlington *Hawk-Eye*'s blaring headline after the 1928 election: "Thank God, America Saved—Rum, Rome and Ruin" that indicated the tenor of the times.

The isolation of moderate Republicans began in earnest during the Reagan administration. Then along comes an unusually low-key 67-year-old Republican moderate with guts and a lifelong background in the Republican Party of his ancestors. On the basis of principle and conscience, he determines he can "no longer live with the extremism of the Bush agenda." In the process this unassuming Republican delivered a stunningly effective critique of Republicans and the president as no longer standing for "moderation, tolerance, and fiscal responsibility" in a party increasingly excelling in the politics of meanness.

George W. Bush was supposed to have been a different kind of Republican, a "uniter," he kept telling us, not a "divider." But the hardcore conservatives and sanctimonious religious righters controlling the party aren't interested in any new kind of Republican. An affable front man who could raise tons of money was fine, but they didn't want any of that moderation stuff.

The door really slammed on any moderation when Bush got Richard Cheney as vice president. Cheney was the ultimate right-winger as a Wyoming congressman casting votes against fair housing legislation, the Safe Water Drinking Act, federal support for AIDS testing and counseling, and even against Head Start and funding school lunches for poor children.

Those who thought Bush's loss of the popular vote and more than three million more Americans voting for Gore and Nader than for him would cause some conciliation, moderation and governing in a centrist fashion with the Senate split 50-50 were disappointed. Instead, the extremism and arrogance that characterizes the GOP took over with its close-minded leaders in control.

This drove Sen. Jeffords away from the party of his ancestors. As a headline in the national newspaper *USA Today* read: "The Vermont moderate didn't leave the Republican Party. Rather the rightward-marching GOP left him first"—after he was isolated, shunned, humiliated and even threatened by the heavy-handedness of the Bush White House and Republican leaders.

Sen. John McCain, R-Ariz., who has felt the wrath of fellow Republicans, said it well: "If you're going to threaten retaliation and revenge against people if they don't vote the way you want them to, there is going to be a price." He added a truism: "Tolerance of dissent is the hallmark a mature party, and it is well past time for the Republican Party to grow up."

So it is a measure of the fanaticism infecting the GOP that the party leaders would actually risk loss of the Senate and jeopardize the president's entire agenda simply to punish a senator who at times strayed from the party line.

It is difficult not concluding that the GOP is a party whose leaders are slow learners who let their party be a party of sore winners, as they continue self-inflicted gunshot wounds. Remember when Newt Gingrich, then Speaker of the House (for a short time before he was ousted) told a group of Young Republicans: "I think one of the great problems we have in the Republican Party is that we don't encourage you to be nasty." The GOP still hasn't given up the politics of meanness that continues to backfire with the loss of a highly respected senator and with him control of the U.S. Senate.

Jeffords summed it up by saying he decided to become an independent "to best represent Vermont and my own principles," dismissing all other explanations as "spinning." He simply and bluntly said: "I cannot be what I am not."

Some background:

Pennsylvania Republican Gov. Bill Scranton was a personal friend supported by our western Pennsylvania newspapers, not because he was a Republican, but because he was a genuinely good governor for all the people. Same for U.S. Sen. Jim Duff, a Republican—"Big Red" had many golden retrievers and wanted to give me one but died before it could be delivered.

We also supported Democrat Gov. David Lawrence, probably Pennsylvania's most effective political leader ever. Two editorials in one week indicated our approach. One highly praised Lawrence for the nation's best highway safety program. The other one hit him hard for appointing an incompetent political hack as Commissioner of State Police.

Inconsistent? Certainly not, because we were right both times.

All this simply underlines the independence of our newspapers. And at election time, I'd remind our editors and reporters that no candidate was as good as his friends claimed nor as bad as his opponents maintained.

Incidentally, I've never voted a straight ticket in my life, and our newspapers backed candidates of both parties. It's irrational to believe that any one party has all the good guys or all the bad. Like a wise man said, "The person who says there are two sides to every question grossly over-simplifies it."

August 8, 1994

Whether it's news-papering or ranching, or any business or profession, it seems there are always those who say, "This is the way we've always done it" or "We've never done that before," or maybe "They wouldn't like it that way," whoever "they" are.

Perhaps this resistance to new ideas and better ways of doing things is why real progress is so difficult. The thinking of so many of us and our leaders is "inside the box," while being creative requires thinking "outside the box."

A Georgetown University management professor, Robert Bies, said that the "box" is a set of rules we impose on ourselves when we think about new ways to approach problems and get things done.

It was a wise philosopher, Rudolph Flesch, who said, "Creative thinking might simply mean the realization that there is no particular virtue in doing things the way they always have been done." So many of us are unable to understand this. The fundamental truth is that the only certainty is the certainty of the constancy of change—in our lives and in our world.

Evidence is abundant that in many areas and on many levels, we have boxed ourselves in with worn-out answers and outdated responses to critical problems—and because of this, we repeat mistakes. And yet we wonder why so many things remain wrong in our communities and in the world around us.

The beloved Will Rogers, whose homespun wisdom and philosophy is timeless, sums it up best: "Even if you're on the right track, you'll get run over if you just sit there."

A sign posted at the American Press Institute back in the 1960's, when it was at Columbia University, read: "Change, adapt, or die." While it was admittedly somewhat dramatic and blunt, more of us need to heed this advice.

It doesn't take much application of these truths to understand why most nations are locked in mindless arms races that drain scarce resources, piling up needless red ink and creating more problems for all of us.

Or why we're boxed in old ruts with outdated thinking that is depleting our country's natural resources and lousing up our environment to the point that we're all at risk. So many of us are unaware of what is happening around us in our one world.

Meanwhile, many have insulated themselves from how other people think, with false assumptions and self-imposed constraints. They have built walls around themselves and have a dangerously stupid stance that smacks of "Don't confuse me with facts because my mind already is made up."

Sadly, this cut-off of communication leaves no opportunity to get new ideas from people who can see problems from different perspectives. And it ignores the old Chinese proverb: "The more lines you cast in the water, the more likely you are to catch a fish."

Maybe a lot of us need more healthy skepticism and a proneness to ask "Why?" And the curiosity and questioning of a child would help, too. If we could do more of this, we could shed a lot of bad habits and useless rules—and do things better than they've ever been done before.

Georgetown University has a great Jesuit saying that goes something like this: "It's a lot easier to ask forgiveness than to ask permission." And along the way, a lot more good could be done.

CHAPTER 3

Medium Grades for the Media

Typical of his mode of operation, Simon, in his December 2, 2001, column develops his thesis, in this case a harsh condemnation of corporate ownership of media, by providing significant chunks of the hidden news which corporate media prefers to keep hidden. Failure to report demonstrations against terrorist training at the School of the Americas takes center stage as evidence against big media effectiveness and integrity.[1] Thus the corporate-owned media fails in its duty to inform the public. Note again, in making his case, Simon relies on hard facts—enlightening and valuable in themselves—from prestigious and verifiable sources. The second column selected, February 27, 1995, continues the same thesis, in this case lamenting the passing of MacNeil/Lehrer News Hour to Liberty Media of TCI.[2] Simon's October 27, 2001, criticism of media extremists who thoughtlessly parrot the government line, can be seen in retrospect as a prescient warning of America's current floundering in the morass of ill-conceived wars in Afghanistan and Iraq, frightening parallels to our Vietnam disaster in too many respects. And always Simon maintains perspective, here by employing de Tocqueville as a telling touchstone.

---

1. Belles lettres not infrequently does a better job than the mass media: on Salvadoran fruit of School of the Americas efforts, see the grim harvest described in the fine novel by Manlio Argueta, *One Day of Life*, New York: Vintage International, 1991.

2. "At least until television itself, in whatever evolving form, becomes a battleground of criticism and debate, it will remain an essentially conservative technology: isolating, narcotizing, trivializing, commercializing, reflecting a simpler moral universe." Jeffrey Scheuer, *Sound Bite Society*. New York: Four Walls Eight Windows, 1999, p. 190.

December 2, 2001

In previous columns, "Think about It" has infrequently cited instances where the establishment press has fallen on its face in reporting crucial events, and in the process denied the people's right to know.

A glaring recent example is the upwards of 10,000 citizens of conscience who assembled Nov. 17-18 at the gates of Fort Benning in Georgia to protest the U.S. Army's infamous School of the Americas based there. Anyway you cut it, this was a major news event.

Recently renamed the Western Hemisphere Institute for Security Cooperation in an attempt to shed its unsavory past, this "school" has trained many thousands of Latin American soldiers in counter-insurgency tactics, as too many have become "killers in uniform."

U.S. and international human rights organizations have documented the hundreds of SOA graduates who have participated in widespread terrorism, civilian-targeted-torture, disappearances and killings. The record confirms this has happened mostly in Guatemala, El Salvador, Columbia, Chile, and other countries in Latin America when those countries were controlled by repressive dictatorships supported by American tax dollars.

Compared to the 8,000 that demonstrated last year, this was the 12th annual march commemorating the massacre of six Jesuit priests in San Salvador killed by SOA graduates. SOA products were also responsible for murdering Salvadoran Archbishop Oscar Romero, champion of the poor, as he celebrated mass in his cathedral. What the protestors from all over the country were demanding was closure of this "terrorist training camp in our backyard." Known as the School of Assassins throughout Latin America, and taxpayer supported, it has produced hundreds of killers who have returned to their own countries to crush fellow citizens striving for democracy and a better life.

But here's the gut point: Did any of you learn any of this from our TV networks or the establishment corporate media? Nada: This reality makes a mockery of American ideals and principles we should cherish, and it sabotages the people's right to know. Such news suppression does not make for a healthy society or an informed citizenry.

Analysis of the why of such censorship, which is increasingly happening in controlled coverage of the supposed war on terrorism that has become a war on Afghanistan, would require many columns. But here are a few basics to think about: During my 30 years of newspaper publishing in western Pennsylvania, and also Arizona during the 1960's, the majority of the U.S. newspapers were independently owned and operated. Today such private control is becoming the exception. The media now is dominated by 10 corporations. They control most of the nation's newspapers, magazines, television stations, radio outlets and even movies and publishing houses. An eye-opening exposé of all this is revealed in *The Media Monopoly* by respected and widely known journalist giant, Ben H. Bagdikan.

Until the mid-1980's, our major TV networks were all independent companies that regarded their news divisions as prestigious adjuncts to commercial programming, and not sources of revenue. Who can forget the excellence of CBS's Edward R. Murrow and Walter Cronkite. But all that changed between 1986 and 1996, as the giant conglomerates took over. Now NBC is owned by General Electric, CBS by Westinghouse and ABC by Disney. In this transition, TV news ceased being an obligatory public service and became a profit center geared to "Infotainment" so as to enhance corporate balance sheets.

Harvard's Sorenstein Center reports that along the way program time devoted to international coverage dropped from 45 percent in the 1970's to less than 14 percent in 1995, and lower today. En route, freedom to report fully and objectively ownership's vested interests took a nose dive. So is it surprising that when General Electric was cited for substantial padding of overtime on a defense contract, NBC didn't carry what happened to taxpayer money, and the other networks closed ranks.

Why do you think opposition to the war (not against terrorism but against Afghanistan), while growing in this country, has surged upwards in Canada, the British Isles and in Europe? The highly professional CBC and BBC are independent non-profit public institutions not beholden to corporate underwriters. They rely on hard fact gathering and critical objectivity. Their reporters aren't becoming "stenographers" dependent on the government's versions of news with its doctored handouts that allow only what Big Brother wants you to know. Rarely does this include the strategic military blunders, mounting civilian deaths from indiscriminate cluster bombs that can shatter eardrums and burst lungs of innocents within a wide range of hits or misses. The news is not sanitized by CBC and the BBC.

When Defense Secretary Rumsfeld and Pentagon spokespersons either deny or cast doubt on civilian casualties, and come up with stuff like "We really didn't want to bomb the Red Cross food warehouse again but we heard the Taliban was stealing the food," it doesn't enhance your democratic right to know the facts nor make for a healthy functioning society. So there'll be more than seven million Afghans heading for starvation this winter.

People overseas aren't getting doctored versions of the news nor are they subject to "the military wants to do journalism" that John MacArther, a *Harper's Magazine* editor, reported in his excellent book, *The Battle of Lies.*

February 27, 1995

Chalk another one up for further deteriorations in the quality and objectivity of the news available to the American people.

The respected MacNeil/Lehrer NewsHour isn't going to be like it used to be. Public television's flagship news program soon will be controlled by a private, for-profit, right-wing media conglomerate that could be labeled reactionary.

Liberty Media, a subsidiary of TCI, the nation's largest TV system operator, is buying two-thirds of MacNeil/Lehrer Productions, the News-Hour's producer.

TCI isn't just another media conglomerate. *The Rocky Mountain News* in Denver reported in December that "Regulators, independent cable industry consultants, consumer groups and lawyers representing cities, complained that TCI employs a ruthless policy designed to muffle criticism, smother competition and saddle local governments with huge legal bills."

The article described the boss of TCI, John Malone, as "a predator with the compassion of a great white shark."

So is it any wonder this entrepreneur has a well-earned reputation for Machiavellian business tactics?

Further, TCI has been called "the worst discriminator in the telecommunications industry" by the League of Latin American Citizens and the NAACP.

Malone is known for his open hostility to any government regulation, and he supposedly joked about "shooting the head of the FCC."

An example of his tactics is a memo Malone sent local TCI cable operators instructing them to raise cable rates and "blame it on re-regulation and the government."

This was reported in the Washington *Post* in November 1993.

But what makes all this dangerous for the cause of truth and the public's right to know is Malone's announcement that the radical right-wing cable channel, National Empowerment Television, will have increased access to TCI cable systems, giving it the opportunity to reach a potential 13 million new viewers. And Malone praises the likes of Rush Limbaugh, especially noted for his "reign of error."

National Empowerment Television, the newest far-right channel noted for its extremism, reaches millions of homes across the U.S.

The NET channel boasts Newt Gingrich's weekly TV show, and his objective of gutting public broadcasting underlines the fact that a program such as NewsHour can be absorbed by a right-wing corporate media conglomerate.

What is superficially perplexing about Malone's TCI taking over a public television news program is his statement last fall on ABC World News Tonight.

He said: "Nobody wants to go out and invent something and invest hundreds of millions of dollars of risk capital for the public interest. I mean, one would be fired as an executive of a profit-making company if he took that stance."

If no executive would invest money in the public interest, then why is Malone investing in a money-losing show such as the MacNeil/Lehrer NewsHour?

The answer is rather obvious: Influence, power, access, control of decisions made in Washington.

And one wonders what will happen with the Federal Communications Commission's ongoing investigation of anti-trust charges against Malone's TCI? Will this be a dead duck with help from Gingrich?

What's deplorable is that none of this seems to bother PBS, which apparently greeted the corporate takeover of its flagship with enthusiasm.

PBS president Ervin Duggan called it "a welcome infusion of capital into the NewsHour."

October 27, 2001

Perhaps the paramount lesson mankind could and should have learned from wars, especially those of the bloody 20th century, is that their greatest casualty is truth.

It may be well to also recall Alexis de Tocqueville's warning of nearly two centuries ago that "war is the surest and shortest means to the destruction of democracy." Wisdom of the French political genius has been reaffirmed many times.

Our president tells us that we are now a nation at war. But the war we are now involved in is essentially different from any before—and with more at-home vulnerability than Americans have experienced.

Another incongruity is that in a real sense this "war" could be called a police action, which recalls the police action of 1950 in Vietnam that went on to become a war claiming 58,000 American lives.

As with the Gulf War, there's more of a need now than ever before for a broad coalition that is willing and enthusiastic. But this objective is on shaky ground with a coalition that is so unnatural its survival is questionable. Evidence already indicates elements of reluctance and uncertainty confronting coalition members fearful of strong currents in their countries. None of these problems will be improved by mistaken bombings of Red Cross centers, U.N. food depots, homes and possibly a hospital, along with tides of starving refugees who have already been victimized by years of war and devastation in their country. All this could be dangerously exacerbated by extremists in and out of government who are the "nuke 'em" variety.

Actually aiding the terrorists and gaining them support are those like New York *Post* columnist Steve Dunleavy, who in effect demanded oceans of blood when he said: "As for the cities and countries that host those worms, bomb them into basketball courts."

There are area far-outs who have indicated similar beliefs. Such advocates of indiscriminate violence would be very compatible with Adolf Hitler's Nazis and their policy of guilt-by-association that wiped out innocent civilians and little people who chanced to be in a town with a few snipers.

Another wild extremist example is Bill O'Reilly who night after night on cable television has been banging his loud drum for indiscriminate reprisals. He proclaimed on Fox News Channel (that seems to go for this stuff), "Unless the Taliban quickly hands over Osama bin Laden, the U.S. should bomb the Afghan infrastructure to rubble—airports, power plants, water facilities and roads… We should not target civilians, but if they don't rise up against this criminal government, they starve, period." For good measure, O'Reilly urged that the U.S. "extensively bomb Iraq and Libya," saying, "Let them eat sand." It is certain Osama bin Laden will be pleased with results of this.

It is not difficult to understand how such venal stupidity, in its stark contrast to genuine American ideals and principles, plays in the Arab world and also with our would-be allies. It's a winner for the extremists.

Since the war in Vietnam ended badly for all involved, the military has used and abused newspapers and television to tell and show American citizens stories that have ranged from "carefully controlled" to plain old "making it up," a nicer way of saying "lies." Reporters and cameras are not wanted to get too close because things might be reported about military efficiency that would upset taxpayers who are paying for missile misses and stealth photography.

If too many reporters are reporting for duty, saluting the commander-in-chief and awaiting orders, then a news profession that is vital to a democracy is in effect morphing into PR fakery for the government. This is not in the best interests of a healthy democracy and can be fatal if carried too far. News reporting that is best for America should be impeccably accurate and operate on a without-fear-or-favor basis.

CHAPTER 4

Refuge of Scoundrels

Patriotism is one of those problematical "virtues" which can so easily bleed off the skepticism necessary to pulse through the healthy body of public thought, a virtue which can, in excess, produce jingoism. At its most cancerous, patriotism joins with fear to feed on the healthy body politic, a psychological reality Nazi propagandists well understood.[3] In his column of May 15, 1995, Simon explores the "patriotic" militia movement as a manifestation of this danger. But perhaps "patriotism" has been more dangerously exploited following the September 11 attacks: in his November 24, 2002, column Simon contrasts the immediate post-9/11 patriotism, "its noblest sense of community and coming together" with the subsequent patriotism of "enforced conformity as it sacrifices civil liberties for an elusive security and imperils our cherished Bill of Rights." Further warning against blind red-white-and-blue thinking in his column of January 24, 2003, Simon writes presciently that Bush's policies "will kill tens of thousands of innocent people and untold numbers of our own countrymen. This war will... destabilize the region for years to come, but worst of all, it will confirm for all the world our country's growing reputation as an irrational and undisciplined bully..."

May 15, 1995

If the armed militias known to exist in more than 40 states are "very patriotic," as Gov. Gary Johnson was moved to protest in behalf of the New Mexico militia, then why don't they utilize the political process and the ballot box, the legitimate tools of a democratic society?

Do genuinely patriotic groups that truly believe in the democratic pro-

---

3.   "Before it establishes its worldly dominion, fear's empire colonizes the imagination." Benjamin R. Barber, *Fear's Empire*, New York: W.W. Norton & Company, 2003, p. 215. (Barber's study examines the dangerous, self-defeating empire of fear constructed in the wake of the 9/11 attacks.)

cess form paramilitary groups, stockpile weapons and practice camouflage soldiering in the woods as they spew anti-government rhetoric getting ready to "take back our government?"

So is it difficult to perceive that some militia leaders already envision themselves as future heads-of-state or dictator—in a society that would not be democratic?

After one realizes the evidence of the hate-mongers, racists and white supremacists, neo-Nazis, fanatical extremists, assault weapon zealots and yes, the far-out kooks drawn to militia movements, it is difficult equating this with patriotism and America's basic principles of tolerance and respect for differences.

Is much imagination needed to comprehend that armed zealots bound by paranoia and fear, who are disseminators of a virulent anti-government philosophy, can help plant thoughts of insurrection in someone's head who doesn't have much exposure to reality?

Was Timothy McVeigh, who had militia connections, "pushed over the edge" into the violence in Oklahoma City? It doesn't take a psychologist to savvy that bitter words and excessive language have consequences, and when you mix armed groups with hate you've got a recipe for disaster.

What about these militia leaders? John Trockmann, co-founder of the "souped up" Montana Militia, known as one of the most extremist, has links with the white supremacist Aryan Nations based near Hayden Lake, Idaho.

Mark Koernke, "Mark from Michigan," is a leading propagandist for the militia movement. Until early this month he had an hour-long short wave radio show over World Wide Christian Radio. (Yes, "Christian.")

Robert Pummer of the Florida State Militia exhorts his members to "Buy Ammo Now." Steward Webb, leader of Guardians of American Liberties at Boulder, Colo., has a history of anti-Semitism and regularly appears on right-wing radio shows spouting his conspiracy theories. James Roy Mullins, founder of the Blue Ridge Hunt Club in Virginia, was arrested in July and charged with possession and sale of short-barrel rifles and unregistered silencers. He formed his "club" to "arm its members in preparation for war with the government."

These are just some of the "patriots" leading militia movements who actually believe, among other things, that the salt mines beneath Detroit hold a division of Russian troops ready to take over the U. S.; that Amtrak repair yards in Indianapolis will be used as a huge crematorium to "fry" political dissidents; that the United Nations plans to conquer the U.S. using the National Guard and Los Angeles gangs to disarm the public; that black helicopters are buzzing Western states on surveillance missions for invading U.N. troops... and on and on.

No, this isn't meant to be funny. This is just some of what many grown adults and otherwise sane people in the militia movement actually believe is true.

A politically knowledgeable friend recently asked a pertinent question: What would be our country's reaction if armed groups of black men were parading around in the woods in about 40 states spouting anti-government rhetoric and in effect preparing for revolution?

What would your reaction be? Now be honest about it.

Just a thought: There's no doubt some well-meaning good people belong to the militia movement. But with national awareness of it surfacing since the Oklahoma City bombing, the word already is out, some of these are leaving the militias.

November 24, 2002

Many will remember learning in school long ago about America being a "beacon to the world." I still feel the thrill of reading that about our country and the far-reaching effect of its principles and ideals on the world that made America so much admired.

But that was long ago and it's different now. Any reading of the foreign press, listening to overseas broadcasts such as the BBC, and maintaining contacts with friends in other countries conveys a different picture that can make you flinch. (Some of those contacts resulted from study missions as a journalist that took me into 49 countries during the 1950's, 1960's, and early 1970's, mostly conducted by the U.S. Society of Editors & Commentators.)

The different U.S. image emerging abroad depicts an arrogant bully insensitive to others, strutting its long superpower status with a might-makes-right approach, and a self-righteous get-'em-dead-or-alive attitude, spoiling for a fight. An old cowboy friend would call this "throwing your weight around." He was the one who asked, "When are we gonna pick on someone our own size?" None of this represents the real America that became great because of its principles.

Thus it is understandable that even our allies consider us morally obtuse and politically naïve, at risk of laying ourselves open to further terrorist attacks because of a simplistic one-dimensional approach to terrorism as if it's something suspended in outer space as an abstract phenomenon. To put it mildly, in the opinion of our friends overseas, Americans do not have a monopoly on political wisdom and good judgment.

Not incidentally, the establishment media is not reporting these realities or the massive demonstrations building in many countries and across America against war in Iraq. As with heavy civilian casualties in Afghanistan, the U.S. media is not providing the complete picture. And how many of you know about the hundreds recently demonstrating against the war at Secretary of Defense Rumfeld's Taos home?

The resurgence of anti-Americanism around the world finally caught attention of the Bush administration enough to cause the U.S. State Department to recently hold a two-day closed-door conference on the spread of anti-American attitude in virtually all other countries. That "closed-door" means the conference was held at an undisclosed location on an invitation-only basis restricted to 20 scholars and 50 government officials.

Examples of the growing anti-Americanism are endless. One need not go beyond our allies to get the thrust, such as *The Guardian* of London saying "an inarticulate president with a right-wing agenda and a traumatized public, attempting to govern as though these divisions (an American split down the middle politically) do not really exist." And ending a 9/2/02 article with "The problem with America is its government. What they, and we, need is regime change."

Then there is the previously reported poll by *The Independent* of London showing that over half the British named President Bush as the 3rd biggest threat to world peace after Osama bin Laden and Saddam Hussein.

Yes, would that we could see ourselves as others see us.

Much of this anti-Americanism is resulting from the administration's obsession to attack Iraq and "get Saddam" ostensibly because he has weapons of mass destruction (as do 17 other nations, including some not our friends)... and maybe because "he tried to kill my daddy." It couldn't be because of oil?

What the gung-ho war hawks in the Bush administration (who dodged military combat) are unable to comprehend is that a U.S. invasion of Iraq unwittingly plays into the hands of al-Quaida and militant Islamists, giving them a new lease on life.

Evidence mounts they are already positioning themselves to capitalize on the coming war that would swell their ranks with recruits for militant causes—and provide employment for endless new terrorists.

Inevitable civilian casualties in a country already shattered by 22 years of bombing and sanctions have made it a nation of have-nots. Impoverished Iraqi families rely on emaciated children to beg and peddle so they can eat. UNICEF reports document the physical and psychological suffering of deprived children. Hundreds of thousands are struggling to survive midst surroundings marked by malfunctioning sewers, inadequate water, electricity that usually doesn't work, hospitals sorely in need of medicines and basic equipment, and massive deterioration everywhere. Yes, sanctions have taken their toll.

In a nation that prided itself on its schools and universities where parents from around the Arab world used to send their children to study, literacy has plummeted from 87% in 1985 to 45% in 1995 (most recent year statistics available), as growing numbers of children can no longer attend school because of multiple hardships.

Those who think it's patriotic and a credit to America to further pulverize a suffering people need to check their credentials as true Americans.

And if our leaders lack the ingenuity and ability to get one man without turning loose a military juggernaut that could wipe out a nation, then maybe *The Guardian* is right about a needed regime change.

As there are usually more than two sides to every question, so are there different faces to patriotism. Its noblest sense of community and coming together showed America at its best in the inspiring initial response after the Sept. 11 attacks. But there's a less pleasant aspect showing now that is equating patriotism with an enforced conformity as it sacrifices civil liberties for an elusive security and imperils our cherished Bill of Rights.

"Patriotism" is even blinding Americans to the "why" behind the "what"—why our country so admired in so many ways is becoming so detested. Meanwhile, Bush's vacuous repetition of "They hate our freedom" inanely puts us out of the ball park and increases our isolation.

January 24, 2003

In stark terms of what is happening in America and to our country, as its government pressures war on Iraq, it is getting past time to stop tip-toeing around realities and recognize the downright dangerous wrong of the world's mightiest military power gearing for an onslaught on an already tattered country that will further the misery of its people and kill even more of those already suffering from 12 years of sanctions and bombings.

This is a frightening time for our country, but if we cannot speak out of Christian conscience and conviction in the great American tradition, and stand for the best of America against an attorney general-foisted culture of "patriotic" intimidation—that is suspending our constitutional liberties and stifling dissent—then we will have forfeited our citizenship forever to a moral silence.

If the government's definition of a "good American," who blindly goes along with the powers-that-be in a my-country-right-or-wrong mentality, then all of us and the better America will lose. "Patriotism" then will become narrow, partisan, jingoistic and opportunistic, as is already happening with massive cashing-in on the supposed war on terrorism and the cash-cow bonanza to insiders in any war. What then will become of duty to think for ourselves, to speak, to dissent and to demand a better case for compromising our most fundamental principles as Christians and citizens?

Think about this: Many of us have seen the bumper stickers reading "God Bless America." But are we so ethically blind and naïve as to believe that God will bless America if America does not bless what delights God nor play the game according to God's rules?

Many Americans have agonized over the perplexity of "Why do they hate us?" But if our chicken hawks are so gung-ho for war and make it the first rather than the last option, then we'll soon find out as the avalanche hits us and the answer will be terribly manifest. "Going to war to keep the peace" won't wash with the world's people either, nor with God.

Yes, our country now more than ever needs a better relationship between love of God and love of country… And a better excuse for war than oil or revenge for "he tried to kill my daddy."

So when Bush II says, "I'm getting sick and tired" (with the peace process and UN inspections), it makes any good American wince, realizing that such reasoning will kill tens of thousands of innocent people and untold numbers of our own countrymen. This war will not only do far more harm than good, destabilize the region for years to come, but worst of all, it will confirm for all the world our country's growing reputation as an irrational and undisciplined bully acting not because it should, but because it can, making its own rules as it goes. Real patriots love their country too much to see it trapped in its own worst stereotype.

Bush II's speech last year at West Point's military graduation unveiled his new pre-emptive war strategy. In effect this means Bush wants to knock off any country he suspects might want to do us in before that country maybe gets around to it. Already the sharp contradiction of administration policy toward North Korea and Iraq has made a mockery of the Bush pre-emptive "policy," as he has muddied the waters with our South Korean ally, whose people now consider the U.S. a bigger threat to peace than North Korea, as a Gallup poll there proved. Thus a question: If North Korea was rich in oil and Iraq didn't have any, would the Bush policy toward each be different? 'Nuff said.

But there's another kind of pre-emptive action burgeoning in America. This is a faith-based opposition to the Bush-Cheney-Rumsfeld rush to war on Iraq. It is rapidly becoming an ocean wave and, surprisingly, it is mostly religious leaders and congregations of mainline Protestant, progressive evangelicals and Catholics in the U.S. and England that have been the most vocal and visible in raising the alarm.

Just as surprising is the fact America's churches are on the move much sooner than they were in the Vietnam War of the 1960's, when they were slow to wake up. Catholic Bishop Thomas Gumletom of Detroit, who has been in Iraq many times since the 1991 Gulf War, bluntly said: "What we are doing must be condemned without equivocation. It is morally bankrupt, totally depraved." Significantly the Bishop said this before the World Association for Christian Communicators at their two-day workshop last April on "The News Embargo on Iraq."

Rev. Edward Rowe, noted pastor of Detroit Central United Methodist Church, told the Michigan *Christian Advocate*: "We can't sleep through the rush to war. Killing innocent victims makes us the terrorists we hate."

Incidentally, both Bush and Cheney, allegedly Methodists (as I am), have refused requests by leading bishops of their own church for meetings. Seems they're too busy readying America's children to kill Iraqi children to talk about Christianity and peace.

With its integrity at stake and realizing it is bearing Christian witness, the religious community across America is energizing a moral debate on the administration's pending war on Iraq.

Every major religious denomination in America, except the Southern Baptist, has issued proclamations questioning unilateral action by the U.S. And the Archbishop of Canterbury, head of the Church of England, has vehemently positioned his church against policies of the Tony Blair government—which just might be heading for a regime change.

The churches' message might get through: "War is not the answer," as was spotlighted by hundreds of thousands protesting the Iraq war in our nation's capitol this past weekend, as more demonstrations build across America.

CHAPTER 5

Courage from Clarity, Hypocrisy from Murk

Perhaps in mind of Kierkegaard's The Attack on Christendom *and Dostoyevsky's* The Idiot, *Simon, in his September 24, 1979, column provocatively queries what might happen if our "Christian nation" lived Christianity. Simon's September 13, 1993, column explicitly lauds the informed clarity of San Francisco Mayor Jordan's challenge to the NRA, while implicitly saluting Jordan's rare courage. Simon's column of December 28, 2003, provides shameful instances of obfuscation and hypocrisy.*

September 24, 1979

Are you interested in asking yourself an intriguing and provocative question? If so, try this one. It could start the wheels turning.

"If you were on trial for allegedly being a Christian, would there be enough evidence to convict you?"

How many people do you know who would be convicted on the basis of the actual evidence if they were charged with being Christians? Would you be convicted at such a trial?

Those are some pretty good questions.

It seems we sometimes forget that Christianity is a way of life, seven days a week, and not just on Sundays or in church. It is how we treat our fellow man and conduct our daily lives. It is the way we play the game and run the course. It represents the ground rules used along the way.

It is not spelled out merely by the motions we go through or by manmade or man-interpreted dogmas. Christianity is not represented by just what we believe, which is important, but even more by what we do, in our daily lives, in the market place, and everywhere, all the time.

Yes, I think most of us will agree that Christianity has not been tried and found wanting: rather it has been wanting and not tried. There's nothing wrong with Christianity but there is something wrong with many of those of us who profess to be Christians while not letting Christianity permeate our daily lives and conduct. Christianity requires more than lip service for it to fulfill its potential and have the effect so sorely needed in this troubled world—a world so full of "man's inhumanity to man" and unchristian acts perpetrated by self-proclaimed Christians and so-called Christian nations.

You see, there are really "no other hands but thine" to express Christianity here on earth and make it work. Some call this God working through man and through people. But can you go to a meeting and distinguish those in attendance who are Christians from those who are not? Can you tell the difference? And I'm not referring to those religionists who have all the final answers and wear their "Christianity" on their sleeves with a holier-than-thou attitude.

Probably most everyone would not argue the point that all of us know how to be better than we are. But somehow it just seems to never really work out that way. We can't seem to pull it off. We can't seem to get there from here!

Then there's the point that Christianity or being a Christian does not just involve what we don't and should not do, but it also involves our sins of omission as well as commission. It involves what we aren't doing that we should be doing. That's the one thing that bothers me somewhat about the Ten Commandments. They are mostly don'ts in Thou Shalt Not form. There's nothing wrong with this, but perhaps we need Ten Commandments, or ten hundred Thou Shalts... things we should be doing, acts and conduct that would make us be judged guilty of being genuine Christians.

You see, real Christianity is not a passive thing to be parroted by rote on a schedule when convenient. Rather it is an active, vibrant, dynamic concept that, if practiced, could not only change the lives of men and women, but also change the world and truly make it a heaven on earth.

September 13, 1993

Frank M. Jordan is the mayor of San Francisco. He also is the former police chief of the city and he knows his guns.

Last July 9, Mayor Jordan wrote a letter to James Jay Baker, executive director of the National Rifle Association's Institute for Legislative Action. This was just nine days after a man armed with three semi-automatic weapons and hundreds of rounds of ammunition walked into a downtown office building in San Francisco and began shooting. Eight innocent people were killed and six others injured in that killing spree.

Here are some excerpts from Mayor Jordan's letter to the NRA:

After stating his belief that "the officers of the National Rifle Association bear a moral responsibility for the deaths of eight innocent people," Jordan said, "Your organization advocates the legal sale of weapons that have no purpose but to create mayhem." (Such weapons include the two semi-automatic 9mm. machine pistols the killer used in San Francisco.)

"But you do more than advocate—you spend millions of dollars each year on lobbyists and political campaigns at both the national and state-house level to pressure lawmakers against restricting the sale of weapons of war in American gun shops.

"Let me tell you, guns do kill people. And when you insist on legalizing semi-automatic guns with 50 bullet clips like the ones used in San Francisco last week, you are encouraging any demented Rambo to walk into any building in America and kill many people before the first 911 emergency call goes out.

He noted "how much more difficult and inherently dangerous the NRA has made the job of these brave police officers by insisting that the murderous fire of the weapons they faced was just another normal American hunting weapon."

Continuing his letter, Jordan said: "...I cannot believe, sir, that when you face the mirror in the morning, you can tell yourself in good conscience that a 50-bullet clip semi-automatic assault weapon is what every red-blooded American boy needs to go hunting. We might as well start using cluster bombs against deer. Nor can you really believe a homeowner needs such a weapon for self-defense."

Jordan said, "There is no explanation for [such killings], except that the weapons are available. And they are available largely because the NRA has perverted the intent of the framers of the Constitution and twisted the meaning of the Second Amendment into a license for Rambo's to hunt and kill their fellow citizens. There is no answer to it, except to make those weapons of warfare and high-speed death unavailable in our country."

Jordan noted the NRA is a powerful organization because it represents the legitimate interests of sportsmen and defends the primacy of the Constitutional protections of individual liberties.

But he said the NRA has crossed the line from protecting those values to perverting those values.

"The time has come for America to outlaw the weapons of war that make every office building a potential shooting gallery. It is my fervent prayer the NRA leadership has the courage and wisdom to join in this just war and cease lobbying the government to allow guerrilla warfare against our own citizens."

Amen!

December 28, 2003

The abundance of hypocrisy displayed in workings of both Congress and the Bush administration was readily documented by this column recently, based on a continuing ample quantity of factual source evidence.

Prime among the many examples of rank hypocrisy was George W. Bush saying in a London speech Nov. 19 that Iraqis now have the same free speech that is enjoyed by citizens of Great Britain and the United States.

This grand pronouncement was made after U.S. Viceroy Paul Bremer a month earlier in Iraq shot down some Iraqi-run newspapers, radio and television stations for criticizing his authority. And scarcely two weeks before the Bush "free speech" claim, U.S. soldiers handcuffed and taped an Iraqi man's mouth before hauling him away because "This man has been detained for making anti-coalition statements," as Reuters news agency quoted the "incident's" commanding officer.

At the time of these reports, this column had no expectation that even more startling evidence of hypocrisy in high places was about to burst in the nation's news. Biggest of a shocking trio was confirming the disclosure that Sen. Strom Thurmond, R-S.C., longest serving senator in U.S. history, who recently died at age 100, had fathered at age 22 a child by his rich family's 16-year-old black maid. The Thurmond family has belatedly confirmed a rumor that swirled around South Carolina for decades.

As Dixiecrat presidential candidate in 1948, Thurmond thundered there were "not enough troops in the army to force the Southern people to break down segregation and admit the Negro race into our theaters, into our swimming pools, into our homes and into our churches." He electrified segregationist rallies with shouts such as "all the bayonets of the Army cannot force the Negro into our homes." Meanwhile, as governor of South Carolina, Thurmond was taking his hidden mixed-race daughter into his home—but she used the back door.

This legendary white political icon had done what was typical then in the South when the son of a master's family tested his sexuality on a vulnerable girl in the master's house. Thus he was a racist by day and a hypocrite by night, which could be called "after dark integration." This was hypocrisy at its worst, and a duality that is the ultimate lie.

So is it surprising there's a thread of denial running through many southern family trees, making it very painful to face a story that has been so well-controlled for generations?

Perhaps this is why Strom Thurmond, Jr., United States attorney for South Carolina, who acknowledged his half-sister's account, after the media reported it, (she's a 78-year-old retired school teacher) did not return calls for comment. And Luke Byars, executive director of the state Republican Party, said: "We got no comment on the whole matter." (This won't get Luke into *Profiles in Courage*.)

Wonder if there'll be any comment from Sen. Trent Lott, R-Miss., who was Senate Majority Leader and No. 1 Republican in Congress last year when he made this brilliant statement at Mr. Thurmond's 100th birthday party: "The country would have been better off if Strom Thurmond had won the presidency in 1948." Nuff said.

No. 2—Ex-Gov. George Ryan of Illinois drew worldwide notice and made history last January when, in his final hours in office, he emptied the state's entire death row population of 171 prisoners. Gov. Ryan did this then because evidence indicated innocent men had been sentenced to execution, and the Illinois prison system was "broken." (This after a lifetime supporting capital punishment.)

Last week Ryan was indicted by a federal grand jury on charges of racketeering, conspiracy, mail and tax fraud and lying to law enforcement officials. The U.S. attorney in Chicago unveiled a 91-page indictment bearing 18 counts against Ryan. After four decades in Illinois politics, he could face up to 95 years imprisonment if convicted of these charges. The federal prosecutor said: "Basically the state of Illinois was for sale" to Ryan's friends and family. The corruption extended during Ryan's tenure as secretary of state and then as governor.

No. 3—Gov. John G. Rowland, of George Bush's home state of Connecticut, is facing increasing pressure to resign after admitting he took favors and money from friends and powerful business interests. Some of his aides and friends are currently at the center of a widening federal investigation into awarding of state contracts.

Recent polls in Connecticut show widespread dissatisfaction with the governor and half the state's voters believe he should resign.

During his recent speech before the Middlesex Chamber of Commerce, Gov. Rowland said he "had no interest in blaming others or pointing the finger." But then went on to say: "I should have paid more attention to people around me, people who I trusted." The governor refused to take questions from the press.

At the same meeting, the governor's wife delivered a poem she had written that stingingly rebuked news organizations for reporting her husband's shortcomings and the widening federal investigation into his administration. Another example of wanting to kill the messenger if you don't like the message.

Perhaps it should be noted that all three individuals, Strom Thurmond, former governor George Ryan and Gov. John Rowland are Republicans.

PART II

Egalitarian Democracy

CHAPTER 6

It All Starts with You

Simon's commitment to democracy and the democratic dialogue on which its functioning depends permeates all his thinking and his writing, as apparent in columns printed in other chapters as any here; yet these which follow perhaps more clearly focus salient details of this commitment. Simon clearly shares with another agricultural land-based social philosopher a passionate belief in every individual as imperative to democracy's vitality: Wendell Berry writes, "It is understandable that we should have reacted to the attacks of September 11, 2001, by curtailment of civil rights, by defiance of laws, and by resort to overwhelming force, for those actions are the ready products of fear and hasty thought. But... they cannot protect us from what may prove to be the greatest danger of all: the estrangement of our people from one another and from our land."[4] Simon would chorus a mighty "Amen" to Berry's sentiment. The column of July 30, 1979, both testifies to Simon's belief in hands-on democracy and reminds us that he speaks to us from "down on the ranch," rather than pontificates from the beltline "back there." The July 8, 2001 column documents the courage that individual activity in democracy sometimes demands.

July 30, 1979

With the way things have been going in this country, probably more of you than ever before have been motivated to write a letter to your congressman. Doing this could make a difference and do a lot of good if you do it the right way.

Rep. Morris Udal (D-Ariz.), who made a pretty good run of it for the Democratic Presidential nomination in 1976, has come up with some helpful pointers as to how you can make your letter to your congressman

---

4. Wendell Berry, *Citizenship Papers*, Washington, D.C.: Shoemaker & Hoard, 2003, p. 6.

more effective. It is significant when a congressman tells you how to write a letter to Congress.

So, to make each letter count…

- Be sure your letter is addressed properly with title and zip code. For House members it is Washington, D.C. 20515, and for Senators the zip is 20510.

- Be specific in your opening paragraph, especially if you are writing about a bill or issue, such as saying, "I am writing you about food stamp reform…"

- Timing is important, and give your congressman time enough to do his work. Don't wait until the bill has gone through committee.

- Write your own congressman and senators. Most letters from outside the district or state are automatically ignored as organized mail. (The guys know who can vote for or against them!)

- Be brief. A cogent, fact-filled note on one sheet of paper can be more helpful and effective than a long letter.

- Write your own views, not someone else's. A personal letter is far better than a form letter or signature on a petition. Form letters are readily recognizable and often receive form replies. Congressmen usually know what the major lobbying groups are saying. Your experiences and observations are more important.

- Give your reasons for taking a stand. Statements such as "Vote against H.R. 100; I'm bitterly opposed" don't help much. But saying "I'm a hardware dealer and H.R. 100 would put me out of business for the following reasons…" tells a lot more and can be much more effective.

- Be constructive. If a bill deals with a problem you know exists, but you believe the bill is the wrong approach, then say what you think is the right approach.

- If you have expert knowledge, share it with your congressman. No congressman can be an expert on the vast array of complex bills on which he will have to vote.

- Don't make threats or promises. If you feel strongly about a bill, then say why you do. Your reasons might change your congressman's mind, but your threats probably won't.

- Don't berate your representatives. You won't persuade them of your position by calling them names. If you disagree with them, give reasons for your disagreement. And write them a "well done" when it's deserved. (These guys are human, too.)

- Don't pretend to wield political power and influence. Unsupported claims will cast doubt on your views. Write as an individual and not as a self-appointed spokesman for others.

- And don't become a "pen pal." Quality rather than quantity is what counts.

Remember that mail to modern-day members of Congress is more important than ever before. Senators and representatives today rarely get to spend more than two months in a year among the constituents in their districts. Thus their mailbags are their best "hot lines" to the people back home.

So write a letter to your congressman and senator, and make it a good one that will count.

July 8, 2001

Some readers of last week's "Think about It" column questioned the experiences "Granny D" cited of what raw power can do, even in a democracy—unless it is restrained.

But all those events did occur and can be documented. And it was the Capitol Police, acting under orders of then Senate Majority Leader Trent Lott, who handcuffed this 90-year-old grandmother when she was peacefully demonstrating for urgently needed campaign finance reform. As you probably know, Sen. Lott has always been adamantly opposed to any kind of campaign finance reform that would cut the take on "contributions" from giant corporations. Thus, as "Granny D" so accurately said, "raw power can strike swiftly, discrediting proper law enforcement and setting up new ones run by political cronies with prisons and police of their own to suppress and arrest those who dare protest." Yes, it can happen here.

And there's more that you probably are unaware of because Big Media isn't in to reporting such as federal judges sentencing elderly Catholic nuns to prison for peacefully protesting injustice.

This past May in Columbus, Georgia, U.S. Magistrate G. Mallon Faircloth sentenced 26 protesters for trespassing on federal property, and 21 got the maximum six months in federal prison.

Included among the "convicts" now in jail are Franciscan nun Dorothy Hennessey, age 88, and her kid-sister, Gwen Hennessey, 68, also a Franciscan nun. Elizabeth Anne McKenzie, 71, from Sisters of St. Joseph, Miriam Spencer, 75, from Sisters of St. Joseph of Peace.

Then perhaps proving he's an ecumenical person, Judge Faircloth also slapped sentence on two Quakers from Ohio. Bill Houston, 72, got the maximum in federal prison, but Hazel Tulecke, 77, was let off easy with only three months in prison for protesting.

Judge Faircloth apparently relented from that kindness because a man from Mississippi, Steve Jacobs, was "given" two 6-months sentences, which can be called a stretch for the "crime" involved.

Maybe to show he was a compassionate conservative, Judge Faircloth (that name really flips me) told Sister Gwen Hennessey that she didn't have to report to the federal pen at Pekin, Ill. (nearest to her order's Dubuque, Iowa motherhouse) until after she celebrates the 50th anniversary of taking her vows.

The judge also "went soft" when he offered 88-year-old Dorothy Hennessey the option of serving her sentence under "motherhouse arrest" in Dubuque. Sister Dorothy told the judge "no thanks," because she's not an invalid and wanted to be treated the same as her 25 co-defendants. She also said: "If there's time left after we get out, we might want to go into prison ministry."

Incidentally, the Hennessy sisters have 13 brothers and sisters and said their peaceful civil disobedience was an activist memorial to their late brother, Franciscan friar Ron Hennessey, who served 34 years as a missionary in Latin America and was a close friend of Salvadoran Archbishop Oscar Romero, who was assassinated in 1980 during mass in his San Salvadoran cathedral. That murder has since been documented as being master-minded by graduates of the Army's School of the Americas. In fact, any alumni meeting of the SOA would be the largest collection ever of human rights violators, torturers and murderers. Literally dozens of assassinations and crimes against humanity have been committed by graduates of the School of the Americas, as the record now documents. Panama strongman Manuel Noreiga, who was on the CIA payroll and is now in prison, was an SOA graduate.

So what were these courageous and dedicated Christian Americans of principle protesting? Since 1990, when Maryknoll priest Father Roy Bourgeois, a former military officer (who addressed a meeting on the WNMU campus in Silver City a few years ago), and a handful of others, including actor Martin Sheen, began protesting at the gates of the infamous School of the Americas at Fort Benning, Georgia, annual protests have occurred. This "School for Assassins" as it is known throughout Latin America, has recently been misnamed the Western Hemisphere Institute for Security Cooperation, yet another sugar-coated mislabel for nefarious activity.[5]

The protests beginning in 1990 have since grown to tens of thousands every October when priests, nuns, ministers, professors, students, young and old, all Americans of conscience, gather at the Fort Benning gate to protest the school's deadly role that has trained hundreds of killers-in-uniform all over Latin America. Each year more "cross the line" carrying coffins and name placards representing those killed by (taxpayer funded) SOA graduates. These citizens of conscience are then arrested for trespass and sentenced to federal prisons.

So now Judge G. Mallon Faircloth has again protected us and made the world safe from religious women of conscience by jailing senior Americans. Is our society better because these nuns in their 70's and 80's are behind bars?

Yes, it did happen here in America.

---

5. The details of George Orwell's *1984* and Aldous Huxley's *Brave New World* can no longer be dismissed as distopia fantasies: the "misnaming" of this school for terrorists, for many years now funded from Washington and operating on American soil, is a stellar example of Orwell's "Newspeak."

CHAPTER 7

Democracy under Threat

In an American era of disillusionment with many of our institutions—fed by election fraud, influence-buying by special interests, corporate, governmental, even church corruption, a faltering and inequitable economy producing new ranks of poor and marginalized, all signaling a possible breakdown of the social contract—faith in the democracy that carried our nation through two centuries to world pre-eminence seems at low ebb. Undeterred from criticism wherever it is justified, Simon ever tenaciously clings to the essence of democracy as it was framed for us by the Founding Fathers. Writing for September 23, 1996, Simon decries big-money interest-buying, a major threat to that democracy. Earlier in a July 16, 1979, column he lamented another bloat debilitating democracy, the bureaucracy, especially the extravagantly expensive military bureaucracy, its member benefits representing what might be ironically described as the most lavish functioning socialism. Writing for January 21, 2001, Simon describes what for many Americans was, perhaps, the most disillusioning event of our lifetimes, the 2000 presidential election. Note again the channel Simon opens up to foreign press and opinions.

September 23, 1996

Republicans long have been referred to as the country club set, but since Pat Buchanan launched himself more recent references to country club Republicans have sought to distinguish the well-to-do establishment types from Buchanan's blue-collared crowd who want to shake up the established system.

Regardless, what could be called a new country club has taken root and is flourishing. This club is made up of wealthy, high-powered donors to both political parties. Representing mostly big corporations, they are pouring increasing billions of dollars into the coffers of the Republican and Democratic parties to in effect buy what they want. In return, these big-money donors reap billions from government subsidies, business deals, tax-break provisions and regulatory reforms. The hundreds of thousands and often millions of dollars they give are a form of political insurance to make sure they are at the table when agendas are set, bills written, votes cast and appointments made.

All this makes the big money system a means to the contributors' ends and strictly for their benefit. It also means these huge contributions to buy influence are fueling a political arms race and a spending war that has escalated since a Republican Congress came to power. The crowd now running the show has given a new dimension to the booming big money game in Washington.

Deplorably and dangerously, it also has corrupted the nation's political system and, in effect, puts the government up for sale to the highest bidder. It also blurs policy differences between the two major parties. Eventually, it could fuel growing interest in alternative political parties, as perhaps the only way to correct a shady system that is harming America.

These mostly corporate club members, in a dollar-driven system that corrupts and puts the special interests in the saddle, might be many things but they sure are not us. These biggies pushing their self-interest are not among the 99.97 percent of Americans who don't make political contributions of more than $200.

Their club membership fees are big soft-money contributions that are nothing more than political money laundering designed to bring illegal contributions into federal elections. If you don't pay, then you don't belong to the club. Simply said, money talks because big contributions buy political clout, and there are plenty of congressmen with their hands out.

This big-money system has so permeated and corrupted the political system that it is making the government a market place where you can buy a law, buy an amendment or a regulation. The bigger your pay-off the more certain your buy.

An example is the United States Sugar Corp. which gives generously to both parties. The result makes it beneficiary of huge government handout programs that leave U.S. consumers paying twice the world price for sugar. Likewise, the giant Archer Dainiels Midlands Co., "super market to the world," is the top recipient of corporate welfare, funded by taxpayers. No wonder that ADM sold a Florida condominium to Elizabeth Dole for a bargain. Do you wonder why husband, Bob, protects the ADM tax-funded subsidies?

As proof that in this corrupted system there are no permanent friends and no permanent enemies, just permanent interests, the Republican and Democratic parties now are largely corporation-funded, even by the same corporation. Fifty-nine double-donors have given each party at least $100,000 since 1991.

Playing both sides are four giants who make each party's list of the top 10 soft money givers. These are Archer Dainiels Midlands, oil conglomerate ARCO, Lindner's American Financial Corp., and alcohol giant Joseph Seagram and Sons.

Underlining the system are two multi-millionaire sugar barons, Cuban refugee brothers. Alfonso Fanjul backs President Clinton, and brother José is a key fund-raiser for Bob Dole. But these Fanjuls, who have contributed hundreds and thousands of soft money to Republicans and Democrats, won't be able to vote for their presidential favorites. You see, they're not U.S. citizens and don't pay taxes.

Despite all these realities, congressional Republicans continue to vote against campaign finance reform.

P.S. Try not to be cynical.

July 16, 1979

If you want to enjoy soft living, go along comfortably in sort of a rut and retire early with a fat pension, then get a federal government job and become a bureaucrat.

This might seem like a strong statement, but there are plenty of facts to back it up.

Since 1970, there has been a 97 percent increase in federal personnel costs. Military pay and benefits have increased 43 percent in eight years, according to the Library of Congress. And U.W. Chamber of Commerce says the average yearly pay for a federal civilian employee in 1977 was $16,201, compared to $11,840 in the private sector.

About 17 percent of all federal blue-collar workers won increases up to 25 percent above local private wages in 1976. Wage increases are almost automatic and come twice a year. To keep pace with inflation, the raise granted last October added $23 weekly to the paycheck of the typical Washington-based federal employee. And since October, 1977, a beginning job at the management or professional level pays $26,022. In 1949 it was $7,600.

The New York *Times* says, "Washington, once considered Sleepy Hollow on the Potomac, has become a boom town for luxury buyers and sellers. And the reason is simple: money, and lots of it." This lush market has brought the most expensive stores and restaurants to the area. And all that monthly civilian Federal payroll in Washington of more than $600 million had produced a standard of living 30 percent higher than the national average.

Then there's lack of control of overtime pay. The Pentagon, also known as the "Defense" Department, which is the federal government's largest employer with 1 million civilian employees, 2,049,000 military personnel, and 2,050,000 it pays "outside the walls," spends about $400 million a year on overtime. But the "funny" part is (this will kill your pocketbook!) that it couldn't tell Congress how many employees were collecting overtime pay or anything about what work they perform! The government's biggest employer, the Pentagon, just didn't know. After all, it's only money that's involved!

The military pension system is the most liberal and outlandish. It is costing taxpayers about $10.2 billion a year, and is expected to reach $35.7 billion before the year 2000. After 20 years service a retiree can get half pay, and 75 percent after 30 years, plus cheap medical costs and commissary privileges denied the average citizen.

The most discouraging fact about today's bureaucracy is how dead, uninvolved, and downright indifferent it is. The prevailing attitude is don't rock the boat or make any waves. One government agency head told the *Saturday Review* magazine, "I don't think I've seen a new idea since I've been here, not even a bad one."

But you know, this isn't funny. Certainly not when the bureaucratic monster we have created, which isn't working very well, is consuming your tax dollars that are steadily increasing as a continuing inflation eats them all away. No, there isn't anything funny about this at all.

January 21, 2001

Would that we could see ourselves as others see us.

Yes, it does take imagination to adequately do this, and imagination is a wonderfully effective entrée that can open many windows, enhancing one's awareness of the world around us.

All this was triggered for me when I read an e-mail communication from a relative in Australia. Most everyone has imagination to some extent, so let yours consider what a Zimbabwe (Rhodesia) politician advised the children of his country to study closely because it shows that election fraud is not only a Third-World phenomena. There it is:

Imagine that we read of an election occurring anywhere in the Third World in which the self-proclaimed winner was the son of the former prime minister (the senior Bush) who was himself the former head of that nation's secret police (CIA).

Imagine that the self-declared winner lost the popular vote but won anyway, based on some old colonial holdover (Electoral College) from the nation's pre-democracy past.

Imagine that the self-declared winner's victory turned on the disputed vote in a province (Florida) governed by his brother (Jeb Bush).

Imagine that the poorly drafted ballots of one district, a district heavily favoring the self-declared winner's opponent, led thousands of voters to inadvertently vote for the wrong candidate.

Imagine that members of the nation's most-despised caste, fearing for their lives and livelihood, turned out in record numbers to vote in near universal opposition to the self-declared winner's candidacy.

Imagine that hundreds of the most-despised caste were intercepted on their way to the polls by state police operating under the authority of the self-declared winner's brother.

Imagine that six million people voted in the disputed province and the self-declared winner's lead was supposedly only 327 votes, fewer certainly than votes not counted and the county machines' margin of error.

Imagine that the self-declared winner and his political party opposed a careful by-hand inspection and recount of the ballots.

Imagine that the self-declared winner, himself a governor of a major province (Texas), had the worst human-rights record of any province in the nation and the most executions of any other province and virtually all countries of the world that execute their citizens.

Imagine that a major campaign promise of the self-declared winner was to appoint like-minded human rights violators to lifetime positions on the high court of the nation.

What would be your reaction reading this about some strange country elsewhere in the world? Would you think it another pitifully sad tale of an undemocratic country suppressing the rights of its citizens?

Little imagination is needed to understand the significance of these views from abroad about our recent presidential election:

"America has succeeded in electing a dead man as senator of Missouri, but not a president. The failure of the 2000 presidential race tarnished the image of a model democracy fiercely proud of its institutions and loyal to its Constitution," said *Liberation*, Paris, France.

"The foremost world democracy misfired...A doubt was cast upon the most sacred document, the U.S. Constitution," said *Izvestia*, Moscow, Russia. This article cited the lively debate among Russians as to who would be better for Russia, Bush or Gore, and that everybody in Russia was rooting for Bush.

"For a considerably long time, the United States has projected itself to the rest of the world as the beacon of democratic elections and orderly transition. Malpractice, irregularities, deception, unfairness and fraud are steamy clouds beneath which election results in other countries outside the west lay hidden…Yet virtually every one of those lurid epithets has been applied in the state of Florida, ironically, the home of Mickey Mouse," said *The News*, Lagos, Nigeria.

"The scuffle over votes in Florida and the difficulty in choosing a president, as *La Republica* of Rome said so clearly, is proving devastating to the principle of legitimacy based on reciprocal recognition that electoral results are a numerical approximation of the national will," said *Clarin*, Buenos Aires, Argentina.

There are dozens of other similar commentaries from newspapers around the world, including many cartoons poking fun at Florida and the American electoral process and election results.

Finally, from U.S. Supreme Court Justice John Paul Stevens: "Although we may never know with complete certainty the identity of the winner of this year's presidential election, the identity of the loser is perfectly clear. It is the nation's confidence in the judge (and courts) as an impartial guardian of the rule of law."

Think about it.

PART III

Equality in Economic Opportunity

CHAPTER 8

Big Oil Rules

Simon's column of December 24, 1979, serves to remind us of the ubiquitous power of oil as a corporate player in forging and perpetuating that increasingly extreme and dangerous cleavage between top and bottom of economic opportunity and realization so strongly characterizing America through and in the aftermath of the Reagan years, what Kevin Phillips termed "that second Gilded Age."[6] The column serves as a footnote commentary on what Philips described in 1990 as "the new political economics, intensifying inequality and pain for the poor, the unprecedented growth of upper-bracket wealth, the surprisingly related growth of federal debt, global economic realignment, foreigners gobbling up large chunks of America, the meaninglessness of being a millionaire in an era with nearly a hundred thousand 'decamillionaires.'"[7] Indeed, if Phillips' almost-20-year-old formulation of American political economics sounds more than ever accurate of America at the end of the George W. years, so even more does Simon's almost-30-year-old alert to the menace of big oil power. (In reading this column note Simon's fondness for gentle satire and his strong reliance on generalization from verifiable facts, including statistics. And, no, that "dollar gas" is not a misprint!) Of course we are today familiar with an even more astronomically incomprehensible soaring of those oil profits subsequent to the giveaways of Bush, Cheney, Inc. So, also, are we familiar with flourishing Bush administration and corporate culture creations of alternate "realities" through lies and evasions. In his column of April 15, 2001, Simon focuses on the self-interested practice of this propaganda by Big Oil.

---

6. Kevin Phillips, *The Politics of the Rich and Poor*, New York: Random House, 1990, p.xviii.

7. *Ibid.*, xxii.

December 24, 1979

Here we go again!

OPEC: the oil-producing sock-it-to-'em-frequently nations have again kicked off another round of price increases. Only this time it's a sort of free-for-all: any nation can charge whatever it wants.

This is all the "encouragement" Big Oil in this country needs for jacking up those prices at the pump. (That's our supporting role... pay for it!) The facts indicated it's not difficult for our patriotic oil companies to substantially further increase their profits in the process, and still use OPEC as the excuse.

One doesn't need to be a genius to figure out what happens to profits on domestically produced oil and that coming down the Alaskan pipeline that was supposed to solve all our oil problems: at least that was the story when the pitch was made for the pipeline. You see, none of this domestic oil is controlled by OPEC prices, and yet the way those prices go up at the pump you'd think it all came from OPEC instead of just a portion—less than half. Just look at what's happened to oil company profits since OPEC started socking it to us... with the apparent cooperation of Big Oil. Come to think of it, guess the oil companies had to put out money for bigger adding machines with enough digits to handle the swelling profit figures.

One of the major problems for citizens today is figuring out the truth about energy issues, especially oil and gasoline prices. We're bombarded with TV and radio commercials, newspaper and magazine ads, news interviews with business executives, all giving the oil companies' version of the "facts," and all paid for with the money we spend on gasoline, fuel oil and natural gas to heat our homes.

It's my belief that most Americans recognize this one-sided, self-serving oil company propaganda as being far from the truth. Just because the oil industry's message is repeated constantly and expensively does not make it any truer.

The polls show that Americans of all philosophies know that rapidly rising energy prices mean much more profit for the oil companies with little or no new energy or other benefits to the public. And I like to think that Americans see the drastic cost increases in fuel oil, gasoline and natural gas as a major cause of the inflation that is hurting every American family and devastating too many of them.

Meanwhile, Big Oil and the energy companies are prospering more than ever, declaring profit percentage increases in the hundreds, using their windfall profits to buy other corporations, and in many cases actually producing less oil and gas. Just like the Arabian oil sheiks, they're trying to find places to put their excess money. Examples: Mobil spent $800 million to buy Montgomery Ward. And Exxon just paid more than a billion dollars for an electric motor company. Do you know where that money came from? It came from you and me.

The earnings and growing financial power of the oil companies were indicated by Rep. Charles Vanik (D-Ohio), a ranking member of the House Ways and Means Committee. In 1976, before the companies really became flush with profits, 19 of them paid about $3.3 billion in U.S. federal taxes on a worldwide income of $27 billion: that's only a 12.2 percent tax rate, far less than most of us pay the government: Deducting that $3.3 billion and $12.2 billion in foreign taxes, those 19 companies had about $11.5 billion remaining at the end of 1976 for distribution to stockholders or new investment... tidy sum! And remember that $12.2 billion paid in so-called "taxes" to foreign governments was largely royalty payments labeled as taxation.

The point is that the after-tax income of 19 American oil companies in 1976, which was a cool $11.5 billion, clearly indicates that the industry has sufficient resources to maintain a strong research and development program for additional sources. And the tax advantages for the oil companies existing in the law, which is patently unfair to the rest of American industry and especially to the taxpaying consumer, shows that the oil companies are creating capital to an extent grossly disproportionate to all other sectors of our economy... and they're basically doing it at the expense of the guy at the pump; that's you and me. Who's covering our losses and our increased costs? Where and how do we inch up our prices every time OPEC and the oil companies want more billions?

Seems to me it's about time for President Carter and Congress to stand up to the oil interests. Maybe it's about time for the people to blow the whistle on this.

Anyway, whether it's dollar gas or no gas, Merry Christmas tomorrow! May it be a good one for you and yours.

April 15, 2001

After carefully assessing all available facts about what the Bush administration has already done and intends to do to our environment and wellbeing, the conclusion becomes unavoidable that there are people in Washington and the White House who are losing it.

If they aren't losing their senses, then is it subservience to Big Money

vested interests now dominating national policy with their greed for profits?

Never mind that polls have consistently documented the strong majority of Americans are deeply concerned about all aspects of their environment and want it to be better in every way. After all, this does involve
where we all live.

Here's the most recent example to back up the above. The White House
and its Senate leaders have made drilling in the Arctic Refuge the center-
piece of a new energy bill already introduced in cahoots with the powerful
oil lobby that is waging a well-orchestrated campaign to push it through.

Consider the composition of the President's Energy Transition Advi-
sory Team involved in all this with its 63 officials who just happen to have
contributed $8 million to the Bush campaign. (Payback time?) Dominat-
ing them are 27 representatives from Big Oil and Gas, and another 23 big
wheels from major coal, nuclear and other energy suppliers. This is the
crowd putting out the bum dope that drilling in the Arctic Refuge will be
a cure-all for America's admitted energy problems.

This claim is completely misleading and flat-out wrong. Credible experts, backed by the U.S. Geological Survey, estimate the Arctic Refuge
has only about 3.2 billion barrels of economically recoverable crude oil.
That is less than our country consumes in six months. Wrecking a national
treasure and the crown jewel of America's remaining wilderness, a unique
19 million-acre environmental cathedral where mountains meet the sea,
for only six months of oil is obscene, stupid, and it's un-American, too.

Even over its estimated 50-year lifetime, it would provide less than one
percent of the oil we consume. All this is enough to make Teddy Roosevelt,
our most environmental president, turn over in his grave. And he was a
Republican, too—back before the mutations set in resulting in the current crop of bought-and-paid-for congressional extremists now pushing
the GOP out of the mainstream.

Is it surprising even conservative analysts like Marshall Whittmann
of the Hudson Institute are warning that administration actions are leaving the president and right-wing Republican congressmen vulnerable to
charges the GOP is controlled by and beholden to Big Business and likely
to pay a price for this in the 2002 elections?

Contrary to Big Oil propaganda about boosting energy supplies and
lowering gas prices, Arctic Refuge oil would take at lest 10 years to begin
reaching West Coast refineries and, even at peak production of 150 million barrels, will have no impact whatsoever on gasoline prices which are
determined by overall global supplies. And Big Oil knows this.

A lot of hogwash has been dished out that new technologies make oil development possible without harming the environment. That's what Big Oil told us before going into Prudhoe Bay on the North Slope west of the Arctic Refuge. Instead it has turned a thousand square miles of once-pristine wildlife habitat into an industrial wasteland that produces twice as much nitrogen oxide air pollution as does Washington, D. C. –almost as bad as Houston, Texas, that became America's most polluted city while Bush was governor. Prudhoe produces a thousand tons of drilling waste per well and some 400 spills each year of crude oil, diesel fuel, acid, and other hazardous materials.

Big Oil propaganda, echoed by its congressional lackeys, claims oil drilling would be confined to only 2,000 acres. But they don't tell us these would be spread across far-flung sites requiring construction of roads, pipelines and processing facilities extending over hundreds of square miles of fragile land at the biological heart of America's most important nursery for numerous Arctic wildlife.

Why isn't the Bush administration smart and honest enough to acknowledge these truths:

- Improving the quality and reducing the friction of replacement tires to match those that come standard with new cars would save 5.4 billion barrels of oil over the next 50 years, which is 70 percent more oil than can be economically taken from the Arctic Refuge over the same period.

- By simply increasing average fuel efficiency of new cars, S.U.V.'s and light trucks from 24 to 39 miles per gallon over the next decade—which can be done—we would save 51 billion barrels of oil, which is 15 times more oil than the likely yield of all Arctic drilling.

- Investing in energy-efficient lighting, heating, air conditioning, and process control systems would substantially increase available energy and make oil from the Arctic Refuge look like peanuts.

Are we going to let all this go down the drain and sacrifice the price-less Arctic Refuge for the passing profits of a few oil titans who currently have oilmen Bush and Cheney in their hip pockets? To do so would be a slap in the face to the majority of Americans, of all political parties.

CHAPTER 9

"The Rich Get Richer and the Poor Get Babies"

Toward the end of his 1990 The Politics of Rich and Poor, *Kevin Phillips wrote, "By the time of Bush's inauguration in January 1989 the triumph of Upper America was both complete and precarious—precarious because its success was becoming so obvious."[8] In his column of November 20, 1995, Simon documented details of what was obvious. By the time he wrote for April 29, 1996, arguing for an increase in the minimum wage, the emergence of two economies in America—that of the minority rich and that of the majority poor, ever nibbling away the middle class—had become increasingly apparent. As Carol MacLennan's essay, "Cost-Benefit Analysis and U.S. Democracy" made clear, the American majority was to be increasingly held out of the loop of decision-making: "Democratic influence is increasingly barred from two of the most important sources of power that affect American life: technology and the global corporation."[9] Simon's April 2, 2002 "Opinion" challenged the "economic recovery" announced by a Bush administration preparing to export American armies to "spread freedom and democracy" around the world, what would prove to become a tragic confirmation of Noam Chomsky's contention that "freedom without opportunity is a devil's gift."[10] Writing for October 2, 1995, Simon scorned the "trickle down" theory, as mythical as the fisherman's flounder.*

---

8.   Kevin Phillips, *The Politics of Rich and Poor*, New York: Random House, 1990, p. 210.

9.   Carol MacLennan, "Cost-Benefit Analysis and US Democracy," in *Meanings of the Market—The Free Market in Western Culture*, James G. Carrier, ed., Oxford: Berg, 1997, p. 221.

10. Noam Chomsky, *Profit over People*, New York: Seven Stories Press, 1999, p. 91 (excerpted from the annual Davie Memorial Lecture delivered at the University of Cape Town, South Africa, May, 1997).

November 20, 1995

It's not only getting tiresome to report this, but downright disgusting, because income in our country is increasingly redistributed to the rich. It should be a national embarrassment because it can greatly harm America's health.

The building blocks of a decent future for millions of our citizens are being destroyed by congressional action, as our country's leadership proves we have a greed surplus and a justice deficit.

In the forefront of this is the GOP leadership. It makes one feel like intelligent Romans undoubtedly felt as Nero fiddled while Rome burned.

There's a veritable array of documentation to back up this depressing assessment. Here are just a few examples:

- Millions of Americans work longer, harder and more productively, as they become poorer, in the world's richest nation. From 1988 to 1993, worker productivity in the private sector increased 5.9 percent, while average hourly earnings declined by 4 percent during the same time. By 1993, the typical family lost $1,400 of the buying power it had in 1991.

- Worker's average inflation-adjusted weekly earnings plunged 6 percent between 1973 and 1993, which put them below 1967 levels. The Economic Policy Institute reports that since 1990, college graduates have been losing ground at the same rate as workers with less education.

- Among the reasons is that jobs, wages and salaries are being downsized in the leaner, meaner world of global corporate restructuring. Corporations are aggressively automating amid their merger-madness as they shift operations without regard for people, between cities, states and nations in a continual search for lower taxes, bigger public subsidies (at taxpayer expense) and cheaper labor. The Third World and eastern European countries already have proven that cheap labor does not mean low-skilled labor.

- Profits of Fortune 500 corporations jumped 54 percent in 1994. Wealth is not trickling down because it is flooding upwards. *Business Week* magazine reported the average chief executive of a major corporation earned 149 times more than his or her workers in 1993, and it has risen since then. In 1960, it was 41 times more.

- This helped make the United States No. 1 in inequality among industrial nations. One out of four children is born into poverty in the world's wealthiest nation. The richest 1 percent of American families have nearly as much wealth as the bottom 95 percent. This inequality smacks more of an oligarchy than democracy.

- If the House GOP spending reductions are fully implemented, the poorest fifth of families with children would lose $15,521 in 1996 government benefits, 11 percent of their income. The poor would fall further behind on the tax side, too. Poor people aren't going to benefit from GOP's capital gains tax cut. And about a third of all children live in families with incomes too low to pay federal income taxes, which makes them ineligible for the Republicans' vaunted tax credit of $500 for every child. Also, 10 million low-income families would lose some or all of their earned income tax refunds.

- Half of the individual tax breaks passed by the Republican-controlled House will go to those making more than $100,000 a year, and the upper 1 percent will get more in tax breaks than the bottom 60 percent; for the lower middle class there will be virtually no tax reductions. By contrast, 20 percent of United States families with income in excess of $79,056 will receive by the end of this decade more than 60 percent of the tax relief under GOP plans.

- The Children's Defense Fund reports that current Senate legislation would cause the number of children in poverty to increase by 11 percent, boosting the poverty rate in America from 14.5 percent to 16.1 percent. The biggest increases in poverty are occurring among young white families headed by married couples who are high school graduates.

- Meanwhile, billions of tax dollars for corporate subsidies and welfare continue untouched, with billions more for corporate tax credits. And the GOP-controlled Senate and House voted $17 billion and $9 billion more, respectively, for armaments and the military than even the Pentagon requested in its 1996 "defense" budget.

As to the corporate downtrodden the GOP is protecting, the nonpartisan General Accounting Office reports that 37 percent of large U.S.-controlled multinational corporations, with assets more than $100 million, did not pay a single dollar in federal taxes in 1991. And the GOP Congress socks it to the little guy, the poor, elderly and children.

It's a sickeningly obscene situation. The well-being of our country cries for an updated Economic Bill of Rights—before it's too late.

April 29, 1996

It seems rational to say that anybody who works a 40-hour week should have a wage providing enough money for them to live on. It's difficult to imagine any fair-minded, intelligent person who would disagree with this.

With Republicans in Congress touting the importance of ending welfare dependency and getting poor families off welfare, one would think the GOP leadership would be gung-ho for raising the minimum wage to be consistent with their position.

Instead, they are dead-set against raising the minimum wage from $4.25 an hour to the $5.15 as President Clinton proposed. When the minimum-wage issue was raised in the House, the GOP leadership took measures to block it. And over in the Senate, Majority Leader Bob Dole used his 35-year knowledge of the legislative process to block even any negotiation of a bill he is unwilling to debate. When Senate Democrats tried to force votes on minimum wage and Social Security, Dole pulled bills to avert a vote. He didn't want representatives of the American people to register their opinions. Is this democracy and a willingness to make the hard choice? Is this the kind of leadership we would get from a President Dole?

To their credit, 20 moderate House Republicans broke ranks and agreed to a $1 minimum wage increase to $5.25 an hour, 10 cents above the Clinton proposal. None of these moderates was among the Gingrich Storm Troopers.

April 1 wasn't April Fools Day when it marked the fifth year since the last federal minimum wage increase. There have been 17 increases in the 58 years since 1938, and not one caused any long-term economic pain.

During the last five years, with no minimum wage increases, congressmen have three times voted themselves raises making $41,000 a year, so they now make $133,600 yearly, without counting the extra perks. Every

16 days, a congressman gets more money in pay than an average working American makes in an entire year.

The GOP suggestion that most minimum-wage workers are teenagers flipping hamburgers is a lot of baloney. The reality is that 47 percent are older than 25, two-thirds are adult, and four in 10 minimum-wage workers are the sole bread winners in their families. Could you support your family on $4.25 an hour, which is 30 percent below the poverty level for a family of three? It also is highly questionable that "there are going to be a lot of young people who lose their jobs," as the all-but-anointed Republican presidential candidate recently said in opposing a minimum-wage increase.

The best known study on this was conducted by two Princeton University professors, David Card and Alan Krueger, who surveyed 331 fast-food restaurants in New Jersey when that state raised its minimum wage by 80 cents to $5.05 an hour in 1992. Ten other states already have minimum wages above the federal level: Alaska, Connecticut, Delaware, Hawaii, Iowa, Massachusetts, Oregon, Rhode Island, Vermont, Washington, along with the District of Columbia.

The Princeton study showed that even after the restaurants gave the 19 percent increase to their minimum-wage workers, the higher minimum wage did not cause a drop in the restaurant's number of employees.

Another authoritative study just released documents that the pay of chief executives of United States corporations, with stock options included, soared 311 percent in 1995. This was the highest jump in a decade and put the CEO's medium pay at $5 million annually. Of course, many of these are contributing heavily to GOP congressmen and support their position opposing any increase in minimum wage.

A higher minimum wage, which even at the administration's proposed $5.15 an hour is well below the official poverty level for a family of three, would at least be a step in the right direction of lessening the growing gap between rich and poor in America, which is worst among industrial democracies and a national embarrassment. It might even be a way of lifting all boats, and not just the yachts.

With the wage gap growing as a public issue, and three-fourths of Americans supporting an increase in the minimum wage, it is incredible that the Republican congressional leadership is adamantly opposed to any minimum-wage increase. Or do those lush "contributions" from the big boys mean that much to them?

April 13, 2002

Something doesn't jibe, as the big money media begins to declare an economic recovery based on indicators. Maybe an apt label would be: There's more to unemployment figures than meets the eye.

Yes, the question is real because those indicators have little meaning for average working people. No proof exists the so-called recovery signs will be meaningful to average workers. In fact, the reality of recovery declarations shows a callous disregard of America's little people.

Ironically, as big media parrot the line we're into an economic recovery, along comes the collapse of Kmart and its announced intention to drop 20,000 of its workers.

If there's actually an economic recovery going on, try telling that to the 650 Silver City-area mineworkers laid off by Phelps Dodge Corp. Or try convincing the tens of thousands of people knocked out of their jobs because of mergers and downsizing after giving the best years of their lives to the companies now casting them aside.

Most recent unemployment figures for February put the official rate at 5.5 percent. This translates to 7.9 million people who have no jobs. Try telling these unemployed workers there's an economic recovery.

As Paul Harvey would say, here's the rest of the story, as reported by the Labor Department's Bureau of Labor Statistics: beyond these 7.9 million unemployed, there are 4.4 million American workers who are not counted in the official unemployment figures. You could call these disappeared workers who have become discouraged but want and need jobs. They have given up for a variety of often economic reasons, including transportation problems and children's day-care necessities if parents work.

There are also another 4.4 million people who are working only part time but who want and need full-time jobs that are not available. None of these are counted as unemployed.

Beyond all these are 9.2 million officially self-employed workers, who understandably are often working only sporadically. And this work can often be something of a feast-and-famine existence.

Apart from this total of nearly 26 million workers who are unemployed or are just scraping by, there are 7.3 million workers, as reported this past February, who are multiple job-holders out of necessity. These 7.3 million people can't make a go of it without working more than one job. It is startling that just one year ago there were less than 4 million American workers holding more than one job. This is nearly a doubling in one year.

Do you think these multiple-job, hard-working Americans believe there isn't a recession going on or that we're having an economic recovery?

The reality of many millions of unemployed and underemployed workers seems to indicate an over-supply in the labor market, with its resulting downward pressure on wages and benefits.

As with the growing gap between rich and poor in America, it also indicates the chasm existing between ordinary working Americans and those encased in their own little world of privilege, as they question if any recession even existed. So is it surprising such people have a callous disregard for the plight of the working people and their struggles? This contrast is emphasized when the establishment media proclaims recovery from recession amidst the unrelenting human suffering from unemployment and the struggle to make a go of it because of inadequate income.

Celebrating economic recovery before any significant drop in unemployment is registered makes for a glaring contrast between the haves and the have-nots in our country.

The unawareness at the upper end makes for a scary blindness that spells danger ahead. Meanwhile, the so-called signs of recovery contain no evidence it will mean anything of significance to the majority of American workers and the little people of our country.

One need not be a genius to understand what all this portends for the wellbeing, health and future of our society. This reminds of an apt saying: "Would that the blind could see."

It becomes even more distressing when contemplating the dominance of big money, big business and the ultra wealthy in the Bush administration. Such people seem insensitive and even oblivious to the dangerously growing wealth gap in America that bodes no good for our nation's genuine security.

As the title of the book written by Max Lerner long ago phrased the problem: *It's Later Than You Think.*

October 2, 1995

The magazine *Business Week* recently carried an upbeat article about the state of the nation's economy, labeling it "an economy that's just right." This assessment is buttressed by the fact production is way up, profits are soaring and executive pay is skyrocketing to all-time heights. *Business Week* enthused that "the economy should at least live contentedly well into 1996."

But wait a minute. Then why is job insecurity simultaneously so rampant among American workers, and why is there so much anxiety lingering just beneath the surface?

Secretary of Labor Robert Reich calls these workers the "anxious class." They are working harder and longer but no longer getting ahead. Their paychecks don't go up much, and far too many of those checks go down. Meanwhile, the cost of almost everything goes up and up, such as cars, college, medical bills, retirement and the children's braces. En route, this anxious class breathes a sigh of relief when they are spared in the latest round of layoffs from corporate downsizing and mergers but worry they might be next. And with good reason, as many companies with rising profits are laying off people anyway.

During the Reagan years, we heard a lot about "trickle down" that could be called an apologist argument about growing profits at the top somehow trickling down to the workers below. Is it strange that we rarely hear that argument today? A recent item in the San Jose (Calif.) *Mercury News* noted that "unlike past economic growth periods, many Americans cannot count on their employer's rising profits trickling into their paychecks."

Could this be part of the reason, as reported by Mark Shields of the Washington *Post* and TV panels, which starkly illustrates the workers' steadily declining share of their production: In 1960, the average pay after taxes for CEO's of the largest U.S. corporations was 12 times greater than the average wage of their workers. By 1974, it had risen to 35 times more than the average wage of those workers. Today it is 135 times greater and the highest in the industrial world.

With that kind of spread in the division of wealth produced, should we be surprised that after-tax income of the richest 1 percent of the nation equals the total wages of the bottom 40 percent? And that 40 percent includes the most productive workers in the world.

Another perspective: From 1983 to 1989 (the Reagan years), in a span of six years, the richest 500,000 American families increased their net wealth by $1.8 trillion. That increase was more than the entire net wealth of 55 million working class families, whose wealth declined during those years. Seems trickle down got frozen.

So here's a rather brutal incongruity that our political leaders and too many of us don't seem to be thinking about enough: Our nation has the wealth, the science, the technology, the energy, the brains to do virtually anything it wants to or has to do. Yet, it has sickening racial problems, a rampant drug crisis, horrible slums, shocking poverty that is growing, deteriorating cities, inadequate schools, overloaded hospitals, water unfit to drink in nearly a third of its cities and air so foul that it's almost choking some of the largest cities. And our endangered environment is more at risk than ever before because of recent congressional action.

Doesn't all this say loud and clear that both political parties have their priorities messed up and are not confronting the truly critical problems facing our nation? Have you heard any would-be presidential candidate say anything meaningful about these crucial realities threatening our country? None have. Jesse Jackson alone addressed some of them, but he hasn't declared as a presidential candidate for 1996.

Yes, it's a sad and dangerous commentary on the state of our country's leadership, and it underlines that those in power don't deserve to be there.

CHAPTER 10

A Rose by Any Other Name:
Globalization and Corporate Greed

While "globalization" and corporate greed were American realities long be-
fore the Supreme Court elected George W. Bush our president and before Osama
bin Laden assured W.'s "success" and his re-election, Bush's "War on Terrorism"
accelerated implementation of neo-conservative policies and temporarily jug-
gernauted most opposition out of their path. Writing for March 9, 2002, Simon
documented some of that acceleration. Earlier, on February 20, 1995, Simon
focused attention south of the border where corporate greed was taking aim at
the Zapatistas, in this case documenting a specific detail of what Noam Chomsky
generalized: "There are many factors driving global society towards a low-wage,
low-growth, high-profit future, with increasing polarization and social disin-
tegration. Another consequence is the fading of meaningful democratic processes
as decision making is vested in private institutions and the quasi-governmental
structures that are coalescing around them, what the Financial Times *calls a 'de*
facto world government' that operates in secret and without accountability."[11]
Again focusing on the specifics which speak most loudly, Simon wrote for March
17, 1997, on hunger and starvation in a world of plenty and greed, and for July
13, 2003, he wrote how that greed is perpetuated by the Bush/Cheney team.
Simon details the ultimate travesty of patriotism on March 16, 2003, detailing
the corporate profiting from the war, including lucrative grabs by Cheney and
cronies.

March 9, 2002

We're getting robbed, you and me and all of us ordinary taxpayers.
Even worse, we're paying those enabling the looting, our congressional

---

11. Noam Chomsky, "The Zapatista Uprising," in *Profit over People*, New York:
Seven Stories Press, 1999, p. 127.

"representatives" with ample administration acquiescence. Sounds crazy, but it's true.

Shamefully, this looting of tax dollars from our country's treasury is going on under cover of the flag as the corporate perpetrators previously proclaim "United We Stand," while spouting their patriotism in fighting terrorism.

Meanwhile, the establishment media trumpets a jingoistic call for all Americans to rally round the flag, which in this instance, means supporting legislation legalizing the looting.

Disgustingly, the "skullduggery" of this greed-o-rama began within hours of the 9-11 attacks, and is continuing with a rush.

One columnist can only cover the tip of the iceberg, so here's part of the ongoing rip-off that has already surfaced, with many ties for first in the "me first" line. Bush's "economic stimulus" package is loaded with blatant corporate giveaways.

Boeing, America's largest aircraft maker, will reap extra millions after its attack force of 34 in-house lobbyists and 50-plus for hire, went after those big bucks they knew would flow from the war buildup. Example: The Pentagon's December appropriation bill requires the Air Force to lease 100 Boeing wide-body 767 commercial jets for use as refueling tankers. Price $20 million per jet per year for 10 years. That's $20 billion, far more costly than buying all of them. The Air Force must then spend another $3 billion of taxpayer money to convert the 100 planes to tankers. Then, after 10 years, taxpayers must pay another $3 billion to restore the planes for commercial use.

The Air Force doesn't even want these pricey planes, and there was not a hearing, not even a vote on them.

The entire deal was slipped into the Pentagon bill at the last minute, along with another bauble: a 10-year lease of four 737's for use as executive jets to ferry Pentagon brass and junketing congressmen hither and yon—in the name of national security.

Washington's most powerful lobby, the drug makers, with 625 registered lobbyists (90 more than total congressmen) spends about $100 million yearly to lobby for what they want. The big drug companies "invested" $26 million in the 2000 campaign and "gave" $625,000 to Bush's inaugural, and it paid off big. Bristol-Meyers, Eli Lilly, Pfizer, Squibb and Merck are part of the "nation's defense system," as Bristol-Meyers' CEO, Peter Dolan, boasted. Here's what they're doing in the name of national security: blocking generic drug companies from making less expensive versions, immunizing drug companies from lawsuits by Americans made sick or dead from using drugs sold to fight terrorism.

The drug bigs even want FDA rules waived that require drug testing, quality control standards, and notification of serious illness and injuries caused by their products—all in the fight against terrorism.

Within days of the 9-11 attacks, airline CEO's were in front of the grab line raking in the $15 billion bailout that, with White House backing, killed all provisions that allocated even a dime for any benefits to devastated families of the 140,000 laid-off workers. The bailout also assured top executives could continue collecting bloated salaries, which tax money spared the CEO's any personal sacrifice, as they whacked off workers and canceled their severance pay.

During the 2000 campaign, George W. thumped his chest declaring that he would end money-laundering run by global banks.

Then, his treasury secretary, the Paul O'Neill who bragged that Enron shows "the genius of capitalism," quietly cut a deal with the Cayman Islands that shields U.S. banks like Citigroup with secret accounts in the Caymans for their shady clients.

As a notorious haven for tax cheats, Cayman private banks have some $800 billion stashed for wealthy Americans, many of whom are patriotic flag-wavers.

Biotech giants, like Monsanto and Dupont, had their lobbyists hand Congress a ready-to-go demand list as part of Bush's $3 billion bill to "defend America against bio-terrorism."

Its provisions include limiting the industry's liability from any adverse effects of bioengineered products they make, and severely restricting the money courts may award to anyone who suffers or dies from their "biomedicines." It even requires us taxpayers to defend the companies in court and pay any judgments against them for injuries or deaths caused by products they sell under the label of battling bio-terrorism.

There are enough dozen of other examples of big corporations' grab bag under the guise of fighting terrorism to fill this page. Maybe these warrant another round because you're not getting the real story from the establishment media.

February 20, 1995

It is now evident that a war party is gathering in Wall Street led by Chase Manhattan Bank, one of the powerful bigs in American banking.

The Emerging Markets Group of this giant bank has billions at risk in Mexico. When the Mexican peso suddenly was devalued Dec. 20, that crash drastically shook the investor confidence behind those billions. It was this direct hit that got things moving at Chase.

The bank's "Political Update on Mexico," dated Jan. 13, bluntly states, "The government will need to eliminate the Zapatistas to demonstrate their effective control of the national territory and security policy."

Here we have a major U.S. bank urging another country (Mexico) to wipe out the Zapatistas, an indigenous rebel movement. Bluntly stated, that means to kill them. This is another reprehensible example of moneyed interests focused on their investments attempting to dictate policy of another country—even if it means killing that country's citizens.

Chase's Mexican memo continued: "While Chiapas (the poverty-stricken southern Mexican state), in our opinion, does not pose a fundamental threat to Mexican political stability, it is perceived to be so by many in the investment community." If the "investment community" perceives something to be, that's what is paramount, regardless of reality.

All this causes one to question if the fundamental consideration of the recent NAFTA agreement wasn't the security of foreign investors. Too many times in our history it has been the dollar that determined policy even if it meant eliminating obstacles, including humans. This is why we played ball for years with the ruthless dictators in Haiti so we could keep labor cheap and the country "safe" for foreign investors.

Author of the memo is Riodan Roett, now serving as a Chase advisor while on leave from his position as director of Latin American Studies at John Hopkins School of Advanced International Studies. While known as a conservative right-winger, Roett was considered a rather rational sort in academic circles.

What has embittered Roett is the hit he took when President Zedillo devalued the Mexican peso. Having known and worked with Zedillo for a decade, Roett assured Chase executives that Zedillo could be counted on to do the bidding of foreign investors. The bank substantially increased its Mexican investments, but then took a berating when huge trade deficits forced Zedillo to devalue the peso.

So now Roett wants Mexico to wipe out the Zapatistas. And this ties in with the stepped-up Mexican Army campaign against the indigenous rebels in Chiapas—with human rights violations and atrocities taking place.

The state of Chiapas is the poorest in Mexico and was exploited for decades. Illiteracy among adults is three times higher than the national average; 42 percent of the people dwell in housing without sewage; 35 percent are without electricity; social justice, democracy, schools, decent living conditions, human rights and freedom have not been the lot of the majority poor in Chiapas. And the peasant rebels there will not wait longer for the fruits of their 1910 revolution when Emiliano Zapata fought for the *compesinos* and gave them hope.

And why should they wait? Read these words: "The disheartened world of field work, the laborers whose sweat waters their disheartened state as well, cannot wait longer for their dignity to be recognized really and fully—a dignity no whit inferior to that of any other social sector."

Pope John Paul II, not known as a friend of rebels, said those words in an address to *compesinos* in Oaxaca and Chiapas on Jan. 29, 1979.

The U.S. government should be on the side of these struggling people if it is to be true to genuine American ideals and principles. Far too many times in our history we have lined up with the oppressors. It is time for our country to be on the right side, even if the big banks want it otherwise.

March 17, 1997

Most of us have heard or read about hunger in the world and there are many thousands of people, especially in Third World countries, who are starving to death.

Who hasn't seen TV news broadcasts showing those walking skeletons along the roads of Africa?

Millions more on every continent are suffering from severe malnutrition.

It's happening here, too, in the world's richest nation where more than one in every four children is raised in poverty and most have inadequate diets. Half a million are hungry enough to be on the brink of starvation.

This suggests there isn't enough food to go around. But this isn't true. There's enough food in our world, and collectively, we have the capacity to feed everyone.

So what is causing the starvation and hunger? It is because of a scarcity, but the scarcity is one of justice, humanitarianism and real democracy—with no scarcity of greed.

There are many examples. In Central America, where 80 percent of rural children are undernourished, and thousands of peasant children die without adequate care, half the cropland is used to grow coffee, bananas and sugar for urban consumers and for export, and to raise beef for fast-food chains in the United States.

Particularly in Brazil, there are cattle-growers knocking down rainforests for more pasture to raise more beef so they can sell it for hamburgers in the United States.

In the process, they uproot native people, and too many times the government backs them.

Even worse, evidence underlines the probability that the persons profiting from all this are strongly opposed to any democratic reforms and violently opposed—often paid thugs—to any of those leftists trying to give the little guy a fair shake.

It's happening in India, too, where millions go hungry, and farm workers survive by eating rats, while government soldiers stand guard over millions of tons of surplus grain awaiting export, for the profit of the few.

In sub-Saharan African countries another pattern is playing.

Even during bad years of drought and famine as thousands die of starvation, billions of dollars of locally grown beef and vegetables are shipped to European and North American markets.

To compound this ghastly problem, American government aid and World Bank assistance, along with much private charity, too often is funneled through the same corrupt and repressive regimes that are responsible and perpetuate the economic and social injustices that created the problem.

Just as a tool is only as good as the person using it, foreign aid only can be as good as the recipient government controlling it.

Unfortunately, the bulk of U.S. aid goes to only a few governments, of which too many are harshly opposed to reforms that would benefit the hungry and thus possibly endanger those governments' hold on power.

A peasant in El Salvador pinpointed it when he said that you will never understand violence and rebellion until you understand what happens to a parent who sees his children die of hunger. And he added this perspective: "When my children were ill from hunger, they died with a nod of sympathy from the landlord. But when the landlord's dogs were sick, he made me take them to the veterinarian."

Meanwhile, thousands of jobs in our country are being downsized to temporary and part-time so employers don't need to provide benefits or pay for full-time work.

Temporary agencies are the fastest growing businesses in America. Only 60 percent of U.S. workers are employed full-time, as documented by economists Bennett Harrison and Barry Bluestone in their book *The Great U-Turn*.

I wonder if any of this was included in what Ronald Reagan meant when he said, "It's morning in America"?

July 13, 2003

Those of you who are "well-fixed" enough to get some benefit from the Bush tax cut probably have stock portfolios, which could be helpful enabling you to cash-in on what Bush is doing mostly for those who don't really need help. Thus you probably are aware of the significant fact about the market's ups and downs: Every rally has been to lower high and then back to lower low.

If Bush gets all of his tax cuts—$364 billion over 10 years already pushing deficits sky-high—it will mostly go to the wealthiest Americans, and equal 1½ times the size of Department of Education budget and nearly nine times the size of Environmental Protection Agency budget. Both these realities tell something scary about the Bushies' skewed priorities.

Trying to bring the mass-mess of tax figures down to everyday understanding, households with incomes over $1 million will receive an average cut of $90,222. Taxpayers who earn $35,000 or less a year will get a $27 tax cut. Despite these facts, George II says his tax cuts "will help average Americans"!

In his State of the Union address early this year Bush said: "The way out of this recession, the way to create jobs, is to grow the economy by speeding up tax relief so people have more money to spend." Those 27 bucks will really help the little guy! But since the Bush tax cuts to help the economy, job loss has surged higher than ever and unemployment is at its highest level in nine years. Results are proving the opposite of Bush's claims, and he's on track for the worst unemployment record of any president since Herbert Hoover, the Republican in the White House during the 1929 stock market crash that brought on the Great Depression of the 1930's.

Meanwhile, the $5.6 trillion surplus Bush inherited from Clinton is rapidly becoming a $2 trillion growing deficit with every tax cut making it worse, and our nation's fiscal stability hanging in the balance.

Compounding potential pending disasters to our country from Bush policies is a continuing corporate crime wave showing no sign of slowing. The Boston *Globe* in May reported that "the FBI is opening three to five investigations a month of suspected fraud of $100 million or more by executives of publicly traded companies." These are the Big Money boys funding Bush campaigns.

Reactions from the White House and "reforms" in Congress remind of an old Indian proverb: "Big noise up the trail, nothing come down."

The SEC's anemic $1.4 billion settlement with Wall Street, compared to the many billions involved in fraud, was a slap on the wrist and insult to millions of small investors, pension holders and retirees who lost hundreds of billions in life savings.

It was this misleading information and phony corporate accounting supported by conflicted bankers, brokers and stock analysts who played the game that caused the rip-offs.

There's another major scam robbing the U.S. Treasury (us) of billions of tax dollars—and will force us taxpayers to pick up the bill because of bursting budget deficits. And this from the party that used to preach fiscal responsibility!

This tax dodging robbing our nation's treasury is corporate offshore tax havens. These allow U.S. corporations to move their headquarters offshore (usually to the Bermuda Triangle) by mere paper transactions.

The one redeeming aspect of Bush's shameful tax cut was a single decent provision that closed the disgraceful loophole costing our country billions of dollars in much needed revenue—but it was stripped behind closed doors at the last minute.

The patriotic draft-dodger who maneuvered this deal against our country's welfare was Vice President Cheney, who brokered the deal off-stage at a last minute closed House-Senate conference committee meeting.

Shafting us ordinary tax-paying citizens even more—during a time of much flag-waving (all these guys wear the flag in their lapels), is the fact these tax-avoiders continue to receive lucrative government contracts, and under the Bush regime without competitive bidding.

Another shameful scam now running rampant is excessive distribution of stock options to top corporate executives that has fueled an epidemic of fraud and abuse at major corporations.

The staid *Financial Times* reported the 209 executives from 25 largest U.S. corporations, who filed for bankruptcy between January 2001 and July 2002, walked away with gross pay packages of $3.3 billion, mostly from stock sold before their companies collapsed.

It is significant that virtually every corporate disaster in recent years had a stock option component.

And Warren Buffet, a renowned and decent investment group chairman, who despite his great wealth opposes eliminating inheritance and estate taxes, said: "We have seen more misdirected compensation in the last five years than in the previous 100."

Because these top executives set their own pay with rubber-stamp boards, they have a special conflict of interest to "cook the books" and manage their companies with shortsighted goals raising stock prices so they can cash out even if the company collapses beneath their greed. It is this that has caused loss of tens of thousands of jobs and ruined livelihoods of countless human beings.

All this is becoming an epidemic under the corporate-dominated regime of George II, with Vice President Cheney as USA CEO and power-behind-the-throne.

March 16, 2003

National Public Radio let the cat out of the bag. Even before it invades Iraq, the Bush White House is dealing out lucrative contracts to its Big Money corporate cronies to rebuild what it will further tear down in that already crippled country where 14 million humans (60% of Iraqis) barely survive like refugees on government provided food rations.

It's more payback time for big corporate campaign contributors already circling like vultures to cash in on Bush's war. And you-know-who will provide the bucks to fund those lush government contracts? It won't really be "government money" because the government hasn't any that doesn't come from us little taxpayers.

Senate Foreign Relations Chairman Richard Lugar (R-Ind.) is upset because this sneak deal was done behind Congress' back, especially since it is Congress that under our system must provide the money to fund both the war and reconstruction caused by that war. Bush's new allies like Latvia and Bulgaria won't be kicking in any money.

This latest end-run by the Bushies reminds again that to this administration and its corporate backers the bottom line on Iraq is the bottom line. There's money to be made from war and little things like logic, alliances, morality and even mass murder don't interfere with the single-minded pursuit of profit. Modern moralists would call this "situational ethics." That's a convenient code perfected by the Bush White House (or is it the Cheney White House?) that allows you to do what you want to do when you want to do it and still feel good about it the next morning—when the Bible might get read (but skipping the passage about "Blessed are the peacemakers").

Vice President Cheney's example aptly shows how you can have it both ways, cashing in both coming and going. When he was Defense Secretary during the Gulf War, Cheney presided over the pulverizing of Iraq's infrastructure, and okayed that slaughter on the now infamous Highway of Death when defenseless fleeing Iraqi soldiers were mowed down like rabbits by the tens of thousands. Then Cheney echoed the president's line when Bush I labeled Saddam "Hitler revisited."

When George I couldn't lick Clinton for the presidency, Cheney moved to the private sector and things suddenly warmed between him and Saddam. With Cheney as CEO of Halliburton Corporation—right after the rape of Kuwait, his company became Baghdad's biggest supplier and wrangled a $73 million contract to reconstruct Iraq's war-torn oil industry.

During the 2000 campaign, when Cheney was confronted about his chumminess with Baghdad and the huge profits he made working for Iraq, Cheney flatly denied it all. But the facts cry out so loud that you can't hear what Mr. Cheney says. When it comes to making a Buck, the Vice President had no qualms about doing business with the "Butcher of Baghdad" and "Hitler revisited." It worked very profitably for him, too. Oversee the destruction of a country and then make big profits rebuilding it.

This also reminds of Defense Secretary Donald Rumsfeld's cuddling overtures to Saddam back in 1983, despite gassing of the Iranians. Experts at rationalizing, the Bush people covered that with "the enemy of my enemy is my friend." (Temporarily at least.)

Another significant aspect of what might be termed "maneuvers for profit," is the fact that in 2000, just short months after pocketing his $34 million Halliburton retirement package and then joining the GOP ticket, Mr. Cheney was lobbying for an end to UN sanctions against Saddam. But that was then and this is now.

Halliburton, Enron and other corporate giants aren't alone in cashing in on war. Hewlett-Packard and Bechtel armed Saddam back in the 1980's— and UN inspectors are still looking for their stuff. Boeing, Lockheed-Martin, Hughes Electronics and Loral Space helped China acquire rockets and missile secrets—and some of these long-range nukes are pointed our way. Does that show you don't let patriotism interfere with profits?

Lest we forget, Cheney and his staff had secret meetings last October with Exxon-Mobil, Chevron-Texaco, Conoco-Phillips and also Halliburton, to decide who gets what from Iraqi oil. And the V.P. is still stonewalling about who attended those meetings dealing with the people's business that affects all Americans.

Yes, to the victor goes the spoils, or is it sp-oil-s?

CHAPTER 11

Smoke Screen

One of the most outrageous sagas of corporate greed and mendacity has been played out by the tobacco industry. On June 28, 1993, Simon reported on the subsidies long supporting that industry. By the time of Simon's column of May 12, 1997, the smoke screen propaganda the industry had for decades blown in our faces had been penetrated: they and their allies had been legally cornered by concerted legal action of 22 states' attorneys general. Writing on August 12, 2001, Simon decried the exporting of "our national tragedy" as the industry could no longer deny its long-time role as "merchant of death" to American tobacco users.

June 28, 1993

If there ever was a subsidized "private enterprise" on the dole, it is the tobacco industry. And if there ever were suckers for being had it is you and I.

To back this up, cigarettes cost the American economy more than $100 billion every year.

This translates to more than four bucks for every pack of cigarettes sold. That's a $4 per pack tobacco industry subsidy!

And this is on top of some $40 million doled out each year in direct governmental assistance to the tobacco industry—all paid by our taxes!

You and I, and all the non-smokers, are shelling out that $4 per pack subsidy in higher taxes to pay for unnecessary health care costs under Medicaid, Medicare, veterans' benefits, in higher health insurance costs because smokers require much more health care but usually pay no higher premiums, and in higher prices to cover increased costs due to smoking-induced permanent disability and absences from work.

Even if you include all the money collected from all cigarette excise taxes, the total is still only about 10 percent of the added costs smoking forces on us taxpayers.

The tobacco industry, of course, and many smokers are already hollering about the $2 per pack increase in the current federal cigarette tax being proposed by the Clinton administration.

Two bucks a pack may sound like a lot of tax increase but it's actually chicken feed compared to the crushing burden in health care and other spin-off costs the tobacco industry and smokers are imposing on all of us.

Further, it is a lot lower than the cigarette tax in virtually all major countries, and it is historically low even by U.S. standards.

For example, in Canada the tax is $3 per pack and Denmark nearly $4. In Germany, Great Britain, Sweden and Norway, the tax per pack is above $2.

Here in the U.S., percentage-wise the tax on a pack of cigarettes has actually been going down. In 1962, a tax of eight cents a pack was 30 percent of the total price.

In 1992, 30 years later, the per pack tax was only 11 percent of the price. Translated, this means those cigarette companies have really been socking it to you smokers!

As to state cigarette excise taxes in cents per pack, there are 18 states with a higher tax than Pennsylvania's 31 cents.

Tops is Massachusetts at 51 cents, and the District of Columbia and Hawaii tax a pack 50 cents. And guess which states tax a pack only a few pennies?

You're right, the tobacco-growing states of Virginia, Kentucky, North and South Carolina... as they and the federal government further subsidize the industry with taxpayer dollars.

Responsible studies have shown that a $2 per pack tax increase would likely cause about eight million smokers to quit.

But this would force two million of them to save their own lives!

It would also save tens of millions of dollars in health care costs every year, and undoubtedly reduce the need for higher taxes all along the line.

If more smokers had the guts and brains to kick the habit, it also would save a lot of lives—and not just their own.

About 435,000 human beings die every year because of smoking and another 96,000 die because of passive smoke exposure.

This compares to about 43,500 deaths caused by auto accidents, 105,000 deaths because of drinking, and murders causing 24,000 deaths yearly and smokers are way ahead of the cocaine, crack, heroin and morphine users who eliminate only about 4,450 of themselves every year!

It is also meaningful that the more education a person has the less likely that person is to be a smoker.

It is the same with income, as those who can least afford it irrationally smoke the most.

This all means that smoking in public could tag you as less educated with a lower income level. That's not very impressive!

So how do all of you, and especially you non-smokers, feel about being forced to continue subsidizing the tobacco industry to the tune of four U.S. dollars for every pack that goes up in smoke, and doing it with your tax money?

While you're thinking about this, be advised that kissing a smoker is like licking out a dirty old ashtray.

I tried it once, just once, long ago.

May 5, 1997

It couldn't happen to nicer guys!

That's what I thought as I read more about concessions tobacco companies are making in their collapsing position as they scramble to make the best deal possible.

You see, the legal and political scales that have long been heavily weighted in favor of cigarette makers began to tip the other way after the attorneys general of 22 states filed suit to recover monumental health costs caused by smoking. Seems that made the big boys reverse course as it sort of gave them religion.

After decades of deceiving Congress and the American people about the hard evidence that cigarettes kill people, after years of lying about it under oath and keeping the evidence hidden, the tobacco barons have moved from the bunker to the surrender table.

This is an industry that is ethically bankrupt and financially sound. But they're still probably laughing hysterically all the way to the bank, because when the possibility of a deal involving immunity hit Wall Street, tobacco company stock prices surged upward. Translated, this means a lot of American investors are willingly putting their money into something where the price tag includes human lives and death.

Fewer people were killed by atomic bombs that destroyed Hiroshima and Nagasaki than are killed each year in the U.S. by the tobacco companies and their cigarettes. These kill more people every year in our country than the total who die from murders, car wrecks, AIDS, disease and drugs of all kinds.

It has been amply documented and repeatedly confirmed by industry defectors, and the Liggett Co.—smallest of the Big 3, that recently jumped ship—that it is the intensely addictive quality of nicotine that puts such a stranglehold on smokers. That's how the cigarette companies reap their billions because nicotine keeps the customers coming back for more.

Is it any wonder that tobacco companies are feverishly opposed to nicotine being declared a drug? But it is a drug, pure and simple. People with their heads fastened on hope the Food and Drug Administration will so declare it.

Thus these shysters and hucksters of death-dealing products have the gall to pressure the Congress of the United States to pass a law granting them immunity from all their lousy deeds, past, present and future. The cigarette makers are pressuring for total absolution with an impenetrable legal shield against all lawsuits for all time! If our representatives grant that, they sure aren't representing us. But maybe the tobacco companies have enough bought-and-paid-for politicians in Congress to swing it for them.

This is the same outfit that sent a solemn assemblage of top executives before Congress to swear under oath that they did not believe tobacco and its nicotine was addictive. That ludicrous testimony earned the ridicule it deserved and convinced a lot of people these businesses and their executives respected neither facts nor fairness and don't give a damn about their fellow Americans. Fortunately, such testimony also created a public-relations disaster that the worst enemies of the tobacco barons could not have desired.

But there's a joker in the deck, and one can be justified in being pessimistic about our Congressmen plugging it. This is the reality that already the cigarette makers' growing profitability is coming from unregulated foreign markets where they freely advertise and lure new generations into nicotine dependence. Allowing the tobacco companies to continue this is abetting a crime against nations and peoples worldwide because it's killing people.

How can Congress ignore that?

August 12, 2001

There is a lot more to the tobacco story than what was reported in this column last week. And there are far-reaching implications from the Republican congressional leadership in effect being in Big Tobacco's hip pocket, as the record so decisively documents.

From the days when the extremely successful Marlboro Man advertising made multiple millions in profits for Philip Morris—even though the Marlboro Man rode off into the sunset and never returned because he died from lung cancer, the company's direction has become increasingly contradictory.

Many will remember when Big Tobacco never hid its cigarette lights under a bushel—and heads of the Big Five swore under oath before a congressional committee that smoking and tobacco are not addictive (I thought you went to jail for perjury).

More recently, we're aware of the excessive campaign to overhaul the image of Marlboro Man Inc. from corporate bad boy to a wonderful global citizen doing an array of good deeds everywhere for the environment, arts, AIDS, and humanity. The motto for all this is "Things are Changing," as designed to convince us there's no more big bad tobacco company causing people to reach the Pearly Gates ahead of schedule. But are the cigarette giants really changing, or is it more of the same under a different banner?

So from a stance that denied the deadly effects of smoking (which was like spitting into the wind), the tobacco giant has shifted overseas to an incredible position of in effect bragging about cigarettes killing people rather than denying they do! This is being justified by touting the financial benefits of smoking that outweigh the costs. And this is based on the grisly position of the "indirect positive effects" from early deaths!

In the process, with help from a friendly Bush administration, a nation that admirably committed itself to reducing death and disease worldwide, is wiping out that splendid American public health legacy by spreading worldwide our growing national tragedy from smoking. In the process, these merchants of death are dramatically underlining the tremendously urgent need for strong international controls on the marketing of tobacco products... before more than the four million people public health figures say will die from tobacco this year. If the present rate of increase continues, by 2025, 10 million people will be dying yearly because of smoking.

This lethal direction surfaced in the Czech Republic where Philip Morris took over the old state-run tobacco business and now sells 80 percent of what Czechs are smoking. With either morbid humor or a cynical and brazen disregard for human life, the Philip Morris Company is now bragging about the many "positive" economic effects of smoking. The main source of these supposed economic benefits comes from "health care cost savings due to early mortality." This was actually cited as the reason in the report commissioned by Philip Morris as done by the consulting firm Arthur D. Little International.

So now we have the spectacle of a cigarette company whose past strategy either denied or avoided any reference to the murderous aspects of its products, now trying to market as a good thing the lethality of cigarettes. Can this actually be the result of sane thinking by responsible human beings?

To put it bluntly, Big Tobacco is bragging about saving the Czech government millions in pensions and health care costs by bumping off a portion of its population!

As *The Wall Street Journal*, that stalwart friend of the working man, recently reported: "The premature demise of smokers saved the Czech government between 943 million koruna and 1.19 billion koruna ($23.8 million to $30.1 million) in health care, pensions and housing for the elderly in 1999."

The Journal also said, referring to the Philip Morris-commissioned report, that it "calculated those costs of smoking such as expense of caring for sick smokers and people made ill by second-hand smoke, as well as income taxes lost when smokers die." *The Journal* concluded that "weighing the costs and benefits, in 1999, the government had a net gain of $5.82 billion koruna ($147.1 million) from smoking." Just think of all the money smoking saved the Czech government! Tremendous!

No wonder a Czech public health specialist and opponent of smoking, Eva Kralikova, sarcastically suggested that under the Philip Morris-Czech government reasoning, "the best recommendation for the government would be to kill all people at the time of their retirement." Doing that would really save money.

And a British anti-smoking activist called doing this "an extermination program for the newly retired."

Or should we call this the Philip Morris plan for saving the safety net without bankrupting governments? Or maybe it's their budget cruncher!

Is this what the giant cigarette company means when it proclaims, "Working to make a difference" as it spreads our national tragedy everywhere? And the current Philip Morris motto is "Things are Changing."

PART IV

Defense of Individual Rights

CHAPTER 12

The Least of These

Accompanying the paradoxical success of modern medicine in extending life spans, and well before the first arrival of Baby Boomers had begun swelling the ranks of senior citizens, Simon had assumed his advocate's role for the elderly, here on September 10, 1979. Indeed, some of Simon's most impassioned criticism of the government is occasioned by policies which cause deprivation and suffering to the most vulnerable in our society and abroad. December 19, 1994 focused Simon's indignation on the waste of money in campaign coffers, money which should be feeding hungry children. Writing for April 20, 2003, he castigated Bush and the Republican Congress for pursuing a "homeland insecurity" policy which disregarded suffering of children and the poor, and he presciently predicted the disaster to which that policy has led us. Focusing on our urgently needed national health insurance, Simon on July 22, 2001, writing out of his accustomed ability to cut through the distracting flim-flam to the heart of the matter, castigated the Beltline brouhaha over "a 'Patients' Bill of Rights' without the right to health care." Finally, on November 30, 2002, Simon wrote to set the record straight on the Republican attempt to redefine "liberal" as a dirty word, Simon reminding us of the protections past liberals have provided for "the least of these" and all of us.

September 10, 1979

There is an American tragedy unfolding in how the world's most affluent nation cares for its elderly. This fact is doubly significant because the "elderly" are burgeoning in numbers.

There are now 22 million Americans 65 or older. In less than 30 years there will be 60 million, one of whom could be you. And this compares to the four million over-65 group back in 1900 when they represented only 4 percent of the population. That percent has almost tripled and is increasing rapidly as the younger age groups decline in numbers.

While most elderly Americans live independently, there are about a million who are spending their last days in nursing homes. Another million are forced to live in "geriatric boarding houses" or "hotels" for the elderly. These numbers are skyrocketing and will double or triple within 25 years. This means more and more families are making anguished searches for nursing homes, special residences or other homecare services.

Meanwhile, long-term care for the aged is fast becoming one of the biggest items on the country's health agenda. There are more patient beds in the nation's 22,500 nursing homes than in its hospitals. One third of the federal health budget is spent on the aged and 40 cents of each Medicaid dollar goes to nursing homes... and this figure is certain to increase with the oncoming tidal wave of people over 55.

A big problem is that care for the aged lies outside the mainstream of American medicine. The elderly are "modern" medicine's stepchild. Bur for a few notable exceptions, the medical profession has given comparatively little attention to diseases associated with aging. As a result, the quality of medical treatment in nursing homes has suffered.

The reprehensible part of all this is that brain disease, which accounts for 75 percent of institutionalized patients, is too often misdiagnosed and inadequately treated. An estimated 30 percent of the blank-faced men and women in our nursing homes and boarding houses have treatable dementia caused by anemia, poor nutrition, metabolic changes or simple depression that IS reversible—IF diagnosed and treated properly, which treatment they probably will never receive. And so doctors continue to diagnose arthritis and senility as "the price of old age."

It was against this background of desperate need that the great boom in nursing homes took off in the 1960's with the advent of federal aid. Since then, the nursing-home industry has gone from a $500 million business to one of $13 billion last year. The industry itself is dominated by enterprises run for profit. Yet the nurses and aides who work in nursing homes are among the lowest paid with the fewest benefits, and their turnover rate is high. Those were among the reasons that 9,000 nursing-home employees in New York City went on strike last year. Further, the fuel of federal funds through Medicare and Medicaid has given rise to abuses, profiteering and outright rip-offs.

So along the way when you reach an age arbitrarily set by insurance companies and bureaucrats, whether it be 62, 65 or 70, you will probably be forced to retire from a job you've held effectively for many years. Then you may discover that the pension fund into which you've contributed most of your savings is either bankrupt, or will pay you far less than you thought. And those Social Security payments are inadequate in our highly infla-tionary economy.

You'll also be stereotyped as outdated, slow, sexless, senile and unemployable. Thus the rest of society can avoid dealing with you as a person. If you are the one old person in 10 who will require extended care, the whole dehumanizing process will reach rock bottom for you in a nursing home or "retirement" hotel.

All this is why the Gray Panthers, founded in 1970, are leaders in an exciting movement with growing political effectiveness that has already been proven on a national scale with enough Congressional votes to raise the mandatory retirement age to 70 and to strengthen the Social Security system.

While the Gray Panthers are effectively concerned about nursing home reform, they are also translating their concerns about runaway inflation, forced retirement, the American pension system, public transportation, drug abuse and attitudes toward aging into effective action at the state and national level.

In Kansas City, they ran a workshop to inform state legislators about proposed nursing home reform bills they had drafted. In Massachusetts, local Gray Panthers won an increase in the Medicaid monthly personal needs allowance for nursing home residents. In California, Gray Panthers successfully fought to keep the state's largest nursing home open because relocation to another site would have endangered the lives of many of the residents. California Gray Panthers also pioneered in the long needed training of nurses' aides and other nonprofessional personnel in extended care facilities.

On the national level, they are working to bring out of committee a bill that puts teeth into the patients' rights section of the Medicaid program... which bill is strenuously opposed by the nursing home industry. The Gray Panthers also filed a lawsuit against the Department of Health, Education and Welfare to change regulations that drain the life savings of Medicaid patients' families causing extreme hardships and even death. And their political clout is showing in support for U.S. Representative Ronald Dellum's (D-Calif.) proposal for national medical-quality standards and emphasizes preventative health care.

So while you're thinking about all this, remember that aging happens to everyone.

December 19, 1994

When one thinks about the obscene amounts of money candidates spent in the recent elections and then realizes the desperate needs of people throughout the world and in our country, it makes one almost gag with the utter wastefulness of it all.

And what does it say about our priorities when self-interest political action committees can shovel out hundreds of thousands of dollars to, in effect, buy congressmen and senators so their vested interests will be protected by lawmakers who are supposed to represent the people?

At least the money-talks maxim didn't hold true for the two candidates who outspent all others. Michael Huffington in California got defeated in his U.S. Senate bid despite spending $27 million. And Oliver North couldn't con Virginia voters although he had a weak opponent and spent more than $12 billion in what had been considered a sure-thing run for the U.S. Senate.

With 15 million American children living in poverty, with millions of our citizens without basic medical care and with continuing acceleration of the poor getting poorer that began with a vengeance in the Reagan years, the examples are endless of what a difference money wisely used could make in the lives of so many of our fellow Americans. And what a difference those wasted political dollars could do for people around the world who are dying of hunger and disease by the millions.

A staggering current example of tremendous need is Haiti where, despite the naysayers, Clinton administration policy has freed a long-oppressed and brutalized people from their crushing yoke. At least Haitians can sleep now without being terrorized by killings, beatings, raping and stealing. But an almost impossible situation with nothing to build on has a long way to go until the future is secure.

The western hemisphere's poorest country, born of a slave revolt, during its 190 years of existence has experienced successive governments that have taxed, stolen, extorted and preyed upon its people. No wonder a Haitian scholar at Wesleyan University labeled his country "a predatory state that preys on the population at large."

Two-thirds of Haitians are illiterate and have been degraded for decades by grinding poverty, malnutrition, disease, violence, corruption, overpopulation, rapid urbanization, deforestation and serious soil erosion, all to an extent that survival is in doubt.

About 40 percent of the population has no access to safe water. Half the population is malnourished; 15 percent of the children die before they are 5, and curable diseases such as malaria and tuberculosis are widespread. Basic services such as roads, schools and water were not provided by Haiti's rapacious rulers. In fact, the only smoothly paved road in the country stretches a little more than a mile to the house of the capital's former police chief, where the macadam abruptly ends at his property line! And we let Lt. Co. Michel Francois, a killer, and his ruling cronies leave the country with their stolen millions, after they pillaged government offices of everything of value.

There are only six doctors per 200,000 people in Haiti, and there is only one maternity hospital in its capital, Port-Au-Prince, which has a population of two million. As with the few hospitals throughout Haiti, there is no running water or ambulances, and 80 percent of the hospital's equipment does not work.

Just let your imagination think about what those millions of dollars disgustingly blown away in our last election could do in situations such as those to which the Haitian people are subjected.

April 20, 2003

With the nation's attention riveted on the Iraq invasion, and eyes glazing over when those billions tossed around in Washington surface, we aren't focusing on a ticking time bomb with a shortening fuse here midst our growing homeland insecurity.

This reality is etched out in the administration's budget passed by the House. It belatedly reminds us that scant attention has been paid to the human consequences and costs to our homeland of Bush's war plans that have spent months and billions of dollars concentrating on Iraq and war.

The House budget plan already passed is a gruesome recipe for domestic disaster that slams the needy poor while giving unstintingly to the already rich. While giving the wealthy $1.4 trillion in tax cuts, it demands billions of dollars in deductions from programs that provide school lunches, food stamps, health care for the poor and disabled, veterans' benefits, student loans and even temporary assistance to needy families.

The non-partisan Center on Budget and Policy Priorities found that proposed cuts in child nutrition programs would eliminate school lunches for 2.4 million low-income children—who usually come to school hungry because there isn't enough food at home.

The Republican-engineered House plan mandates that $265 billion be cut from entitlement programs over 10 years, of which $165 billion would come from programs that assist low-income Americans who are hurting more than anytime since the Great Depression of the 1930's. This urgently growing need is spotlighted by reports from the nation's mayors that city shelters and soup kitchens are being overwhelmed with people in need like never before experienced.

The forced cuts in Medicaid would eliminate 13.6 million children if it were achieved by reducing the number of children covered. These are the poor and needy without coverage who have no other place to turn for medical help.

Cuts in foster care and adoption programs could reduce by 65,000 the number of abused and neglected children eligible for foster assistance programs. The destined food stamp cuts would reduce average benefits from an already lean 91 cents per meal to 84 cents. Can you imagine any of the millionaire plutocrats in Congress wading through a meal costing 84 cents?

These are just some of the cuts mandated by the GOP-controlled House budget bill that will hack and crimp vital services in education, health and welfare for needy deserving Americans.

And with all levels of government afflicted with growing deficits, more of the same is a dangerous inevitable if congressional leaders continue to compound the pain of further tax cuts for the rich, and even insist on restoring the president's tax cut and its runaway retrogressive budget so as to please a wartime president.

The downright idiotic nature of this cut-off-your-nose-to-spite-your-face national throat-cutting comes in focus when House majority leader, Tom DeLay (R-Tex.) blithely says, "Nothing is more important in the face of war than cutting taxes." What world is such a "leader" living in?

Are our government leaders actually incapable of understanding that part of the price of a costly war is giving up unnecessary luxuries like tax breaks for the very wealthy? And with the deficit already spiraling out of control, the burden of paying for the war and rebuilding Iraq could trigger mammoth national discontent as crucial needs in our country go begging.

Flat out, isn't there something downright obscene and dangerously stupid about a millionaires' club like the Senate proposing nearly trillion dollar tax cuts for the rich while their country already has cut and continues to cut urgently needed social programs, runs up huge and growing budget deficits, fights a money-eating war in the Middle East, and continues to spend $1.6 billion every month supposedly fighting the "war on terror"—as our war on Iraq makes even more "terrorists" that will require even more billions of tax-payer dollars to counteract? And while this dog chases its tail, human insecurity at home and abroad escalates and already constitutes a dangerous threat making any security threat from Saddam Hussein seem like chicken feed. Lest we forget, of many reasons, Bush went to war because of Saddam's "weapons of mass destruction" but we're still looking for them.

With the Bush people focused on war and getting bigger bangs for our bucks, scant attention is being paid to humanitarian consequences of their war. A leaked UN humanitarian-planning document outlines this. Two million internally displaced persons (one million already displaced); up to a half million civilians injured and killed; 600,000 to 1.5 million refugees fled to neighboring countries; 10 million Iraqis, including 5.2 million children under 5, pregnant women and women with infants, in immediate need of food and aid; growing public health crises including outbreaks of measles and epidemics such as cholera that follow loss of water and sewage systems.

If the Bush government doesn't have effective answers to these results of its military actions—and do better than it has in Afghanistan—then our country will be in deeper trouble than it already is, both here at home and all across the world where our beloved country is becoming feared and even hated. (You won't grasp these realities from a government flack like Fox News, but you will from unvarnished reports.)

July 22, 2001

Observing the windy baloney that has been going on in the U.S. Senate, where posturing lawmakers have been with straight faces debating whether the huge centers of corporate power that are HMO's should be immune from lawsuits, you would think the right to sue an HMO is the most important health-care issue in America.

This is an insult to the intelligence of any reasonably informed person with a modicum of sense about the issues. There isn't a poll anywhere that says Americans are clamoring for more courtroom tedium to cure what ails them. And those without health-care coverage don't have any insurance company to get frustrated at. Yes, lawsuits do not deliver health care. And it is difficult to believe any of us feel healthier because of bewildering piles of insurance paperwork that goes with our existing deeply flawed system.

Accentuating the phoniness is the fact that in no way is this debate about a "Patients' Bill of Rights." Actually it is a debate about a Patients' Bill for Rights for people who have medical insurance. This excludes a growing 44 million of us in America without any coverage, and even more of us who cannot afford the medicine we should be taking.

Despite this reality, pompous and posturing senators and congressmen are pontificating the issue as though everyone has health-care coverage, when more than 15 percent of Americans don't. And many of these lawmakers are on the receiving end of tons of money ladled out by HMO's they want to protect from legal accountability for actions that can harm Americans.

This gratuitous immunity from lawsuits flies in the face of the HMO power to do great harm to the sick people of our country. It's just plain un-American and yet Congress is striving to do this led by Republican leadership, the same leadership that just blatantly killed sorely needed campaign finance reform. We should hang our heads in shame, from the White House on down through both houses of congress.

Another major reprehensible phony is the bleating that HMO's will go broke from frivolous lawsuits if they don't have special exemption. Then how come, as reported by Families USA, the 25 highest-paid executives of the for-profit health plans raked in a collective $201 million last year. That $8 million-plus each isn't bad pay, and it does not include piles of unexercised stock options. Any congressman pushing that HMO poverty pitch should be disbarred from his money-collecting job.

The fan dance going on in Washington about being able to go to a lawyer when you get sick is en route to making a bad situation worse, as our "leaders" obviously fail to understand that profit-driven bureaucracies such as insurance companies don't deliver health care. And even a dummy knows that if these companies had their way only the healthy would get insurance, and as soon as you got unhealthy you'd be uninsured!

So why can't the people we support in Congress understand that private-sector profits have no place in a business as vitally important as the life and death of human beings. Flat-out market-place medicine has dismally failed to improve either health care or urgently needed coverage of the many who don't have it. The system is a bust and we're the only advanced nation in the world that's No. 1 in this monumental failure. It's a shame on America, the world's richest nation.

A friend who runs the excellent area asset that is historic Faywood Hot Springs hit it dead center with the astute observation that all of us would quickly get good health care if congressmen didn't have the excellent first-class coverage provided by our government and paid for by us taxpayers—with Vice President Cheney being a prime current example. So why do he and the others in government who bleat about "socialized medicine" make it so cruel and cumbersome for the rest of us to have their health-care coverage and what is a given in other advanced nations that have insurance programs covering everyone?

Further, has anyone ever heard any serviceman or military retiree complaining or clamoring to give it up? The U.S. government dispenses health care and medicine to 7.3 million military people, including those on active duty, their dependents and those retired after 20 years, and this "socialized medicine" is the best. Just ask Vice President Cheney. Our country, with its crazy-quilt costly current system, urgently needs nonprofit national health insurance so badly it can taste it. The simplicity of a single-payer plan would reduce the ultra-costly mishmash we now have, reduce excessive administrative overhead and expand coverage for all. Employee health insurance plans are eroding, premiums are soaring, and the number of Americans without any medical coverage is climbing toward 45 million.

So why can't all of us have the medical protection those in Congress, government and the military possess at our expense, and that our elected officials have been denying us? Meanwhile, the president and his Republican congressional leadership are pushing an exaggerated "Patients' Bill of Rights" that is a Bill of "Rights" without the right to health care.

November 30, 2002

After the dishonesty and distortions that mutilated the word "liberal" in the recent election, some factual clarification is much needed.

The fact that negative political attack advertising, such as that spewed out for the Pearce congressional campaign, went overboard with its anti-liberalism attests to "success" (up to now) of rightwing extremists in smearing liberals and making liberalism a supposedly bad word.

The effort to do this originated in the Reagan era and has been pushed by Big Money special interests and their congressional lackeys every since. The irony of all this is its underlining the dearth of understanding of what liberalism actually is and also how many voters have been hoodwinked. It also says loud and clear that the establishment media has mostly fallen on its face in conveying the realities involved.

Any honest study of the record over the years emphasizes the tremendous significance of what liberal philosophy and liberal legislation has done to make America a better country and give its citizens a better life than they had before. And in many instances such as the Great Depression of the 1930's, it made the difference between our country winning or losing at an extremely crucial time of its history.

It's a contemptible irony that so many people today are apparently bashing liberals while benefiting from the salvation of Social Security that liberals got for them during the FDR years. And notice how the anti-liberal crowd are doing their knocking on the way to the bank to deposit their Social Security checks in accounts protected by federal insurance established by liberal legislation after bank failures of the Great Depression wiped out life savings for millions of Americans and ruined many small businesses across the land.

Lest we forget, it was the Republican Party in the 1930's that strenuously fought to kill the Social Security legislation that today is keeping millions of Americans away from poverty. Millions of other Americans, including young children, would still be working 12-hour days without any benefits or protections if it weren't for the success of liberals who wanted something better for their country and its people.

History documents liberal achievements needing many columns to cover. A smattering of these accomplishments include protecting the water Americans drink and the air they breathe; preventing our country's resources from being desecrated by the greed of exploitation that sees no tomorrow; preserving rapidly disappearing great places of America for benefit of all Americans and future generations; having workplaces with enough safety to protect us; being able to enjoy national parks and recreation areas; and without Medicare and Medicaid that liberals got for us when Johnson was president, how would millions of Americans get medical care when they needed it? And if liberals had been calling the shots, millions of us wouldn't have been ripped off by crooked corporate pals of the GOP.

Congressional voting records significantly document that it is the liberals who believe and practice "Leave no child behind." It is not Republicans, who plastered their convention walls with the showy mantra for campaign purposes in 2000—before it soon became a phony pitch.

You want proof? The nation's premier children's advocacy organization, the nationally respected Children's Defense Fund, scored all congressmen on issues that leave no child behind. Results: 47 U.S. senators scored less than 50 percent compared to a Senate average of 60 percent, and all the flunkers were Republicans. But 36 senators scored 100 percent voting for children's best interests and all were Democrats.

In the House, 117 congressmen scored less than 50 percent on issues important to children, and all were Republicans. With a House average of 69.2 percent, and the GOP controlling a majority of its 435 members, only 26 Republicans had voting records for children above that average. But 49 House members had 100 percent voting records, and all were Democrats. Significantly, the voting record of the GOP leader, Speaker Hastert, was 6 percent for children. If you voted for more of that crowd, then maybe you don't like children either.

Regardless, don't take my word for what liberalism means. Combining the New Webster Encyclopedia Dictionary of the English language and Webster's College Dictionary: "Favorable to progress or reform in political or religious affairs; advocating individual freedom of action and expression pertaining to representational forms of government rather than aristocracies and monarchies (and dictatorships); free from prejudice and bigotry; tolerant, open-minded; characterized by generosity; not characterized by selfish, narrow contracted ideas; favorable to civil, political and religious liberty; and often opposed to conservative."

It's obvious the Founding Fathers had to be liberals or we wouldn't have our cherished Constitution and Bill of Rights (now being threatened). Thus there's a clear connection between being "liberal" and a real American. If I were otherwise and a Catholic, I'd be in a confession booth. As to those who derogatorily sling around the liberal label in their ignorance of its meaning, wouldn't a better yardstick be is it true or not and is it good for our country?

CHAPTER 13

Our Liberties: the Cost of Constant Vigilance

Writing of yet "another imperial presidency," Arthur Schlesinger, Jr. observed, "The flag thus incorporates the First Amendment. But today in another national emergency, officials seek to narrow the meaning of the flag, to identity the flag with the president and his war... Let us not surrender the flag to Attorney General Ashcroft."[12] Writing for December 16, 2001, Simon, too, noted the threat each new war levels on our freedoms. Then noting that "all this is still evolving and coming into focus," Simon deferred conclusions, but by May 4, 2003, he was ready to speak out, condemning sacrifice of traditional liberties to secure an illusive security.

December 16, 2001

When John Ashcroft took his oath of office and became our country's top law enforcement officer as attorney general of the United States, he swore to uphold the Constitution. But his actions since then are increasingly making a charade of the oath.

A cartoon in the Deming *Headlight* Nov. 27, aptly caught the thrust of mounting violations of our revered document and its cherished rights and freedoms. The cartoon read: "Ashcroft's since 2001, Fabulous Holiday Savings" and over the Bill of Rights was stamped, "Reduced 60%." This cartoon hit dead center at the emasculations engineered by Ashcroft, an attorney general who was rejected as senator by the people of Missouri in the last election.

Even extreme right-wingers such as Georgia Rep. Bob Barr and very conservative New York *Times* columnist William Safire, a speech writer

---

12. Arthur M. Schlesinger, Jr., *War and the American Presidency*, New York: W.W. Norton & Company, 2004, p. 72.

for President Nixon, have taken up the cry of opposition to Ashcroft's undemocratic actions that are sabotaging our cherished freedoms behind this guise of supposed national security.

It is dangerously ironic that we're supposedly fighting a war on terrorism to make America safe and keep it free, as this administration is taking away by arbitrary unilateral action the very liberties we set out to defend. This sends a terrible message to the world that when confronted with a serious challenge, we lack confidence in the very institutions we are supposed to be fighting for.

But all this is still evolving and coming into focus as opposition grows across the country. Thus "Think about It" will wait for more perspective enabling a more complete and accurate commentary about what is happening to American principles and ideals right here in our country, almost literally under our noses and behind our backs.

So let's digress from Afghanistan this week to yet another example of a top story that's been under-reported by the establishment media—probably because it might be viewed as "politically incorrect"…and freak out the claque still clinging to a Cuban policy that time has passed by. Along the way, both executive and legislative branches of our government have continued to shoot themselves in the foot, as America stands alone in the world with a Cuban "policy" that even our allies do not support.

Wayne S. Smith, a senior fellow at the prestigious Center for International Policy, and former chief of the U.S. Interests Section in Havana, Cuba, aptly suggests that "our long obsolete and woefully counter-productive Cuba policy is beginning to unravel." So here's the highly significant story that suggests the thrust of Smith's observation…

Eleven American students, with 50 more coming on, are enrolled at the Latin American School of Medicine in Cuba. They come from medically under-served communities in the U.S., with their tuition, room and board, and textbooks provided completely free of charge by the Cuban government. But the students must make a lifelong commitment to go back to their home communities to provide medical health care for the people there.

Incidentally, when the first group of American students arrived in Havana, the U.S. flag was flown and the American national anthem was played.

The offer to train U.S. medical students was extended by President Fidel Castro during the visit in June, 2000, to a Congressional Black Caucus delegation organized by the U.S. Pastors for Peace. After U.S. Rep. Bennie Thomson told President Castro about the high infant mortality rate and lack of medical care in his district in the Mississippi Delta area, the Cuban president offered to provide six years of free medical training for up to 500 U.S. students from medically under-served communities in the U.S.

Cuban medical schools are known to be among the world's best, and that country has universal health care for all its citizens. Both of these realities have been commended in the renowned New England *Journal of Medicine*, which is tops in the U.S.

A stark contrast is unavoidable of Cuba's medical schools turning out doctors to serve in needy areas of their own countries, with the Army's School of the Americas turning out "students" who have brought so much misery and death to their countrymen.

The American medical students join more than 4,000 students from 24 nations in Latin America, the Caribbean and Africa in their studies at the medical school. Cuba opened this highly unusual and much needed medical facility nearly three years ago.

Why doesn't our country use its wealth in this way to benefit mankind? And why are some 45 million Americans without any health care coverage?

May 4, 2003

It is ironic and crippling to confidence in government and respect for our leaders knowing that a prime reason for fighting terrorism was to protect out liberties—as our government's actions are stifling these very same liberties in the name of security.

Again it reminds of the Founding Father's admonition that "he who gives up liberty for security ends up with neither." And the drumbeat of heightened threat levels and security concerns are no excuse for undermining the foundations of our democracy. Hitler used such tools to launch the German people into a repressive dictatorship, as he used the Reichstag fire much as our government is using 9-11 for "cover" in its ongoing "war on terror."

A prime vehicle is the misnamed Patriot Act that right after 9-11 was ready to go and rushed through Congress with no in-depth scrutiny of its consequences. Most congressmen hadn't even read the Act's critical provisions affecting our country and its citizens when they voted.

That dangerous legislation and subsequent presidential orders and executive branch actions have already taken away legal protections assured by our Constitution and Bill of Rights—with virtually no notice to the public. These far-reaching actions are furthering a growing climate of fear among

Americans who understand the meaning, are infringing on individual privacy so basic to free society and, even more dangerous, are inhibiting free inquiry and dissent so essential to a successfully functioning free and open democratic system.

There are reasons to believe this curtailment of liberty will be used to abuse, harass and falsely imprison racial, religious and ethnic minorities, along with those who choose to speak out about what is happening to our country and its ideals and principles. This in turn will stifle the right to dissent that has served America well since the days of our Revolution.

According to legal experts, under the Patriot Act, the government can now search people's homes and businesses while they are away without letting them know the search took place. Even more scary, White House executive actions—with no backing of legislation—now allow the FBI to conduct secret surveillance of any American religious, political or civic group even if there is no suspicion the organization is engaged in any wrong-doing.

Shades of the repugnant McCarthy era that so abused the best of America, and what a facile opening for Big Brother to clamp down on any who don't parrot the party line. It's not a stretch, under an Act that almost makes one choke using its "Patriot" name, to visualize the Gestapo knocking at your door. These and the many other erosions of our civil liberties resulting from the Patriot Act and its follow-up federal government-initiated actions are making it seem like Osama bin Laden and the terrorists are winning because of the self-inflicted harm being done to America—which must be making them very happy with the help they are getting.

The ongoing curtailments warping the Bill of Rights are being piled on, too. New legislation just unveiled further increases the government's ability to intrude into people's private lives and take away fundamental rights supposedly guaranteed by our Constitution. This new draft Bill, gaggingly called the Domestic Security Enhancement Act of 2003 (or Patriot Act II), creates 15 new death penalties. Bush's record as governor of Texas, known around the world as the "killing state," documents this stuff was his specialty with executions (mostly minorities) ranking right up there with Communist China and Saudi Arabia.

This new hit on our liberties would increase the federal government's ability to search homes and wiretap phones, conduct secret arrests, and strip people of their U.S. citizenship for supporting organizations labeled as "terrorist" even if that support was for lawful humanitarian activities. Also, non-citizens can be deported, or indefinitely imprisoned as undocumented aliens.

Results of similar inhuman imprisonment without charges or right to an attorney are showing up with the shackled prisoners from Afghanistan in Guantanamo cages where upwards of 25 have already attempted suicide (NPR report). This expresses the hopelessness of these human beings.

But there is some pro-American action on the part of Congress. Senate Bill 609, "Restore the Freedom of Information Act," introduced by Sen. Leahy (D-Vt.), joined by Senators Levin (D-Mich.), Jeffords (I-Vt.), Lieberman (D-Conn.), Byrd (D-W VA.), would correct some of the harmful provisions of the Patriot Act that allowed private firms to hide environmental hazards from the public and prevent community activists, environmentalists, local and state agencies and even federal agencies from gaining access to potential environmental hazards dangerous to citizens.

And in the House, HR1157, "Freedom to Read Protection Act of 2003," would remove threats created by the Patriot Act to privacy of library and bookstore records, and would restore congressional oversight of the FBI's use of secret surveillance warrants.

The American people deserve these protections and they warrant support of our senators and congressmen. Jeff Bingaman will be on the people's side of these issues, but maybe Domenici and Pierce need to be reminded, and even told to "shape up or ship out."

PART V

Defense of Human Rights

CHAPTER 14

Brothers and Sisters in Diversity

Over 100 years ago that great American, W. E. B. DuBois wrote, "The problem of the twentieth century is the problem of the color-line,—the relation of the darker to the lighter races of men in Asia and Africa, in America and the islands of the sea."[13] Writing near the end of that century for July 14, 1997, Simon updated DuBois' warning. Then writing for December 11, 1995, Simon turned his attention to the centuries-long violation of the human rights of Native Americans. Finally, out of the tohubohu and self-interested clatter surrounding Clinton's proposal concerning gays in the military, Simon imposed his usual intellectual clarity and order, writing for February 8, 1993.

July 14, 1997

Even Americans who have insulated themselves from meaningful contacts with those whose skin color is different probably are aware that we have a long way to go before our country can have the honor of becoming the world's first truly multi-racial democracy.

It is possible that the lack of contact with those who are different involves enough Americans to deepen our racial divisions, regardless of whether this is by intent or occurs naturally because "that's the way it is." Either way, this isn't the stuff that makes our society better by improving the harmony of our different races—who are all Americans.

Gallop polls provide hope and alarm for this crucial issue that affects all Americans and the country's well-being and future.

Just before the president's significant speech last month at the University of California at San Diego, Gallop's annual poll on race relations found that an astounding 74 percent of black respondents said they were

---

13. William E. B. DuBois, *The Souls of Black Folk*, in *Three Negro Classics*, ed., John Hope Franklin, New York: Avon/Hearst Corporation, 1965, p. 221.

satisfied with their standard of living and the way their lives are going. This is somewhat difficult to understand.

Even more astounding, more whites than blacks—93 percent—said they would be willing to vote for a black candidate for president. Could some of those have so replied because it was "the right thing to do"?

Just as significant was the 61 percent of whites who said they approved of interracial marriages. In 1972, only 25 percent of whites approved of black-white marriages.

On the downside, neither whites nor blacks felt that interracial relations are going to improve. Asked whether they felt that race relations always would be a problem, 58 percent of whites and 54 percent of blacks said "yes." In a 1963 Gallop poll the year President Kennedy was assassinated, the responses were less gloomy, with 44 percent of whites and 26 percent of blacks believing race relations always would be a problem.

So the pessimism of blacks about improvements in race relations has increased more substantially than that of whites. This in itself seems to carry some contradiction with the current 74 percent of blacks satisfied with their standard of living and the way their lives are going. However, this does square with the reality of more blacks moving into middle-income brackets. Nevertheless, the unemployment rate of blacks still is twice that of whites, though it is declining.

On the political side, the determination of the congressional Republican leadership to end affirmative action—not mend it as per President Clinton's cautious strategy—already is showing in the shrinking equality of minority admission programs of universities, especially in California and Texas. California once had the nation's best university and college education systems, but Gov. Pete Wilson and his GOP cohorts have turned that around to something of a near-disaster.

There is something prophetic about the 1963 report of the National Commission on Civil Disorders (also known as the Kerner Commission): "Our nation is moving toward two societies, one black, one white—separate and unequal...What white Americans can never fully understand—but what the Negro can never forget—is that white society is deeply implicated in the ghetto. White institutions created it, white institutions maintain it and white society condones it." Does this imply that America's white hegemony might survive only because nonwhites will remain a minority under influence of the white establishment power that rules today?

The numbers could say something else. Professional projections report that by 2050 whites will be a shrinking 53 percent of the American population. The other 47 percent of Americans will be a mix of other ethnic groups: Black, rapidly growing Hispanic, Asian-Pacific islanders and others.

One thing is certain: Mending the separation of our multi-ethnic society is in the genuine best interests of our one country and every American, regardless of the color of his skin. Accomplishing this would be a winner for all Americans.

December 11, 1995

Once in a while, one encounters a monumentally stupid statement by an elected official that reeks of insensitivity and lack of understanding.

The latest is U.S. Sen. Slade Gorton (R-Wash.), chairman of the Senate Appropriations subcommittee overseeing the Interior Department, which handles the Bureau of Indian Affairs.

Here's what Gorton said: "Native Americans must sacrifice like other Americans." After an incredible crack such as that, the senator urgently needs to be asked, "What other group of Americans has sacrificed as much as American Indians?" The factual answer is a resounding none, including African Americans.

Here is a people, the American Indians, whose ancestors lived in this country, their native land, centuries before our ancestors arrived. Since the arrival of civilization and Christianity, the first Americans have sacrificed their land, their food supply, their timber, water and mineral rights, even their religion, and through the years, millions have sacrificed their lives. Only one indigenous person exists for each 100 who lived in the Americas when Europe discovered the New World in 1492. As for being discovered, it was the Indians who found Columbus when he was lost!

So the historical reality of the enslavement of Indians in Central and South America, and the slaughter, decimation by white man's diseases and degradation of American Indians on both continents makes it difficult to celebrate Columbus Day and Europe's so-called discovery of the Americas.

Through 500 years layered with oppression, cruelty, forced removals, poverty, empty promises and broken treaties, it has been a winter of the soul for the American Indian since the white man came.

There was a time when the native peoples of this land lived in the abundance of the animals they considered sacred. Rivers and streams teemed with fish, millions of buffalo roamed the plains providing food, clothing, shelter, bones for tools, hair for rope and dozens of other necessities. Yes, this very basis of life for Indians was gone in 75 years. With it went a rich variety of cultures and native religions that held sacred the earth and her creatures, because the Indian people consider all life sacred and the earth as the mother of all living things.

An old Lakota Sioux chief, Luther Standing Bear, gave this perspective when he said that "Man's heart away from nature becomes hard," and that "lack of respect for growing, living things soon leads to lack of respect for humans, too."

Ironically, in our nation founded on religious freedom, American Indian religions have been devalued, discounted and considered culturally and spiritually inferior. Suppression of Indian religious freedom has been the official U.S. policy through most of our history.

American Indian religious traditions are rooted in the sacredness of the whole earth. And on this sacred earth are places of significant holiness that are counterparts to churches and temples in Western cultures. To the Indians, these are places to pray, give offerings, seek visions for the good of their people, to commune with the Great Spirit. It is well for us to remember, as a wise Indian said, that the Great Spirit has many names and different faces to different people.

The sacred site is often the spiritual focus and wellspring of faith. But at many of these sacred Indian religious sites across the country, timber highways have been pushed through the altars; hydroelectric facilities and ski resorts have bulldozed through the church and countless others desecrated.

To our shame, today we have a Supreme Court that is openly hostile to the rights and religious liberty of the American Indians, as its recent ruling in the Oregon Smith case abandoned 30 years of precedent that has safeguarded religious freedom for most Americans but not for the first Americans. Thus religious freedom for all of us is potentially in jeopardy.

A once proud and independent people have been reduced to utter poverty and the grim hopelessness of reservation life. So, Sen. Gorton, any government grants or loans are merely a meager repayment of a huge debt owed American Indians, who gave up millions of acres of land and their way of life.

Isn't it time to end the contradictions between American ideals and American practices?

February 8, 1993

The emotionally laden controversy and inflammatory politics of homosexuals in the military warrants some observations.

As the arguments heat up over whether homosexuals should be allowed in the military, it seems that already lost in the noise is the fact they already are there. Undoubtedly there isn't a military service in the world almost back to the beginning that hasn't had homosexuals and will continue to have them. And ours is no exception.

The same goes for our society and those of other nations. It is a fact there are policemen, legislators, athletes, doctors, lawyers, scientists, businessmen, laborers, liberals and conservatives, rich and poor who are, have been, and will continue to be homosexuals.

It is noteworthy that homosexuals through history have included some significant personages. These have included Richard the Lion Hearted, Aristotle, Leonardo Da Vinci, Alexander the Great, and the infamous Joe McCarthy—yes, "Tail-gunner Joe," the U.S. senator.

Today, most of the world's major military services do not ban homosexuals and have steadily lessened discrimination. Australia is the latest nation to lift its ban.

Navy Capt. James Bush said on the PBS MacNeil-Lehrer News Hour, "I never knew a case where a piece of equipment didn't work because it was operated by a homosexual, or a ship that didn't go to sea, or where a battle was lost. A review of military history indicates that there is absolutely no empirical data that homosexuals caused any problem."

So maybe what we're seeing is the last major chapter in the struggle against discrimination in the 200-year-old battle for civil rights. We're hearing now, especially from the military establishment, many of the same arguments that were heard when President Harry Truman ordered the military services to accept blacks. And all the forebodings of doom then just didn't materialize.

One of the opposition's arguments now is about the dangers of promiscuity. But what about the promiscuity of heterosexuals, the so-called "straights"? I can remember when our aircraft carrier hit port during World War II, especially Pearl Harbor, seeing sailors lined up around the block waiting their turn. And one of the younger ones was distressed when he returned because "she was eating an apple." Among the married officers aboard ship, those who didn't "go after it" at every opportunity were among the minority. And you know about the society around us today. So maybe there are already promiscuity problems with the straights.

Further, after learning of the experiences of some female service personnel during Desert Storm, one can almost conclude they had more to fear from their sergeants than they did from Iraqis. And who doesn't remember the ordeal of female officers at the Navy's recent Tailhook Convention?

As to reactions of military service chiefs, one doesn't need to be an astute student of history to know they must always react negatively to any changes and are hidebound by traditions, all of which adversely affects their thinking.

One also wonders about the courage of Gen. Colin Powell's opposition to President Clinton's position that would enable homosexuals to no longer need to lie about their sexual orientation.

When Powell became chairman of the Joint Chiefs he soon outlined a broad range of much needed changes that would streamline the military, cut costs and waste, and make for a much more efficient military force adapted to the times. Then he encountered the usual negative obstruction from the services protecting their turf. So what did our No. 1 military officer do? He caved in and has subsequently pulled in his horns on these long overdue improvements.

Then there's the powerful and pompous chairman of the Senate Armed Services Committee, who is making a big thing out of opposition to his president on this issue. Sen. Sam Nunn was one of the big guns in the Democratic Party who wanted to be president but didn't have the guts to make a run for it back when George Bush was still supposedly riding high. So one wonders how much of his stance comes from sour grapes and resentment that Clinton was able to do what he didn't and couldn't.

Congressional Republicans led by chief hatchet man Bob Dole and little hatchet man Newt Gingrich, obviously are using this issue to hit Clinton below the belt and embarrass him any and every way they can. It's my hunch that if the Republicans in Congress continue their partisan negative obstructionism to virtually every Clinton proposal, they are again going to be misjudging the American people. Considering what our country is up against and what needs to be done, thinking Americans are going to demand more than this from their elected representatives.

So with some 10 million Americans being homosexuals, a good many of them parents and raising children, it is a wonder that more of us don't comprehend that homosexuality is not a matter of choice or preference. Rather it is a matter of genetics.

CHAPTER 15

Death Penalty and Torture— No "Life, Liberty and the Pursuit of Happiness"

Founding his thought, as always, on the rock-solid base of liberal principles, Simon inevitably wrote in opposition to the death penalty, certainly to torture; while his always active compassion may have so dictated, it is the philosophical principles from which he constructed his argument. On May 20, 2001, he concluded several columns dealing with capital punishment, the issue having been especially stirred up by the execution of Timothy McVeigh, convicted of the Oklahoma City bombing. Written before the obscene spectacle of our government debating torture, to which we were later to be treated, Simon's column of April 7, 1997, made his position clear. (This is a sort of potpourri column, of the sort Simon occasionally wrote, touching on a number of topics.) Finally, on March 16, 2002, Simon weighed in on the "terrorism detainees," those victims who continued for years after to confront America with troubling moral and legal accusations. Benjamin Barber instructed us that "terrorism is a function of powerlessness and hurts the powerful only as they allow themselves to be hurt."[14] In this column Simon puts the same matter another way, reminding us that "what goes around comes around."

May 20, 2001

This column dealt with capital punishment and the death penalty last March 11, with the premise being that the Biblical Commandment "Thou Shalt Not Kill" means precisely what it says.

But there are international aspects to America's reliance on the death penalty that need focusing because it has worldwide repercussions and

---

14. Benjamin R. Barber, *Fear's Empire*, New York: W.W. Norton, 2003, p. 218.

growing evidence underlines the fact that the death penalty is becoming a diplomatic liability adversely affecting good relations even with our allies.

America and Europe are separated not only by the Atlantic Ocean but also by enthusiasms for the death penalty. The European Union will admit no country that has the death penalty and most of its members will not extradite suspected murderers to America. Among educated Europeans and government leaders, our use of the death penalty has become an even stronger metaphor for America because it is now led by a man who presided over 40 executions in 2000 alone as governor of Texas, known abroad as "the killing state."

Incidentally, our killingest state ranks right up there with Communist China and Saudi Arabia, noted for its barbaric punishments.

The *Sunday Herald* of Glasgow, Scotland, expressed the typical European view by terming U.S. executions, the McVeigh saga and the media's response as "the latest twisted piece of Americana." Knowledgeable Europeans view the death penalty as a human rights issue and are incredulous that Americans support a punishment that has failed to deter crime, mostly targets those who can't afford a decent lawyer, is used on the mentally retarded, and too often gets the wrong man. Further, European nations stress rehabilitation, not punishment. In its belief that execution is appropriate punishment, the United States virtually stands alone in the community of democracies and civilized societies.

So is it any wonder that Felix Rohatyn, distinguished American ambassador to France during the Clinton administration, says that every time he gave a speech in France or across Europe the audiences always asked him to defend America's use of the death penalty, and usually it was the first question.

Our country is the only enlightened nation in the world that kills the retarded and juveniles. And again, Texas is No. 1 in the killing categories. While the death penalty is mostly used in the American South, and is disproportionately applied to blacks and browns who kill whites, it is also shorthand for race relations in America.

Death penalty supporters in America believe in "an eye for an eye" as justice and view executions as social vengeance. The view is anathema among enlightened Europeans and their parliaments who shun it. This makes us a minority of one among democracies and civilized societies.

Good Americans—the genuine variety—should be and are embarrassed by our country being in the shabby company of those nations that kill juveniles and the mentally defective. Here's the roll call of our likeminded: Iran, Pakistan, Saudi Arabia, Nigeria, Yemen. This does not make us part of a roster of enlightened societies and nations. Why do we stand apart from progressive democracies? And why are we so keen to treat our erring children as adult criminals? In Governor Jeb Bush's Florida they treat even middle-school kids as adult criminals. And by the latest count, there are 74 on death row in the U.S. heading for execution for juvenile crimes.

But we are making some progress. Just 12 years ago only two states forbade the practice of killing the retarded. Now there are 13 of the 38 states with capital punishment, and more are moving in the direction of abolishing the death penalty. New Mexico almost did it last year. Maybe the world's "most Christian nation" is actually moving in that direction and will join the community of enlightened nations of the world.

Capital punishment is always problematic with a system that is deeply flawed and prone to error. It becomes even worse when those subject to the death penalty are mentally retarded. This makes it extremely difficult to determine the level of guilt of offenders with mental handicaps, because the death penalty is supposedly applicable to the most blame-worthy perpetrators of the most heinous crimes, especially when their acts are premeditated. Also, a strong case can be made that "cruel and unusual punishment" is a violation of the Eighth Amendment to our Constitution. There's some evidence the courts are moving in this direction.

It can be readily documented that executions do not deter crime, and not just because most murders are crimes of passion. Even knowledgeable supporters of the death penalty recognize this and no longer even bother trying to make that case because the evidence is definitive. If the death penalty is to be anything more than simple revenge, as a state-sanctioned act of theatrical bloody-mindedness, it must be rooted in a moral argument—and this will take a lot of doing. Meanwhile, killing the incompetent and the uncomprehending in the name of justice shames the word.

April 7, 1997

When you see one of those signs along the highway reading "Abortion stops a beating heart," has it ever occurred to you that an execution does, too?

But there doesn't seem to be anything in Right-to-Lifers' agenda that indicates concern about capital punishment and execution stopping a beating heart. Does this rather obvious selectivity in the right-to-life position perplex you?

Here are some other realities that you might want to think about:

- There are 163 nations that belong to the United Nations. Yet physical and mental torture of their citizens occurs in 120 of them.

But the deplorable cynicism-producer is that in 112 of these countries
there are provisions in their constitutions that prohibit torture.

The contradiction indicates that a lot more than legislative prohibiting
is needed to stop the physical, mental and psychological torture of human
beings. In a so-called civilized modern world, why is there so much evidence of man's inhumanity to man? Maybe we'll get to the point where a
lot of us will have had-it-up-to-here with the myriad examples of hypocrisy in our public and political life and among nations.

In this connection, it's significant that Amnesty International USA is
campaigning for a law that will prohibit torturers from being on the CIA
payroll. Achieving that would cut the ranks in the CIA!

- Do you know what America's newest growth industry is? Building
  prisons. Yes, prisons that towns used to sue to keep away, but now
  a lot of them are fighting to attract.

Prison labor is a lucrative aspect of the booming prison business. It
provides companies with cheap labor, and they don't have to provide benefits or vacations—for jobs that were once held by outside workers, as prison
labor undercuts outside wages and gives scarce jobs to prisoners. Inmate
labor can and has been used as a union-busting tool. TWA did it in 1986,
and other companies are eyeing this resource.

A crazy thing is that while crime rates remained rather steady over
the past 20 years and have been going down more recently, the number of
people behind bars in the United States tripled to 1.63 million.

You see, the prison industry has become a big player, and it needs
prisoners to keep growing, as it successfully fights for stiffer sentences and
more prison spending. So with their growing clout, is it any wonder that
spending at the state level for prisons increased faster than any other cat-
egory of public spending, as education spending shrinks?

An increasing portion of that money is going to private companies
moving in on the bonanza. And despite documented abuses and dubious
savings, with inmates at the mercy of the bottom line, it will be difficult to
slow the momentum of private prisons.

In fact, this business is getting so good that some of Wall Street's largest investment houses, including Goldman Sacks & Co. and Smith Barney,

are competing to underwrite bonds for prisons—as financial analysts are herding investors into Wall Street's latest boom industry.

And it figures that the National Rifle Association moved in on the prison boom. This powerful outfit with 3 million members and a war chest estimated at $149 million is using this chance to change its deteriorating image from pro-gun to anti-crime. You know, yet another in the tired refrain of "get tough on crime."

• It's getting to be a real spectacle the way Republicans are increasingly ganging up on Speaker of the House of Representatives Newt Gingrich.

The latest attack came from U.S. Rep. Peter King (R-N.Y.), who called Gingrich "road kill on the highway of American politics." King said Gingrich has "a public approval rating a few points shy of ecoli virus," and as "the most powerful liberal in American politics, he should be replaced as a speaker because he is killing us." Seems the Democrats are understandably silent on the Gingrich issue, because there is no need for them to say anything with the Republican anti-Gingrich chorus increasing. Beats everything, doesn't it?!

March 16, 2002

In his address to the nation last September 20, President Bush said: "We're in a fight for our principles, and our first responsibility is to live by them."

Every real American cheers such words with the fervent belief this means more than lip service to freedom, equality, justice for everyone, respect for human rights, and a deep commitment to the rule of law. These cherished ideals and principles cannot be compromised, nor adhered to, only when it suits a government's whims, and they apply even during times of national crises. Maybe this is somewhat like consistently being more than a "C and E" Christian, meaning Christmas and Easter.

It is not far-fetched concluding that every time our nation fails in its commitment to truly live by its underlying principles, it thereby feeds anti-Americanism in the world. This can quickly turn violent, and it is growing since excessive civilian casualties and destruction in Afghanistan, and the futile escalating violence in the Middle East, where there is stark terrorism on both sides of the Israeli-Palestinian conflict. Deplorably dangerous, administration "policy" has been a bust in abating the bloodshed and at times even given a green light for Israeli Prime Minister Sharon to turn up the tragic violence and killing in the name of fighting terrorism.

Regardless, all this is the stuff that readily produces terrorists, understandably growing by the dozens because of the bloodshed and killings in that part of the world.

Aren't we overdue in better understanding the most effective policy is practicing what we preach, saying what we mean and meaning what we say? And then get it through our thick heads that violence inevitably produces even more violence and that the different "war" in which we're now enmeshed is the same old stuff, and force of arms cannot lastingly resolve anything or produce a better world by piling up the killings?

Referring to the president's wise words at the beginning of this column, one can better understand why so many Americans are turned off by politicians who say one thing and do another, and whose words are just that, words without genuine meaning. Remember the "leave no child behind" forgotten mantra? Meanwhile the Bush administration is already trading our cherished Bill of Rights for supposed security. And the U.S. is sacrificing justice as it undermines legal safeguards for U.S. residents.

Examples are numerous. Hundreds of detainees are being held in prison or solitary confinement under questionable conditions. None have been charged or convicted of a crime, with no evidence of their involvement in the 9-11 attacks or al-Qaida. And the attorney general's refusal to even release their names because doing so would "violate their privacy" is enough to make one swallow an upper plate.

Administration readiness to try these civilians in military tribunals could boomerang too. Our government has always objected when U.S. citizens abroad are subject to such trials. The State Department annually evaluates other countries for their human rights practices, including the right to "fair public trials," with due process protections. And countries that try civilians in military tribunals are cited in what could be called a black list. Bush administration tribunals are thus hypocritical and fail to meet international standards. They could jeopardize U.S. citizens abroad and hurt human rights around the world.

Realistically, the war on terrorism will never by concluded. Even if our government says we've "won," the "victory" could be pyrrhic for the United States. If this administration continues to gut constitutional protections, then the values of freedom become hollow words that can harm our country at home and abroad. By disregarding international protections and turning its back on needed international cooperation with apprehensive allies, the administration is endangering American troops and civilians who may pay the price when they are caught up in armed conflict. Yes, what goes around does come around.

CHAPTER 16

Corporate Giants of Midget Morality

Writing on October 20, 1997, and on January 17, 2004, Simon set out to excoriate corporate capitalism for violation of human rights through focus respectively on two iconic giants, Nike and Coca-cola.

October 20, 1997

Nike sports shoes are a highly popular footwear and undoubtedly better known than any others. Most of you probably have seen them in advertisements with Nike icons such as basketball great Michael Jordan, Seattle Mariner superstar Ken Griffey Jr. and Brazilian soccer star Romario.

But would these superstars of the sports world and many of the others wearing Nike shoes actually be using them if they knew the real story about the company and how it treats the more than 500,000 workers making its shoes in southeast Asian factories?

Last month, two reports by the Hong Kong Christian Industrial Committee and the Asia Monitor Resource Center documented conditions in four Nike factories on the Chinese mainland.

China's official work week is capped at 48 hours, and China's wage laws decree a minimum of 25 cents per hour. But the reports documented that Nike workers are required to labor 73 hours a week and are paid as little as 15 cents an hour in Chinese factories. An additional two to five hours a day of overtime also is required of Nike workers. If they refuse to work the overtime, they can be docked a day's pay.

The monitoring research groups also found children as young as 13 employed in sewing and cutting, both dangerous tasks, often resulting in mangled hands, and fingers lost in the cutting machines. Ironically, the use of child labor violates Chinese law and Nike's own "code of conduct," both of which are meaningless for Nike workers.

Chinese law requires companies to grant maternity leaves, but at the Nike shoe factories, pregnant workers are regularly fired. And women 25 and older often are let go because they are "too old." To top it off, Nike requires its ill-paid workers to deposit a month's wages with the factory as "security."

All these realities help explain the report that Nike's president, Tom Clarke, gave Sept. 22 to their annual meeting in Portland, Ore. Clarke reported that 1996 had a 42 percent increase in revenues and a 44 percent increase in net profits. And that the share price of Nike stock has increased 30-fold since 1987. Perhaps this is why Phil Knight, the Nike founder and CEO, is now the fifth-richest man in the world.

Bluntly stated, Nike's track record means the company represents many of the nastiest aspects of 20th century capitalism that increasingly has a close resemblance to late-19th century capitalism, which wasn't very pretty.

But reality is catching up with Nike. Clarke admitted at a press conference after the shareholder meeting that the emerging campaign against Nike has made a dent in domestic sales.

Scores of community and campus-based organizations in the United States and Canada are passing out leaflets at stores selling Nike products. Activists in at least nine countries mobilized Oct. 18 in support of Nike workers. Community centers in the Bronx organized a return of Nike shoes to the posh Nike Town store along 57th Street in Manhattan. And people across the country have been sending old Nike shoes to add to the pile.

Last year, fourth-graders at the Hawes School in Ridgewood, N.J., wrote a play depicting the sweatshop conditions under which Nike and Disney products and McDonald's "happy meals" toys are made. The pupils were ready to present their play to the entire school when the principal squelched it. But it didn't stay squelched. It's now going to be produced on Broadway starring the original child authors. The one-night-only performance will be at 7 P.M Oct. 27 at the Round About Theater.

Ironically, and rather reprehensibly, it was Spike Lee who made the Nike commercials aimed at the Far East market, which Nike is going after along with targeting women, as their U.S. market shrinks, and it's a piece of flummery that Nike is on President Clinton's Apparel Industry partnership.

Further, the Securities and Exchange Commission on July 10 upheld a Nike challenge to a sweatshop resolution introduced by the pension board of the United Methodist Church, whose shareholders own more than 100,000 Nike shares.

As a Methodist, I think my church should unload those shares pronto, and, as for me, I wouldn't wear Nike shoes even if I were young enough!

January 17, 2004

Just about every reasonably informed American knows by now that far too many giant U.S. corporations are capable of "cooking the books," defrauding their stockholders, shafting their employees and enabling top executives to grab obscene amounts of money far beyond normal remuneration, all of which underlines "rot at the top."

But how many of you are aware that some of these supposedly respectable big U.S. corporations are involved with systematic intimidation, kidnapping, detention, torture and even murder? This reality shows the extremes some corporations are willing to take so as to keep those huge profits up.

This reality was revealed when the Washington, D.C.-based International Labor Rights Fund and the United Steelworkers of America filed four lawsuits in federal district court in July 2001, on behalf of a union representing food and beverage workers in Columbia called Sinaltrainal. Plaintiffs include five workers who say they were tortured or unlawfully detained for union activities and the estate of murdered union activist (Isidro Gil). These plaintiffs contend Coca-Cola bottlers "contracted with or otherwise directed paramilitary security forces that utilized extreme violence and murdered, tortured, unlawfully detained or otherwise silenced trade union leaders."

Coca-Cola's weak defense argued that it cannot be held liable in a U.S. federal court for events outside the United States, and that it does not "own," and therefore does not control, the bottling plants in Columbia. This position makes a mockery of the fact the 20 Coca-Cola bottlers in Columbia are deeply entwined in Coke's core economic activities and are an integral part of the beverage giant's operations. Coca-Cola provides its bottlers with syrup, and they mix, bottle, package and ship the drinks to wholesalers and retailers throughout Columbia.

Last May, Coca-Cola FEMSA, a bottling company, acquired Pan American Beverages, Latin America's largest bottler, making it the biggest Coca-Cola bottler in Latin America. With shared name, shared executives and Coke's 30 percent ownership of Coca-Cola FEMSA, it insults your intelligence for Coke to maintain it is separate and independent from its bottlers.

Paramilitaries are violent right-wing thugs composed of professional soldiers and common thugs. They maintain bases at some Coca-Cola bottling facilities in Columbia, especially where there is union activity. It's a cinch they aren't doing this for free, and it's another cinch that any disclaimer regarding them by Coca-Cola is a phony inaccuracy.

The many murders of Coke bottling workers are part of the larger pattern of antiunion violence in Columbia. Since 1986, more than 3,800 trade unionists have been murdered in that country, making it the most dangerous place to organize anywhere in the world. Three in every five people killed worldwide for trade union activities are Columbians.

On December 5, 1996, two paramilitary gang members drove a motor cycle into the Carepa Coca-Cola bottling plant in northern Columbia and with 10 shots killed the worker and union activist Isidro Segunda Gil, mentioned earlier in this column. (Gil, 27, had worked there eight years.) When his wife protested her husband's assassination and demanded reparations from Coca-Cola, she was murdered (silenced) by paramilitaries in 2000, leaving their two daughters orphaned. A Columbian judge, apparently bought and paid for, later dropped charges against Gil's killers.

So there's understandably a "Stop Killer Coke" campaign picking up steam that aims for public pressure on Coca-Cola to acknowledge its role in the anti-union killings and stop collaborating with violent paramilitary organizations.

This campaign is also reaching into the issue of lack of health care for Coca-Cola workers in Africa and the corporation's water use in India that is causing groundwater destruction. The campaign is heating up, too, with activists in Australia, Latin America, Ireland and Turkey leading anti-Coke campaigns with "Stop Killer Coke" materials. United Students Against Sweatshops are starting efforts to ban Coke from campuses. University College Dublin, Ireland's largest, voted to remove all Coca-Cola products from campus. Bard College in New York will not renew Coke's contract. Students at Carnegie Mellon University in Pittsburgh started a "Coke dump," spilling the stuff into the streets to call attention to the plight of Columbian Union activists. And United Auto Workers Local 22 in Detroit ordered 4,000 "Coke Float" flyers, explaining the campaign, for distribution to members.

While Coca-Cola has virtually unlimited resources to fight lawsuits, conducts its own media blitz and has years of experience fighting high-profile consumer campaigns, its vast global reach can be breached with the growing international support for "Stop Killer Coke." Maybe the beverage giant's 300 brands in 200 countries, with more than 70 percent of its income coming from outside the U.S., can be affected, and another Goliath hit by a David. (But don't think Coke has been affected by the writer of this column, never buying nor drinking the stuff.)

Note: This column is indebted to *Dollars and Sense* magazine and Madeleine Baran, a graduate student at New York University's Graduate School of Journalism, for the significant basis they provided.

CHAPTER 17

Human Rights Watch Worldwide

Heading this representative sampling of Simon's human rights alerts, we most appropriately begin with Iraq, perhaps the most urgent, and in crisis for the longest duration. Writing for January 3, 2001, well before the American invasion had further devastated the population, Simon decried the painful effects of sanctions against Iraq. As update to that concern, Simon's column of April 13, 2003, documents the further human suffering already visited on Iraq by the American invasion. The poignant question with which he ends this column will certainly haunt Americans for many years to come. Simon decried the long-standing sanctions against Cuba on March 8, 1994. Writing for April 26, 2002, Simon turned to another lasting travesty of justice, Israel's reprehensible treatment of the Palestinian residents of the occupied territories. To end this chapter, the column of March 14, 1994, records Simon's condemnation of the Mexican government's harsh attempt to suppress the Zapatista Rebellion, an indigenous movement reflecting long years of grievances.

January 3, 2001

While most of the rest of the world have been laughing their heads off at the election fiasco in the Banana Republic of Florida (and even Castro and Saddam offered to send mediators), the American and British governments under United Nations auspices have been conducting a largely unreported destruction of a nation that is killing thousands of human beings, including at least 200 children, every day.

It is a gruesome coincidence that four days after Iraq invaded Kuwait, sanctions were slapped on Iraq 45 years to the day (Aug. 6, 1990) after the U.S. dropped an atomic bomb on Hiroshima, Japan, that killed more than a hundred-thousand mostly older people and children, leaving a toxic legacy still affecting the population.

But this carnage pales in comparison to the nearly 10 times more humans who have died in Iraq in the past decade because of sanctions and the war led by the United States and Britain. The Center for Economic and Social Rights reports that more Iraqi children have died as a result of sanctions than the combined toll of two atomic bombs on Japan plus the recent scourge of ethnic cleansing in the former Yugoslavia.

More than a million people have died because of economic sanctions against Iraq that have been in place for 10 years. The lives of ordinary Iraqis have been and are being devastated, as their country is reduced to a "pre-industrial" state.

Why isn't it reported in the media that since May, 1998, the U.S. alone has flown some 37,000 sorties, including thousands of bombing missions over heavily populated southwestern Iraq? This bombing—funded by American taxpayers—is an integral part of the most ruthless embargo in modern history. It has made an entire nation "collateral damage" and reflects on the moral and intellectual contortion common in United Nations Plaza, the U.S. State Department and the British Foreign Office, as justification for destroying a country.

When Secretary of State Madeline Albright was asked if the death of half a million Iraqi children was a price worth paying for sanctions, she replied, "We think the price is worth it." Lest we forget, she was speaking for a nation that professes to be Christian. Albright could have said "the price of oil." Iraq's oil fields are second largest on earth, and whenever there's a bombing blitz the price of oil goes up.

Sanctions supposedly are in place to disarm Iraq of its biological, chemical and nuclear weapons, even though U.N. arms inspectors and other international agencies confirm evidence Iraq has been "qualitatively disarmed." An ironic contradiction is muted that the U.S. and other members of the U.N. Security Council are responsible for the overwhelming majority of arms sales in the Middle East and internationally, and they include the world's major nuclear powers. Even tiny Israel has a nuclear arsenal of over 200 warheads.

The hypocrisy involved in this conveniently ignores the fact that Saddam Hussein was a U.S. ally during the 1980-88 war with Iran. His friends in Washington, London and other western capitals encouraged and supported development of his destructive and repressive capacity. Yet, when thousands of Kurds were gassed in the March, 1988, Halabja massacre, the U.S. government increased agricultural credits to Saddam's regime and even sent a delegation of Washington politicians led by Sen. Robert Dole to encourage better relations between the two countries and to teach how to deal with the American media.

But because Saddam won't play our game, we now want a "regime change" in Iraq. We also want a regime change in Cuba because Fidel Castro marches to his own drummer. We justify this by saying we don't like dictators, yet we have no qualms about playing ball with an array of repressive regimes. There was the Shah of Iran, Suharto in Indonesia, Moutu Sese Seko in Zaire (Congo), and before that Pinochet in Chile, Noriega in Panama (who was on the CIA payroll when the elder Bush headed it), and a collection of other Latin American strongmen. Also seems we have no problem embracing communist China.

The multi-billion-dollar operation against Iraq—funded by us taxpayers—far exceeds the scale of the costly NATO campaign in the Balkans last year, but this has been consciously insulated from public attention by both the Clinton and Blair administrations. According to Pentagon figures, U.S. and U.K. fighter planes have flown more than 280,000 sorties after the no-fly zones were established (that's where most of the oil is). Since the massive escalation of attacks starting in December 1998, the U.K. alone has dropped an estimated 78 tons of bombs on southern Iraq compared to 2.5 tons during the previous six years.

Increasing the hit on us taxpayers is the $97 million earmarked by Congress and signed by President Clinton for the alleged Iraqi opposition, which is a badly splintered and contentious collection based in London that entirely lacks any social base in Iraq. The cover for this charade is the ridiculously named Iraq Liberation Act.

(Note: More needs to surface about all this, so until next week…)

April 13, 2003

As the carnage and deaths mount in pile-up quantities from the invasion of Iraq, a swirling array of haunting questions and what-ifs tumble through one's mind. Even brief conversations with others confirm you're not alone midst these nagging questions, as many others share the same concerns.

Because six of 10 Iraqis (14 million) have long barely existed on government rations, it requires little imagination to project what disruption of supply lines and distribution is doing to these harassed and hungry people. Making it even worse, is the reality that tens of thousands of them have been forced to flee Baghdad and other cities because of the bombing and resulting chaos. Compound this with the mental and emotional stress and agony of leaving your home not knowing if your husband, father, son or brother in the military is dead or alive. How would that exposure affect you and what would be your reaction?

As thousands stream out of the Iraqi capitol in chaotic exodus, how often might this occur as reported in the New York *Times*: A laden car carrying two adults and four children pulls off the median strip leaving Baghdad to avoid heavy armored invasion traffic and because of explosions and shelling, some of which hit their car. So what's your reaction to the father helplessly standing with a bloody little girl in his arms, as one of her hands dangles by a strip of skin? And if by some miracle she could be rushed to a hospital (not the Baghdad maternity hospital mistakenly bombed—collateral damage), where there's no water or electricity, how would you react? Likewise, if your child had a life-threatening accident and was rushed to your local hospital emergency room at night, but there was no electricity there; then what would you do?

The Pentagon doesn't like the media to show the actual gore of war's casualties, and the networks have been warned that too much of that "could adversely affect your bottom line." So very few of the many thousands of dead and injured Iraqi soldiers have been pictured in the U.S. media. What few such pictures have filtered through can cause any human being to think about how many of them are fathers, husbands, sons and brothers of families who love them and are agonizing with the uncertainty of whether they are dead, injured or alive. With phone lines knocked out and chaos all around, answers to these wrenching questions don't come easily.

Would any of you wives, mothers, grandparents and children be able to handle such an ordeal for long? Add to this burden the stress of your city or village being cut off from sorely needed fresh supplies, electricity and water, with you and what's left of your family in dire need of decent food, fresh water and medicine. So how would you feel and react to those causing this pain?

Making everything worse is the reality that, with daytime temperatures in the 90's and 100's and because of the prolonged disruption of sewage and water systems, disease will spread rapidly and take a terrible toll on human lives. Couple this with mounting deaths of civilians caught in the fighting that could turn a military victory into a political debacle as world outrage grows.

With cost of this unraveling war now rising beyond a billion dollars a day, and the further burden of paying for extended occupation and reconstruction, how can any true patriot not be tremendously concerned about the Bush budget that just passed the House? This gruesome measure that mugs poor and helpless Americans, as it unstintingly gives to the already rich, is a blueprint for domestic disaster that has even the few remaining moderate Republicans running for cover. Camouflaged by the war, an assault is happening here at home on our society's most vulnerable citizens that can do great and lasting harm to our country's genuine health and security. Imagine what our tax dollars, going up in smoke in Iraq, could do for making a truly better and safer America for all of us. Meanwhile, our government is shackling our grandchildren with billions of new debt, as it exacerbates pressing health, housing, education and investment needs and ignores growing environmental disasters.

Even minimum attention to world media readily conveys the strongly adverse reaction abroad to our invasion of Iraq. And now there are serious problems involving Prime Minister Tony Blair and the British, who are insisting on UN intervention and participation, which George II doesn't want. Incidentally, polls continue to show substantially more than half the British are strongly opposed to the war on Iraq, which leaves us with about only Israel and the Marshal Islands as supporters.

A thought: Those supposed patriots equating conformity with patriotism, who even call it treason to dissent and not follow the president, should realize how compatible their position would be with Hitler's Nazis, Stalin's Communists and yes, the Batthist Party of Saddam Hussein. If by accident of birth, they had been Germans, Russians or Iraqis, they would have been patriotic stalwarts adhering to the party line.

A question: Why doesn't the world's most powerful and richest nation have enough brains, imagination, common sense, courage and humanity to do it a better way for both itself and all mankind rather than creating a disaster for ourselves at home and abroad?

Think about it.

March 8, 1994

There are many things in world affairs that just don't make sense. A prime example involves Cuba. The United States broke diplomatic relations with Cuba in 1960, and then slapped on an economic embargo that is widely recognized as being in flagrant violation of international law because it proscribes trade sanctions based on political ideology. Our western allies have not followed our lead, and Cuba has relations with virtually every other nation in the world.

Despite evidence documenting the counter-productiveness of this policy with our close neighbor, the Bush administration in 1992 further tightened the 32-year-old economic sanctions with the misnamed Cuban Democracy Act.

Supposedly, The United States' tough policy was justified "because

Castro is a dictator;" but what makes this rationale so wacky is that we had close relations with dictators all over the world, especially in Latin America, and some we've "bought" to do our bidding.

What about China, the world's giant communist nation with whom we maintain full diplomatic relations, and even grant "Most Favored Nation" status in trade relations? Further, the United States maintains normal diplomatic and economic relations with numerous authoritarian, repressive regimes in the Middle East, Asia and Latin America. So who's kidding whom?

The cruelest aspect of our economic sanction on Cuba is the ample evidence that embargoes on food and medicine are dangerous weapons that kill just as surely as bullets and bombs. This is why today thousands of Cuban children are paying a terrible price for our country's economic war against their government. These children are suffering and dying from illnesses readily treatable with proper medication, or preventable by vaccination. All this means an inhumane form of warfare directed at civilians, with children being the main victims as the most vulnerable Cubans. Aren't we supposed to be a Christian nation?

This is why the renowned Dr. Benjamin Spock, and his United States-Cuba Medical Project, are buying and delivering desperately needed medical supplies to Cuba to counter an embargo he aptly termed "illegal and shameful." In January, Dr. Spock celebrated his 90th birthday by personally delivering more than $75,000 worth of pediatric and dental supplies. His organization wants to purchase and deliver sorely needed supplies like vitamin and mineral supplements, antibiotics, painkillers, catheters, insulin, sutures and asthma inhalers. These are urgently needed so that children will not suffer or die needlessly from simple infections and diseases.

One wonders if the winds of change will reach President Clinton, who to his shame during the campaign endorsed the 1992 legislation tightening the screws on Cuba.

Recently the Inter-American Dialogue, the Rand Corp., the 20th Century Fund, the Center for International Policy, and even the Army War College have all advocated dismantling the embargo on Cuba.

Even some of the Cuban exile community living in Florida are against the embargo.

Mutually beneficial, cooperative arrangements and improved political and economic relations with Cuba can speed that country's liberalization of its social, political and economic institutions. But will our leaders in Washington have the common sense and political courage to abandon an unwise punitive policy and replace it with one of peace and justice for the people of both nations?

Wayne Smith, head of a mission for the United States Interests Section in Cuba (1979-82), said it well: "Cuba has the same effect on American administrations that the full moon has on werewolves; they just lose their rationality at the mention of Castro or Cuba."

April 26, 2002

American military personnel, especially those who participated in infamous actions in Latin America during the Reagan and Bush I years, need to ponder what this Israeli army veteran said: "Being a citizen in a democracy carries with it a commitment to democratic values and a responsibility for your actions. It is morally impossible to be both a devoted democratic citizen and a regular offender against democratic values." Major Menuchin capped his position with: "I will not obey illegal orders to execute potential terrorists or firing into civilian demonstrations… or carrying out house demolitions and other acts of repression against the entire Palestinian population."

Recently returned from a hurried visit to Pennsylvania (can't be gone long from a cattle ranch with drought conditions bearing down) where I learned much from the experience of Keren Wheeler, who arrived in Ramallah March 28, the day before Sharon's tanks rolled into the West Bank refugee city. As part of an international delegation intending to meet with Palestine civilian groups, Wheeler, 23, holds dual U.S.-Israel citizenship, as do her parents, who emigrated to Pittsburgh in 1985, and have deep ties to the Jewish state. Mrs. Wheeler said her father lost both his parents and his brother in a Nazi concentration camp.

Keren Wheeler is giving interviews about the "egregious human rights violations" she saw that strengthened her conviction "Israeli aggression is driving Palestinians to commit suicide bombings and not the other way around." She saw Israeli forces destroying streets, houses, water and electric lines with tanks, bulldozers, land helicopter gun ships, and Red Crescent ambulances severely restricted and shot at even though international law says ambulances can move freely in war zones.

Moderate Arab rulers are having a tough time explaining why they should continue supporting U.S. policy, as reaction of their people nears the boiling point. The most violent demonstrations supporting the Palestinians have occurred in the Gulf Emirate of Bahrain, home of our Navy's Fifth Fleet.

The Arab world is aware the U.S. is the world's biggest arms dealer, and that its aid to Israel is $3 billion yearly. We also know our strongest ally in the Middle East is Saudi Arabia, whose recent government telethon raised $100 million-plus for families of Palestinians killed, including suicide bombers. Incidentally, 15 of 19 hijackers in the Sept. 11 attacks were Saudi nationals.

Possible bottom line: Ariel Sharon is not a friend of Israel, as his policies create more terrorists. Stanley Bedlington, counter-terrorism expert with the British Army in Jenin between 1946 and 1948, says fresh images on Arab TV screens are already feeding recruitment drives of Al Qaeda and other terrorist organizations.

For the record: Beginning in late 1940's I've contributed to the worthy United Jewish Appeal more times than I can remember.

While there has been little meaningful coverage in the established media, Jewish voices are being raised against what Prime Minister Ariel Sharon's army is doing to the Palestinians in the West Bank and Gaza.

In this evolving tragedy, "Jenin" has become a rallying cry in the Arab world where it is believed the Bush administration has given the green light to the Israeli leader's army to run amok in Palestinian cities pulverizing buildings and infrastructure as it shatters lives. This rallying cry could become a significant equivalent of "Remember the Alamo."

It is surprising that the Israeli daily *Ha'aretz* quoted Foreign Minister Shimon Peres (a former prime minister) as privately referring to the Jenin incursion as a "massacre" that will "do us immense damage in the eyes of the world." So as international pressure builds, the perspective of Israel's diplomatic isolation deepens, along with increasing difficulty for the U.S. to count on its Arab allies for a future strike against Saddam Hussein. Also, being crippled is the increasingly indeterminate war on terrorism.

Last January an open letter appeared in Israeli newspapers signed by 52 reserve soldiers who had fought for Israel's army, and were still called to patrol the occupied territories. The extraordinary defiance was articulated by their published statement: "We combat officers and soldiers, whose eyes have seen the bloody toll this occupation exacts from both sides, hereby declare that the mission of the occupation and oppression does not serve Israel's defense."

It is extremely significant that, despite threats of demotions and jailings and rapidly increasing violence between Israelis and Palestinians, more military reservists are adding their names to the letter (345 as of 3/18 verification).

Ishai Menuchin, who joined the Israeli army 20 years ago as a paratrooper officer, authored a statement published in the New York *Times* (3/19/02) that strongly said "No" to Israel's occupation of Palestine territory.

He spent 35 days in military prison for his refusal to serve in the occupation, but is now a major in Israel's Defense Forces Reserve and chairman of Yesh Gvul, a strong and growing soldier's movement for selective refusal in a military occupation that already numbers in the thousands. Menuchin said that "over the decades the occupation has made Israel less secure and more inhumane." The escalating violence is evidence of this trend.

March 14, 1994

There's a lot more to the Zapatista National Liberation Army uprising in Mexico's impoverished southern states than meets the eye.

The significance to Mexico, our interests, and to all of Latin America is far greater than most mainstream media have reported.

The Mayan Indian revolt that began the same day NAFTA was inaugurated shattered the illusion of Mexico's political stability and exposed massive social inequalities as well as the exclusion of that country's indigenous population from its vaunted economic development. It undressed Mexican reality at the international level.

So the crucial question for the outgoing government of President Carlos Salinas de Gortari is: How far and how fast will the rebellion spread?

Thus the obvious urgency of the current negotiations and the seeming conciliatory tone the government is now giving them.

Unavoidably in the process, the government finds itself facing almost as much political risk from its tentative peace accord with the armed Indian rebels as if the talks had failed.

The government is aware this rebellion could spur on other groups of poor to violence.

Because of that, the government and its ruling PRI (Partido Revolucionario Institucional) has agreed to political, social and economic reforms in Chiapas state. The PRI also has agreed to clean up its fraud-ridden election system that has maintained it in power since its founding in 1929. National elections will be held in August.

Clouding the negotiations is the specter of the Mexican Army's performance in combating the uprising. Dozens of national and international human rights organizations have documented the summary executions and killings, arbitrary detentions, torturing of prisoners, aerial attacks on civilians and villages, and the cover-up approach of the Army and government.

In Chiapas, the government says 100 people were killed, yet the Catholic dioceses there have verified more than 500, with many unaccounted for.

Complications also resulted from the Salinas government's attempt last year to topple Bishop Ruiz by getting Papal Nuncio Giorlama Prigione to publicize Vatican charges against him. Prigione even pressured the other two Chiapas bishops to attack Ruiz.

Instead they issued a joint statement decrying the region's "centuries-long history of poverty and injustices as being the great destabilizer" as part of their support for Bishop Ruiz.

The Salinas government's attempt to pressure Mexico City Cardinal Ernesto Corripio to satanize both the Zapatistas and Ruiz also backfired when the cardinal issued a statement giving full support to his San Cristobal bishop.

Also supporting Ruiz was Adolfo Suarez Rivera, head of the Mexican Bishops' conference representing the nation's 105 bishops and their auxiliaries.

So, is it any wonder that a writer for the prominent Mexican newspaper *La Jornada*, Roberto Biancarte, said that all this "has served to move progressive theological thinking, personified by Bishop Ruiz, from the margin of the church to its center."

And Jose Alvarez Icaza, respected writer on liberation theology, said: "The church of the poor is in the ascendancy at last and Mexico will never be the same."

As a postscript, Bishop Ruiz later this year must make his five-year Ad Limina visit to Rome to evaluate the work of his diocese before a pope who often has been harsh with those who champion the church of the poor.

They also remember that Emiliano Zipata was betrayed and assassinated by the government in 1919.

PART VI

The Folly of War—
The Wisdom of Peace

CHAPTER 18

A War on Truth

Students of history are painfully aware of war's first casualty—truth—for history is replete with sorry evidence of the slaughter. Considering "patriotism and dissent in wartime" in the wake of the 9/11 terrorist attacks, Arthur Schlesinger, Jr. posed three questions which we might wish to consider here: "The first question is whether a democratic people has a moral obligation to terminate dissent when the nation is at war. And the second question is whether, as a factual matter, our ancestors abstained from dissent when their governments took them into war. These two questions presuppose a third: What is the true nature of patriotism anyway?"[15] Perhaps these questions might hang unanswered as a backdrop while we peruse the following columns. On September 13, 2002, Simon questioned the truthfulness of the message pounded out by Bush's war drums, ending with a haunting prescience, "Think about it. Your well-being and that of your country are at stake." We now know the audacious totality of mendacity which led us into an Iraq quagmire bleeding us of lives, resources and reputation. Writing for February 21, 1997, Simon laid bare the mirage of opportunity through military service. On November 26, 2003, reporting Sister Joan Chittester's commentary on "what matters," Simon concluded with her that truth matters.

September 13, 2002

It has been documented in every war ever reported that the first casualty is truth. That's the way it is, and historical reality is already well on its way in the emerging Bush II war on Iraq—if peace doesn't get in its way.

There's also a precedent for the bull emanating from this administration's gung-ho war hawks. Back in 1990, when Bush I ordered American

---

15. Arthur M. Schlesinger, Jr., *War and the American Presidency*, New York: W. W. Norton & Company, 2004, p. 70.

forces to the Persian Gulf, a major basis for his case was that an Iraqi juggernaut was threatening to roll into Saudi Arabia.

Bush's Defense Secretary Cheney's Pentagon cited top-secret satellite images supposedly showing that up to 250,000 Iraqi troops and 1,500
tanks were already at the border threatening the key U.S. oil supplier. All
this turned out to be pure baloney.

The enterprising St. Petersburg (Fla.) *Times*, protecting the right to
know, acquired two commercial Soviet satellite images of the same area
taken at the same time. The only thing visible was empty desert and no
Iraqi troops anywhere near the Saudi border. But in the tradition of thorough reporting, the *Times* asked two experts to examine the satellite images of the expanded Saudi and Kuwait border areas. One of the experts, a
former Defense Intelligence Agency analyst specializing in desert warfare,
was surprised at no sign of the Iraqis, but did note U.S. jet fighters standing
wing-tip to wing-tip at Saudi bases. When the *Times* contacted Cheney's
office (3 times) for evidence refuting the photos or analysis and offering to
hold the story if proven wrong, the official response was "trust us."

In the present increasingly frenetic scramble to prove their case regardless of facts, administration hardliners have an obstacle—beyond the
growing skepticism of the American people. Rolf Ekeus, head of U.N.
weapons inspection in Iraq from 1991-97, has accused the U.S. and other
Security Council members of manipulating U.N. inspections for political
ends. This revelation by a most respected Swedish diplomat unavoidably
strengthens Iraq's argument against allowing U.N. inspectors back.

It is also highly significant that Scott Ritter, a rugged decorated ex-
Marine and former chief weapons inspector for the U.N. in Iraq, recently
said: "To date, the Bush administration has been unable or unwilling
to back up its rhetoric concerning the Iraqi threat with any substantive
facts."

Ritter also has revealed that weapons inspection has been on occasion
a cover for spying.

It's ironic there may have been panic among administration war hawks
last August 5 when Iraq unequivocally invited Senate and House members, plus some of the best and most experienced weapons inspectors in
the world, to come to Iraq for a thorough inspection process. This is what
the White House has been demanding of Iraq for years. Thus this had
ominous potential because it could derail the war train gathering momentum.

To their shame, bipartisan leaders in Congress scorned the offer and
the media fell on its face. A *USA Today* news story called it "the latest

Iraqi bid to complicate U.S. invasion plans." That is reprehensible reporting when powerful politicians are hell bent on starting a war regardless of the unfathomable human misery and death that involves. So no complications are wanted before the bloodshed begins! What kind of human beings fend off the threat of peace? Let the killing begin, and taxpayer dollars flow to do it.

We've been had before, as in the Bush I Gulf War, and already are being had in the pending Bush II Iraq war. Remember how we all were swayed by tearful testimony of a 15-year-old Kuwait girl, known only as Nayirah, before a congressional caucus in the fall of 1990. She described how as a volunteer in a Kuwait maternity ward she had seen Iraqi troops storm into her hospital, steal the incubators and leave 312 babies "on the cold floor to die." Seven U.S. senators used that story during debate and Bush I invoked it five times, saying that such "ghastly atrocities were like Hitler revisited."

It was later documented that "Nayirah" was daughter of the Kuwaiti ambassador to Washington and had no connection to the Kuwait hospital. She had been coached, along with a handful of others to "corroborate" the story, by senior executives of Hill and Knowlton, Washington's biggest global PR firm that had a $10 million contract with the Kuwaitis to make the case for war.

All this is documented in the book, *Second Front: Censorship and Propaganda in the Gulf War*, authored by John MacArthur, publisher of *Harper's* magazine. The respected and courageous MacArthur warns that considering the number of senior officials shared by both Bush administrations, Americans should not forget lessons of Gulf War propaganda. "These are the same people who were running it 10 years ago. They'll make up just about anything to get their way."

Think about it. Your wellbeing and that of your country are at stake.

February 21, 1997

Many people in the United States fervently believe in a number of myths.

One is the supply-siders' "trickle-down" concept that has difficult experiencing any credibility in the real world. Bob Dole was supposedly converted to this for the span of the recent presidential campaign.

Then there's the time-honored myth that national security can be achieved through armaments and military strength. If this were true, we'd never have whipped the British in the Revolutionary War. A more recent example is Iran under the Shah. He had the biggest, most modern, best-equipped military in the Middle East. But the Ayatollah Khomeini, a guy in a white robe with an idea, brought it all tumbling down in a matter of days.

Yet as the billions being spent on armaments in our country and around the world demonstrate, we still seem unable to recognize that a healthy society, economic stability, the spirit of a country's citizens and confidence in their system of government convey far more national security than the size of armies or money spent on armaments.

A current myth that seems to have a lot of acceptance is the one pushed in military advertisements that project an image of opportunity—such as "Join the Army and Be All You Can Be." Back in my military days it was "Join the Navy and see the world"—but what did we see? We saw the sea! Incidentally, the Pentagon spends $1.9 billion of our tax dollars each year on recruiting and advertising.

When you dig into it, the image of opportunity in the military doesn't withstand sober analysis. Perhaps the best measure of the economic impact of joining the military is whether a person with military experience and background earns more or less than a comparable non-veteran.

A comprehensive overview of 14 studies analyzing this question, by Stephen Barley of the School of Industrial and Labor Relations at Cornell University, found that the average post-Vietnam-era veteran earns between 11 percent and 19 percent less than non-veterans from comparable socio-economic backgrounds. And a 1990 study by Bryant and Wilhite documented that the average veteran will earn 85 cents less per hour, or about $1,700 less per year, than non-veterans.

The Pentagon and its military make a big thing of the training you're supposed to get in the military. Yet Ohio State researchers Mangum and Ball, who receive funding from the Pentagon, found that only 12 percent of male veterans and 6 percent of female veterans surveyed made any use in civilian jobs of the skills learned in the military. And veterans averaged only 1.78 months of training in 31 months of active duty.

Cornell University's Barley concluded: "The evidence on rates of return to training and the probability of finding a job in one's chosen profession strongly suggest that, all else being equal, young people should look to sources of training other than the military if they wish to optimize their careers.

A big thing is also made of ROTC scholarships. But Capt. Muhlenbeck, ROTC public affairs officer, says that only 8,000 people are getting

ROTC scholarships nationwide. This 8,000 is about one-fifth of 1 percent of all college students.

And perhaps the misleading advertising in the GI Bill should be a major concern. To become eligible for the GI Bill benefits, enlistees have to pay a non-refundable fee of $1,000. Only veterans with honorable discharges are eligible to get money back. But according to Terry Memison, spokesman with the Veterans Administration, of all the GIs paying in, only 35 percent have received any benefits. And the *Army Times* in 1993 reported that through this deception the military has taken in $720 million more in fees than it has paid out in benefits.

So what kind of "economic opportunity" is there in the Army? The *Army Times* reports that more than 50,000 unemployed veterans are on the waiting list for the military's "retraining" program. And the clincher is the VA estimates that one-third of homeless people today in America are veterans.

November 26, 2003

Sister Joan Chittister, of the Benedictine Order in Erie, Pennsylvania, is an active member of the International Peace Council. Widely recognized and respected in her work for peace and understanding, she wrote a provocative article that was published in the *National Catholic Reporter* last May, under the title "Is There Anything Left That Matters?"

After considerable thought and even hesitation, for the first time ever "Think about It" devotes a column to what someone else said about a very crucial issue that affects all of us. Here's the essence of what Sister Chittister wrote:

This is what I don't understand: All of a sudden nothing seems to matter. First they said they wanted bin Laden "dead or alive." But they didn't get him. So now they tell us that it didn't matter. Our mission is greater than one man.

(She then continues the same point with Saddam Hussein and the certitude of weapons of mass destruction that didn't exist, as the stated justification for our invasion of Iraq, where many Americans are dying because of lies.)

Except that it does matter.

I know we're not supposed to say that. I know it's called "unpatriotic." But it is also called honesty. And dishonesty matters.

It matters that the infrastructure of a foreign nation that couldn't defend itself against us has been destroyed on the grounds that it was a military threat to the world.

It matters that it was destroyed by us under a new doctrine of "preemptive war" when there was apparently nothing worth pre-empting.

It surely matters to the families here whose sons went to war.

It matters to families in the U.S. whose life-support programs were needed.

It matters to Ali, the Iraqi boy who lost his family—and both his arms—in a U.S. air attack.

It matters to the people in Baghdad whose water supply is now fetid, whose electricity is gone, whose streets are unsafe.

It matters that the people we say we "liberated" do not feel liberated.

It matters to the U.N. whose integrity was impugned, whose authority was denied.

It matters to the reputation of the U.S. in the eyes of the world, both now and for decades to come.

And surely it matters to the integrity of this nation whether or not its intelligence gathering agencies have any real intelligence or not before we launch a military armada on its say-so.

And it should matter whether or not our government is either incompetent and didn't know what they were doing or were dishonest and refused to say. The unspoken truth is that either as a people we were misled or we were lied to, about the real reason for this war.

Either we made a huge—and unforgivable—mistake, an arrogant or ignorant mistake, or we are swaggering around the world like a blind giant, flailing in all directions while the rest of the world watches in horror or in ridicule.

If Bill Clinton's definition of "is" matters, surely this matters. If a president's sex life matters, surely a president's use of global force against some of the weakest people in the world matters. If a president's word in a court of law about a private indiscretion matters, surely a president's word to the community of nations and the security of millions of people matters.

Of what are we really capable as a nation if the considered judgment of politicians and people around the world means nothing to us as a people?

What is the depth of the American soul if we can allow destruction to be done in our name and the name of "liberation" and never even demand an accounting of its costs, both personal and public, when it is over?

We like to take comfort in the notion that people make a distinction between our government and ourselves. We like to say that the people of the world love Americans, they simply mistrust our government.

But excoriating a distant and anonymous "government" for wreaking rubble on a nation in pretense of good requires very little of either character or intelligence.

It may be time for us to realize that in a country that prides itself on being democratic, we are our government. And the rest of the world is figuring that out very quickly.

From where I stand, that matters.

CHAPTER 19

The United Nations:
Better *With* than *Without*

Simon's enthusiastic appreciation for the United Nations has been a constant. Writing for October 6, 1997, he took on familiar know-nothing dismissal of the organization, arguing how necessary is the U.N. in all the ways a know-nothing might never imagine. For December 23, 2001, Simon paid tribute to a U.N. which had responded intelligently and expeditiously to the 9/11 terrorist attacks. Writing for September 20, 1993 and September 5, 1994, Simon documents widespread public support for the U.N., despite the isolationist carping of some members of Congress, and he explores a surprising public support for reform of the U.N. by extending to it some principles of our federalism.

October 6, 1997

It gets rather tiresome listening to the Republican congressional leadership and radical right extremists criticizing the United Nations for a bloated bureaucracy and spiraling costs.

Basically this simply indicates these people's ignorance of realities, a proneness to play to the galleries, or perhaps a searching for currents in our society they can then try to "lead."

Ironically, these hits come from the same crowd that was almost mute during the Reagan-Bush years when government costs and waste spiraled through the roof, the little people in America were squeezed to new lows and the red ink hit new highs.

Here are some realities that are ignored or slipped by our congressional leaders and the U.N.-bashers:

- The Secretariat of the United Nations is operating on a zero-growth basis with a budget of $1.3 billion a year. That's less than the annual revenue of most major corporations. Since 1988,

10 percent of the Secretariat staff has been cut, with more cuts planned, and Secretary General Kofi Annan has cut top posts by 25 percent and set rigorous standards for staff performance. This $1.3 billion budget is about 4 percent of New York's annual budget and nearly a billion dollars less than the annual cost of the Tokyo fire department.

- The entire U.N. system employs less than 54,000 people worldwide. This is about one-third the number employed by McDonald's.

- U.S. businesses benefit substantially from the United Nations. United Nations' purchases from U.S. companies amount to more that $800 million a year. This is far in excess of the U.S. contribution to the United Nations' regular budget, and our contributions are delinquent, making us the world's biggest deadbeat. (Along with being the world's biggest arms supplier.)

- Those befuddled people who want to move the United Nations out of New York City need to know it contributed $3.2 billion a year to the economy of that area. And United Nations expenditures in this region generate more than 30,000 jobs with annual earnings of $1.2 billion. So our regular budget dues of only $321 million a year that we owe makes us look like a piker of a "deadbeat uncle."

- By stimulating economic growth in developing nations, the United Nations system creates and maintains jobs for thousands of American workers. Further, more prosperous developing nations become much better customers for United States products.

Have you ever thought that you couldn't even mail a letter to a foreign country without the United Nations Universal Postal Union that supervises agreements on international mail delivery? And you would be in trouble flying overseas if it weren't for the United Nations International Civil Aviation Organization that sets and supervises air safety standards for international air travel.

If you are one of those chauvinistic nationalists who don't want anything messing with our borders, better ask yourself if environmental pollution, climate change, ozone depletion, global warming, acid rain, hazardous chemicals or those infectious diseases that are spreading because of increased global travel ever respect national borders. They never have and they never will, because they can't.

Just as smallpox in the world was eradicated by the concerted efforts of the United Nations' World Health organization, the work of United Nations organizations is a necessity to making the world a safer place for all of us.

Bluntly said, if you really know the score and are still knocking the United Nations, then you could come across as some sort of un-American kook who is dangerous to the best interests and welfare of our country. Whatsa matter, don't you like America?

December 23, 2001

While the terrorist attacks of Sept. 11 have understandably focused attention on specifics of combating terrorism, and now on the military effort in Afghanistan, something different has emerged that is of great significance.

This is the drastic change in the international landscape that has very significantly transformed the role of the United Nations and America's relationship with it. The speed with which this change and precedent-setting actions have taken place would have been unbelievable prior to 9-11.

Within 24 hours after the twin towers collapsed, the United Nations Security Council met at the call of its rotating presidency—currently Jean-David Levitte of France, to consider a resolution drafted overnight that would define the framework for international response to terrorist attacks. In one hour the Council approved it unanimously, which included the votes of Russia and China, and also those of the Council's Muslim members: Tunisia, Bangladesh, Mali and Mauritius. Significantly, Cuba announced its intention to ratify all the U.N. antiterrorist conventions, as did Syria.

Resolution 1368 described the terrorist attacks as posing a "threat to international peace and security," and raised the unusual possibility of enforcement under Chapter VII of the U.N. Charter. It called on the world community "to combat by all means" this threat, understood by Council members to include possible use of military force.

Unanimous adoption of the resolution astonished international law experts with its boldness in requiring specific actions of member states in their domestic legislation so as to combat the threat the Council identified to international peace and security. This resolution also satisfied the U.S. government that it had the legal authority it needed to rebut criticism of whatever military action it might undertake against Al Queda and similar terrorist networks. The resolution even created a counter-terrorism committee to monitor compliance of all countries and promised to "take all necessary steps in order to insure the full implementation of this resolution."

The United Nations Educational, Scientific and Cultural Organization declared that "acts of terrorism can never be justified whatever the motives." But it did recognize that "intolerance, discrimination, inequality, poverty and exclusion, among others, provide fertile ground for terrorism."

All this unprecedented unity and speed with which the international community responded so strongly to the Sept. 11 attacks, sharply turned around the U.S. government. The Bush administration prior to 9-11 was implementing unilateral go-it-alone policies that failed to recognize the reality that no single nation can effectively resolve problems that are worldwide and know no boundaries. This unrealistic stance increasingly irked our allies and was "turning them off" from cooperation with the U.S. in many areas of concern.

The U.N. General Assembly convened October 1 for a weeklong session to directly address a single-agenda item: Measures to eliminate international terrorism. During that unusual session, 168 representatives and observers from nations around the world addressed the Assembly. This was the most ever to address an agenda item since the United Nations was founded in 1945.

Significantly, the U.S., which under Republican control of Congress, had become the world's biggest deadbeat nation, owing a half billion dollars in delinquent U.N. dues, now actually paid up. Congress did this without the usual inventing new conditions to dodge the issue, which was the pattern when Sen. Jesse Helms chaired the Senate Foreign Relations and did so much harm to America's best interests.

Topping off the new direction was the call Oct. 11 by President Bush—to his credit—for the U.N. to take over so-called "nation building" in post-conflict Afghanistan. This was the first time the Bush administration had ever endorsed peace building by the U.N. or any other international entity. This landmark turn in American policy showed that Bush is learning, as he said: "We did learn a lesson that we should not simply leave after a military objective has been achieved." So there is hope as world realities push the Bush administration to effectively meet them.

Perhaps the frosting on the cake of all these monumental changes is that the famed Nobel Prize Committee has just announced its decision to award the coveted 2001 Nobel Peace Prize to Secretary General Kofi Annan and the United Nations. The citation from the Nobel Committee will read: "The only negotiable route to global peace and cooperation goes by way of the United Nations." The U.N. is the only institution that is uniquely qualified to deliver an effective response to global threats to peace and security of all nations.

It is One World out there and "no man is an island." We all are part of the same family tree and that tree is humanity. Growing American awareness and support of the U.N. and its strengths for world peace could become by far the most productive result of what happened Sept. 11.

September 5, 1994

Since its founding in 1945 out of the ashes of World War II, the United Nations has been supported by both major political parties. A key element in our nation's foreign policy successes has been strong bipartisan support for the U.N.

In recent years, however, bipartisan backing for the world organization has been waning. An example came last May when 24 House Republicans initiated a floor vote that would have prevented the U.S. from paying any assessments for U.N. peacekeeping. Only six Republicans voted against the measure as their party becomes more nationalistic and isolationist in its world outlook.

The perils of this direction were reflected in the unilateral ventures of the Reagan and Bush administrations that replaced multilateral diplomacy and led to a series of failures in Lebanon, Libya, Panama and elsewhere. These misadventures cost American lives and accomplished nothing of substance. But they were accompanied by bitter arguments among the public and Congress. In the process there was severe damage to what could be called our collective civic hygiene. This did not help America.

All this leads to a major irony and contradiction. While congressional support for the United Nations is at an all-time low, public support for the U.N. is at an all-time high.

Documenting this, a New York *Times* poll last April found 89 percent of Americans believe that it is important to cooperate with other countries by working through the U.N. And by a margin of 77 to 21, Americans said the U.N. has contributed to world peace.

Does this add up to yet another example of the American people being smarter than their representatives in Congress and more in tune with the times? Could it mean that congressional Republican leadership is increasingly out-of-touch with voters?

Thus, Congress should either get-with-it or get out of the way in its failure to pay some $800 million in delinquent payments owed as legal treaty obligations to the United Nations.

It is highly significant that probably the most credible figure in America, Walter Cronkite, in July said that now is the time "to re-order our world," as he called upon Americans to realize the dreams of U.N. founders. He gave a ringing endorsement to the World Federalist Association, USA, citing his belief that "federalists have solutions to the global problems haunting us today that cast dark shadows over the world our grandchildren will inherit."

September 20, 1993

The so-called "New World Order" that a pumped-up George Bush trumpeted at the peak of his Gulf War popularity has turned out to be a bust. Most everyone realizes this now, as they do that the current "world order" is actually a world of anarchy.

Individual countries and their leaders have the "right" to do whatever they have the will, money, soldiers and weapons to do. And they've done it: murdering their own countrymen, invading other nations and destroying the environment, with resulting problems that know no national boundaries.

A prime reason for this reality is because the United Nations is weak and ineffective by design—because that's the way the great powers wanted it. By contrast, our founding fathers wisely replaced the law of force with the force of law when they formed our federal system of government. In so doing, they united widely disparate colonies with as many or more differences than many of today's nations.

If our effective American federalist model were wisely adopted at the world level it could lead to abolition of war, hunger, human rights abuses, terrorism, drug trafficking, environment destruction and also save billions wasted on enormously expensive individual defense systems for a supposed security that no longer exists. (Doing this would sure lower the taxes we pay.)

Remember that the Shah's Iran went down the tubes almost overnight while it had the biggest, most modern and technically superior armed force in the entire Middle East—which amounted to zilch when it really counted.

The need today in a shrinking, interdependent world is so obvious one wonders how our leaders and too many of us could be so dumb for so long with our own successful federalist system as an example right at hand.

And the American people are for it. The most recent Americans Talk Issues national public opinion poll reveals that a 62 percent majority of American registered voters favor U.S. participation in a world conference to review and amend the U.N. Charter to give United Nations responsibility in areas where individual nations can no longer solve the problems alone. Significantly, the poll shows only 10 percent are opposed to this with 29 percent neutral. Then a strong 80 percent of voters favor the U.N. having responsibility for international security, with 77 percent wanting a World Court and 67 percent for a global police force.

This revealing poll of U.S. voters also documents that 82 percent want to enable the U.N. to arrest individuals who commit serious international crimes, with only 15 percent opposed.

And these strong majorities support holding individuals accountable to an International Criminal Court for such specific actions as violating human rights.

Our federal system has withstood the test of time for a diverse United States. So why wouldn't it for our little One World, where nations today are more interconnected and interdependent than were the original 13 colonies?

The nations of the world and their leaders are increasingly finding out that no longer in today's world can they effectively hack it alone. We are learning the hard and costly way that solutions that really work just don't happen anymore by unilateral action. All this also documents the utter truth of "No man is an island." And neither is any nation in today's world.

CHAPTER 20

A Specter Is Haunting the World— the Specter of Nuclear War

Like death itself, the nuclear threat—so ubiquitous, so omnipresent in the lives of contemporaries—has tended to be relegated to just another of the unpleasant and threatening but inevitable background noises of our urban existence. But like the city roar of internal-combustion engine traffic, the nuclear threat is not inevitable, can be at least alleviated. So Simon forcefully reminds us on January 28, 2001. Writing for April 3, 1995, in observance of the approaching 50th anniversary of our Japanese atomic bombings, Simon presents the evidence that the bombings were unnecessary to compel the Japanese surrender, a tragedy for Japan, the U.S. and all the world. Simon's columns for July 26, 1993, and January 4, 2004, provide an interesting contrast between two presidents and two attitudes toward use of nuclear weapons.

January 28, 2001

Any American and any person anywhere who believes there is no need to worry about nuclear dangers is suffering from illusions. Collectively these could endanger the lives of all of us, and these threats are around us right now.

Even though the Cold War ended 10 years ago with the fall of the Berlin Wall, our country still has a tremendous arsenal of more than 2,500 strategic thermonuclear bombs that are on hair-trigger alert—and not a single one is fool-proof of accidental catastrophe.

Compounding the thin thread holding us, Russia's nuclear command control is seriously deteriorated and thus at risk of an inadvertent launch. It is deplorably dangerous that neither country seems to have enough imaginative, hard-nosed and brainy leadership to cooperatively be working strenuously to take all nuclear weapons off hair-trigger alert. Unless this is done, there's an accident waiting to happen that would be massively death-dealing to millions of human beings.

A tiny fraction of the $122 billion taxpayer money our government has spent and wasted over the past 40 years trying to develop an anti-ballistic missile so-called defense shield—that continues a failure track record—would be a hundred times more cost effective if it were directed toward cooperation in dismantling the nuclear stockpiles of all nations that have "the bomb." Where's real leadership when humanity desperately needs it?

It is not that we don't have other pressing needs. The respected World Health Organization recently ranked the U.S. health-care system 37th among nations of the world. And this for the world's richest country, as it continues to be the only industrial democracy on earth without universal health care for all its citizens. Even poor Cuba has it for everyone.

We're also the only major nation in the world whose citizens are being ripped off by drug companies charging us many times more for identical medicine being sold for a fraction that price outside our borders.

Despite these realities, the full-scale Star Wars system projected by the incoming Bush administration will cost U.S. taxpayers "easily" another $100 billion. And already for fiscal 2001, $4.7 billion has been earmarked for even more of what has proven a colossally failed system. None of these people's billions will enhance the health and security of Americans, while going begging are an array of human needs, such as assisting families in caring for disabled relatives, preventing the spread of HIV in America and around the world, and evaluating the environmental causes of disease.

Is it surprising that members of prestigious and knowledgeable organizations who really understand the issue, such as the Federation of American Scientists (including 40 Nobel Laureates), the Union of Concerned Scientists, the American Physical Society and the Massachusetts Institute of Technology Security Studies Program, have all rejected the feasibility of National Missile Defense? And every American ally almost uniformly opposes it, mostly because more Star Wars threatens to unravel hard-earned necessary arms control treaties and thus destabilize our security.

Just last week, 400 American physicians and health professionals, representing many thousands more, implored President Bush to "recognize the potential public health catastrophe that could result from your proposed missile defense system." They were speaking for their patients and all Americans "who will be placed in greater jeopardy if the system is deployed."

All these concerned groups and professionals understand the health consequences of nuclear explosions that would be devastating. The blast wave and intense heat generated by just one nuclear bomb would kill everyone with a few miles of the explosion. Thermal and ionizing radiation would inflict lethal injuries hundreds of miles away. The explosion would also cause all objects in the area to become dangerously radioactive, creating a vast nuclear "fallout."

The National Research Council recently concluded that 109 of 144 sites used for the U.S. nuclear weapons program will never be clear of enough radioactive contamination to allow unrestricted public use. Additional ballistic missile and nuclear weapons development from more Star Wars will result in even more environmental damage—and the environment is where we all live!

All military tests of the system to date have flopped, except for the single "success" test that the Air Force finally admitted was due to lowered test standards. That's like lowering the bar so the high jumper can "win." And it has cost us $122 billion, so far, for nothing.

Is the military-industrial complex President Eisenhower aptly warned us about so powerful it can jerk around presidents, secretaries of state and congressmen so as to keep its gravy train rolling? What kind of leadership goes along with this against the best interests and security of the American people?

But you can do something about it. National Call-in Days to the White House have been set for Monday and Tuesday, Feb. 5 and 6. The White House phone is (202) 456-1414, and its address is 1600 Pennsylvania Avenue, Washington, D.C. 20500. Tell President Bush to reduce the danger of accidental nuclear war by working with the Russians and other nuclear powers to get all nuclear weapons off hair-trigger alert. The life you save may be your own.

April 3, 1995

For nearly half a century, the conventional wisdom and politically correct stance has been that "hundreds of thousands of lives were saved" when we became the first (and only) nation ever to use atomic bombs on civilian populations with the bombing of Hiroshima and Nagasaki in Japan.

But with the historical perspective and analysis going on since the August 1945 atomizing of those cities, a different picture is emerging in time for the 50th anniversary of the August bombing.

Yes, things are changing because of what we know now that we did not know then.

Gen. Dwight D. Eisenhower, for one, was deeply depressed when he was informed that the atomic bomb would be used in those circumstances. Ike said, "Japan was at that very moment seeking some way to surrender with a minimum loss of 'face'...it wasn't necessary to hit them with that awful thing."

This is buttressed by a Journal Diplomatic History survey of relevant studies showing that "The consensus among scholars is that the bomb was not needed to avoid an invasion of Japan and to end the war within a relatively short time."

"It is clear that alternatives to the bomb existed" and that "Truman and his advisors knew it." Further, discovery of President Truman's lost diary shows it was fully understood that the shock of the expected Russian declaration of war in early August 1945 would likely end the fighting. Truman privately noted in his diary: "Fini Japs when that comes about."

Adm. William D. Leahy, chief of staff to the president, minced few words: "The Japanese were already defeated and ready to surrender. The use of this barbarous weapon at Hiroshima and Nagasaki was of no material assistance in our war against Japan. In being the first to use it, we adopted an ethical standard common to the barbarians of the dark ages. I was not taught to make war in that fashion, and wars cannot be won by destroying women and children."

U.S. Army Air Forces Gen. "Hap" Arnold, subsequently declared that "it always appeared to us that, atomic bomb or no atomic bomb, the Japanese were already on the verge of collapse." And Curtis LeMay, the flamboyant Hawk who commanded the 20th Air Force, stated publicly in 1945 that the atomic bomb had nothing to do with the end of the war at all... The war would have been over in two weeks without the atomic bomb."

Historians and recent studies suggest the number of lives the bombing might have saved has been grossly exaggerated. The consensus of specialists studying the 1945 documents is that the maximum estimate of lives saved is roughly 46,000 "if" there had been an invasion, and most believe that by August 1945, this was only a remote possibility.

All this is confirmed from information the United States had because we had broken the Japanese codes. Thus, we knew that a minor modification of the unconditional surrender formula allowing Japan to keep its emperor-God in an innocuous role like that of the Queen of England probably would end the war.

Yes, things are changing. A well-known military hard-liner, Paul Nitze, recently suggested that "for the first time, we might reasonably contemplate making nuclear weapons largely obsolete for the most practical and fundamental strategic weapons."

And we'd better do it, and fast, for our own safety. Besides England, France, China and Russia, these other nations have a potential nuclear capability: Korea, Israel, Ukraine, India, Pakistan, Argentina and Brazil.

This year's Nuclear Non-Proliferation Treaty should be renewed, and it should include every nation in our world—while we and the other great powers have the clout to do it.

July 26, 1993

It was a real close squeak…

The nine-month moratorium on nuclear testing was set to expire July 1. So the ever money-hungry Pentagon, the Joint Chiefs of Staff, nuclear weapons laboratories, the departments of Defense and even State, and a rapacious weapons industry mounted a massive campaign to resume nuclear testing (and keep the big bucks rolling their way).

That congressional moratorium back in the fall of 1992 was the result of an outpouring of broad-based citizen support for arms control and a nuclear test ban that received strong backing by the arms control, religious and peace organizations throughout the country. And it was two Oregon legislators who initiated it: Rep. Mike Kopetaki (D) in the House and Sen. Mark Hatfield (R) in the Senate—to their everlasting credit.

But this past June rumors were circulating in Washington that the Clinton administration was going to resume testing.

While it would have meant a fight with Democrats in Congress, President Clinton had the guts and sense to stand up against the big boys in the armament crowd and scrap plans for nine underground nuclear tests. This extended the moratorium through September 1994, unless another nation starts testing first.

The window dressing rationale for resumed testing by the gung-ho crowd was to "improve safety features" on nuclear warheads. But experts say the components can be tested without explosions.

The joker in this is that these bombs are far safer than we are! It goes beyond the frontiers of the unreal to renew testing to be sure weapons are safe! And yet the Pentagon wants to continue testing the primeval ovens that put more innocents in peril.

It could be said the only nation on which we have declared nuclear war in 50 years is the United States! We have exploded nearly a thousand nuclear bombs in Nevada. A dirty nuclear secret is there are people down-wind of the test site who have lost up to 16 members of their extended families to radiation-induced cancers. And Nevada ranchers can tell you what has happened to their sheep and cattle.

An Air Force colonel who flew radiation monitoring missions across the country and into Canada and Mexico said, "There isn't anyone in the U.S. who isn't a down-winder!" And when the Atomic Energy Commission reported "no radioactivity east of the Mississippi" they didn't say there were no radiation monitors east of the Mississippi!

You taxpayers and voters who don't like to shell out and want government to spend less of your money should know that each nuclear explosion costs us $50 to $100 million; the Defense Monitor prices it at only $30 to $60 million. Either way, it's only taxpayer money!

A key factor that goes right by the nuclear crowd is that the Soviet Union, before it went down the tubes, conducted about 600 tests as compared to our nearly 1,000. Thus the U.S. is far ahead of any nuclear nation in technical superiority and a lasting test ban would freeze this superiority and keep the U.S. No. 1.

An urgent and long overdue halt to the spread of nuclear weapons is what a test moratorium is all about. Thus had we irrationally resumed testing, then the genie would be out of the bottle all over the world—and you would have to dig deeper in your pockets for more tax dollars to feed the monster, as the deficit accelerated!

There is no question that Russia and France, now observing test moratoriums of their own, would resume testing along with China and Britain, as India, Pakistan, Brazil, Ukraine, North Korea, Israel, and others are ready in the wings.

And how could the U.S. irrationally continue telling the non-aligned nations to refrain from any nuclear weapons and tests—in line with our non-proliferation policy—while we ourselves resumed testing that triggered others in the nuclear club to do the same? More testing would send the wrong message everywhere and put all mankind at risk.

As it is, the non-aligned nations, who comprise more than two-thirds of the 157 countries in the Non-Proliferation Treaty, are rightly fed up with the hypocrisy and procrastination of the nuclear powers, who have been in effect saying, "Do what I say, not what I do."

They are also rightly demanding that the 1963 Partial Test Ban Treaty negotiated by Kennedy and Khrushchev after the Cuban missile crisis be converted into a total test ban treaty. Doing this would be a boon for people everywhere—and it would sure help your family budget and pocketbook!

Any nuclear testing is a dangerous anachronism in a world of potential proliferators, with ever more nations ready to "get the bomb." Thus a multilateral, comprehensive test ban on all nuclear weapons everywhere is a must for humanity and a safe Earth, where we all must live.

January 4, 2004

As we begin our journey into another year, it is urgent and overdue for all of us citizens who love our country to become aware of a great danger that is sneaking up on us. Failure to do this could be fatal to us and to our future.

With the trademark secrecy and closed doors of a regime that has turned its back on democratic openness, denying the people's right to know, the Bush administration has underhandedly embarked our country on an extremely costly and dangerous multimillion dollar expansion of America's nuclear arsenal. Already this has prompted growing fears across the political spectrum that we are leading the world into a new and suicidal arms race.

The Bushites, with their arrogant certitude, are pushing ahead with development of a new generation of nuclear weapons dubbed "mini-nukes" that will be enhanced radiation weapons and "bunker-busters." These are supposedly low-yield nuclear weapons that are causing professional skepticism about use of the word "mini" to describe them.

Unfortunately for the people who are compelled to pay for all this, this arbitrarily dangerous thrust is being done without serious congressional input and the open public discussion so necessary for wise policy in a healthy democracy. Even worse, a dishonest regime is well on its way to transforming its wacky Strangelovian nuclear war-fighting ideas from dark ambition into stark reality. In the doing, the Bush regime is spurring a destructive global arms race because of its development of a new generation of nuclear weapons.

What makes all this utterly irrational, as if administration planners are losing their marbles, is this same administration pressuring countries such as Iran and North Korea to abandon their nuclear plans. Is this yet another example of the Bushite stance of in effect saying, "do as we say, not as we do"? In their blindness, Bush policies are having the opposite affect of containment by erasing the taboo on use of nuclear weapons. Russia has already responded that it will develop new "tactical" weapons, and it would be naïve to doubt our enemies will follow suit.

Even worse, this emerging nightmare being engineered by the Bush administration is sapping our country's moral authority by demanding other countries stop violating the Nuclear Non-Proliferation Treaty when our government has already abandoned that agreement! Is there any sanity in such "policy"? And what does this do to the vanishing respect for America that is surfacing around the world, as the Bush regime bases its foreign policy on the ancient and outdated precept that "might makes right"? (The "might" part is right because U.S. military spending already tops that of all other major powers' military spending combined, and Bush aims to up it even more—with you-know-who footing the bill.)

Under the phony guise of "defending our nation," (a phrase milked *ad nauseum* since 9-11), instead of genuinely protecting our country and enhancing our security, the Bush regime's go-it-alone preemptive war doctrine and callous abandonment of protective international treaties is actually increasing dangers to America and adding to global instability.

Another stupidly dangerous by-product of the Bush policy getting even more nuclear weapons and underlining its willingness to use them is the blurring this does to differences between nuclear war and conventional conflict. Doing this is both dangerously unsettling and provocative, like a drunk in the bar preaching temperance while he orders another round.

Even GOP hawks are getting upset by the radical armament provocations of the Bush administration. Rep. Joel Hefley (R-Colo.), a senior member of the Armed Services Committee, said in an interview: "We don't need new weapons, and in fact they do more harm than good in our relations with other countries and in our moral position on nuclear proliferation. I think they're almost obsolete."

Rep. David Hobson (R-Ohio), chairman of House Appropriations Committee's energy and water subcommittee that controls the nuclear weapons budget, said, "I'm concerned about our image in the world when we're telling others not to build these things, and then we push these new programs."

As it radically reverses a decade of nuclear weapons restraint, Bush II's policies are setting our nation and the world on a dangerously life-threatening course making the nuclear threat more insidious than ever before, as it eliminates safety of the entire non-proliferation program. And because of its approach, this vitally crucial issue is clouded with misinformation, lack of democratic debate, and false patriotic fervor.

All these harsh realities underline how the extremist bluster, dishonesty and arrogance of the Bush regime is seriously endangering peace around the world and weakening the national security of all Americans.

Yes, the arrogance, dishonesty and accompanying greed of its Big

Money supporters is not only weakening national security and threatening world peace, it also underlines a key element missing from this administration's repertoire toward achieving genuine peace and justice so necessary to real worldwide security. It is integrity.

CHAPTER 21

The Costs of War

Americans—and the corporate media which control so much of America's thinking—are not prone to commemorate our national hero, Martin Luther King, with quotations from his New York's Riverside Church speech of April 4, 1967, a year to the day before his assassination, a speech in which he termed his country "the greatest purveyor of violence in the world today." But we can perhaps no longer ignore the cost of that violence. History is replete with lessons of war as a failed policy, a no-win/no-win equation, from the parallel tragedies suffered by Greeks and Trojans on the plains of Ilium to the tragic loss of Ancient Greek greatness out of the Peloponnesian War to the prostrate Iraq and gravely damaged America emerging from the most recent U.S. incursion into the Middle East. The costs of war are ultimately incalculable, certainly to those who pay its ultimate cost—extinction—but also to those fortunate—or unfortunate—enough to be left to pick up the pieces. Nor can the wisest of historians tally up all the costs. Perhaps Barbara Tuchman comes nearest in documenting "the march of human folly." In Simon's first column reproduced here, that of October 18, 1993, he reminds us that war is not the American way. Writing for June 7, 1996, Simon laments the cost to citizen-wellbeing caused by the waste on military budgets. As early in The Bush/Cheney Iraq War as his April 6, 2003 column, Simon revealed the "shock and awe" which would even more dismay us in later years—the cost in human lives; the dollar cost of destroying, then rebuilding a nation; the cost of the ongoing guerrilla war in Iraq distracting from the real "war on terror;" an incalculable cost, the diminution of our own precious liberties; and the cost to our democracy, the erosion of public trust fed by the administration's lies and double-speak—all the "shock and awe" which we would feel even more intensely through the long years of war which were to follow.

October 18, 1993

Who said this? "Standing armies in time of peace are inconsistent with the principles of republican government, dangerous to the liberties of free people, and generally converted into destructive engines for establishing despotism."

Go ahead, take a guess. It was a statement by the American Continental Congress in 1784, as it debated the relationship of the military and democracy in America.

And George Washington had something to say about it, too. Our nation's first president said this in 1796: "Overgrown military establishments, which under any form of government are inauspicious to liberty... are to be regarded as particularly hostile to republican liberty."

Even the Declaration of Independence, in 1776, made the point as it sensed the clash of values we're experiencing today... "The present King of Great Britain has kept among us, in times of peace, Standing Armies, without the Consent of our legislatures. He has affected to render the Military independent of and superior to the Civil Power."

That last sentence underlines why our Founding Fathers firmly believed that the best way to safeguard democratic values and institutions is to keep the pursuits of war, and the instruments of war, distinct from pursuits of peace.

This year our country will spend $291 billion on the military. This huge amount is only a fraction below Cold War budgets and, almost incomprehensibly, that bundle of taxpayer dollars will include spending for an array of Cold War weapons, many that are no longer needed or virtually obsolete. Meanwhile, our foreign policy has been militarized.

Does all this underline the truth of President Dwight D. Eisenhower's stern warning of the dangers of America's "Military-Industrial Complex"? Does it reflect his apt statement in 1953?: "Every gun that is made, every warship launched, every rocket fired signifies—in the final sense—a theft from those who hunger and are not fed, those who are cold and not clothed. This is not a way of life at all, in a true sense. Under the cloud of threatening war, it is humanity, dangling from a cross of iron." Dwight Eisenhower deserves credit for a wisdom that history has not yet granted him.

While our military has repeatedly shown what can be done with its obedience, discipline, conformity, dedication and loyalty, this is at odds with the values of the colonists—who came to America because the military ethic is basically anti-individualistic.

So there is a conflict of values with our cherished principles of individuality and freedom of choice. We Americans want the freedom to pursue social and economic opportunity, to worship as we please, to engage in debate and have the right to dissent and to experiment whether we're challenged or not. A healthy skepticism will always be the bedrock of Democracy.

America will not be kept strong and made better if it's always "my country right or wrong." If the Germans under Hitler and the Soviets under Stalin hadn't taken that stance, things might have been better for them and for the world.

June 7, 1996

When one understands what is happening to millions of Americans at the bottom rungs, and then what's going on with military budget, it's enough to make you sick about our country's future.

Will we ever have an administration that puts people first along with the genuine best interests of our country? We didn't have it under Presidents Reagan or Bush, and we apparently don't have it under President Clinton.

The current budget process is being driven by the demand to balance the budget by any means necessary, rather than by careful consideration of national needs. Neither the congressional Republican leadership nor the Democratic administration is asking what it would really take to move people from welfare to work. How can government policies adapt to meet the economic challenges of the approaching century with compassion, justice, fairness and basic respect for the dignity of every citizen so as to best provide for their security? Neither the White House nor Capitol Hill is on to these crucial questions, or seeking real solutions.

Meanwhile poverty is growing in America along with a decline of participation in welfare programs. Children in poverty in the world's richest nation increased from 12 million to 15 million between 1989 and 1993. Yet a declining number of these children in poverty are receiving needed benefits, and the buying power of food stamps declined 26 percent between 1972 and 1993.

Two full-time incomes now are needed in more households: millions of workers are forced into lower-paying jobs with reduced or no benefits; 20 million workers are under-employed as they settle for part-time, temporary or contract work with minimum security or no benefits. And the number of Americans with no health insurance increased 13 percent to 40 million between 1990 and 1993. All this is happening as more Americans live on the economic edge from paycheck to paycheck.

Amid all these harsh realities, Clinton's budget does not improve the lot of our most vulnerable citizens, and GOP funding reductions and reforms will further worsen their plight, as the deficit-cutting hits people programs while exempting the military and armaments. Yet reducing military spending was one of the top four budget cuts chosen by voters surveyed in a 1994 Kaiser/Harvard survey.

Regardless of these crucial needs, Clinton's Defense Department has proclaimed a military strategy of "preventative defense." This is a formula for endlessly expanding military budgets and meddling in the affairs of other nations as the world's policeman, with U.S. taxpayers footing the costly bill. And nobody is taking up the gut question of "ready for what?"

All this means the United States will continue to spend money it does not have to buy weapons it does not need to fight enemies who do not exist.

And the mix of this new crusade for ever more money for more weapons will be dominated, especially in an election year, by politics and pork. Military planning already is being reduced to public relations and political sloganeering.

Sure there are real problems and potential dangers in our world, plenty of them. But these are largely issues of poverty, underdevelopment, population pressures, environmental degradation and the struggle for human rights and democracy in oppressive regimes with whom we do business. Military power is impotent in terms of what it can do to address these real problems confronting our world.

The Department of Defense inspector general estimates that each year the Pentagon pays military contractors about $500 million it does not owe them. The General Accounting Office estimates these annual overpayments at $750 million. So we entrust a growing $250 billion each year to an outfit that Sen. Charles Grassley of Iowa says has its books so screwed up they can't even be audited.

And neither Congress nor the Clinton administration is doing a thing about it.

April 6, 2003

If we didn't know it before, we know it now that war is always tragic, unpredictable and deadly, and with unintended consequences inevitable.

We also are rapidly learning that human beings are already being killed, maimed and traumatized because of our president's attack on Iraq. International aid agencies and the U.N. agree that more than a half million Iraqi children will be traumatized by this invasion of their country. These are children who already are suffering and dying because of sanctions and continual bombings since the first Gulf War. This is about all they've known in their young lives, these children who are about half of Iraq's 24 million people.

Since most of the U.S. media's war coverage is sanitized and censored through the filter of military field commanders, who permit the reports we get from correspondents with the troops, one needs to turn to the foreign media and such as BBC to learn "the rest of the story." Stark evidence conveys the mounting destruction, maiming and deaths resulting from the most devastating bombing campaign ever known, as the country's infrastructure, public buildings and homes crumble. Because Baghdad is, or was, a city of five million people (human beings like you and me and all people on the family tree that is humanity), the carnage there promises to exceed anything known before.

Contemplating all this spotlights a gut question: What does all this killing and destruction of people who have done us no harm, have to do with fighting terrorism? Whatever happened to the war on terrorism? Has it disappeared with Osama bin Laden? Anybody blind and bigoted enough to actually believe the war on terror will be advanced by pulverizing Iraq and decimating its people is in for a shocking awakening when the hatred and "terrorists" this war is producing shifts into high gear.

Getting our forces into Iraq is the easy part compared to the harsh realities and difficulties of getting them out. And when the war's current estimated cost sinks in—before the numbers are upped, its "shock and awe" will surpass that touted by the military brass that already is being shelved as a dud. So watch for the downward trajectory of those poll numbers. Remember when Papa George I was riding the crest of Gulf War popularity with 90-plus approval ratings? Yet in the same year he couldn't beat an almost unknown Arkansas governor for reelection to the presidency.

Another aspect is destined to hit the public's awareness when taxpayers realize they must pay twice for Bush's war. First we're stuck with the cost of pulverizing Iraq and killing a lot of its people—in the name of freedom, because of George II's obsession with "getting Saddam." Then after the country is shattered, we taxpayers must again line up to pay the costs of rebuilding what we've blown up and torn down. Here's where the "bottom line of the bottom line" of Bush's war surfaces. Cheney's Halliburton and other Big Money corporate campaign contributors move in for the kill to grab those lush government contracts courtesy of us taxpayers.

Results of this can become a dangerous debacle for average Americans and our country's neglected urgent needs that make for a genuinely secure and healthy nation. Reality says we'll be facing the bills alone because our president turned his back on the international community and dealt the UN out of the game—which wasn't a brilliant move. Will the likes of Latvia, Estonia, the Marshall Islands and other "international heavyweights" in Bush's "Coalition of the Willing Bought" pay any of the cost? Incidentally, the pervasive silence of who's in this so-called coalition—a condition demanded by their leaders—is because the people in virtually all those countries strongly oppose the war on Iraq. Does this stance make it easier for the leaders to pocket the bribes that brought them in?

The claim by President Bush and his chicken hawk advisers that our forces are there as "liberators" doesn't pass muster with international law, which clearly says their status is that of "military occupiers." This term is not a moral judgment. Rather it is a technical term under international law that describes the status of armed forces which, in the course of the war, end up controlling territory that is not their own.

A military occupation, almost by definition, is not a pleasant experience for the people being "occupied," because it involves being ruled by a foreign military force. Because this "another-crusade" in the Arab world has a Christian nation as occupier of a Muslim country, it makes a setting laden with dynamite, with the probability of endless guerrilla warfare and high casualties for all involved, without even counting its costs.

So as our warlike government plunges on, based on the president's drumbeat-to-scare-us at his rare press conference March 6, when he referred to Sept. 11 nine times and called Iraq a "threat" 16 times—despite any credible evidence to connect—a basic tenet of Bush policy comes into focus. It is that unprecedented vulnerability is absolutely critical to an anti-constitutional program of control. Is this state of siege a tool for maintaining power?

We should remember what the Founding Fathers understood: "He who trades liberty for supposed security ends up with neither."

Is a president upholding his oath of office to protect and defend the Constitution, which he took with his hand on the Bible, when that Constitution clearly states it is the sole power of Congress to declare war? And when instead he unilaterally plunges his nation into a divisive war that is making our country a pariah of the world?

CHAPTER 22

Selling War

That America is the largest arms-dealer in the world today represents a painful contradiction to our profession as peace-maker, a wrenching irony in light of our founding ideals as a Christian, democratic political and social order. Simon's column of February 17, 1997, argues the role of arms-dealers as peddlers of war. His column of September 8, 1997, tallies the cost, in dollars and otherwise.

February 17, 1997

When President Clinton told the United Nations General Assembly earlier this year that drug trafficking and terrorism were the world's most pressing threats, he admittedly cited issues of great magnitude.

But the president could have named more fundamental issues plaguing our world of which terrorism and the drug trade are only manifestations. These include the continued denial of basic human rights and democratic freedoms, increasing poverty and inequality, environmental degradation, the social impact of technological change, slow progress in world health, and corruption at too many levels in too many governments.

Along with these, the president was silent on an extremely crucial issue of great significance that was spotlighted recently by a world-class statesman who won the Nobel Peace Prize in 1987.

Writing in the prestigious *The Guardian* of London, Oscar Arias, former president of Costa Rica (the only country in the Western Hemisphere that has progressed splendidly without an army), focused on a chilling reality that the great powers have avoided confronting.

The reality is perhaps the greatest threat involving all nations.

Here's the essence of excerpts from *The Guardian* article as Arias so very effectively states it:

The United States and Britain stress the importance of spreading democracy so as to create an environment of stability in which crucial problems can be solved. Yet this is a difficult feat to accomplish while they and other industrial democracies continue to provide weapons to dictators throughout the world, thus giving the enemies of democracy the tools for repression of their people.

It is an unsettling fact that the five permanent members of the United Nations Security Council also are the world's five major arms suppliers. This resulted in United Nations peacekeeping missions repeatedly being undermined by indiscriminate arms exports that frequently forced peacekeepers to be confronted by weapons supplied by their countries.

An example is Somalia where (the U.S.) Operation Restore Hope was forced to collect weapons that were sold during the 1980's to the dictatorial Siad Barre regime by the American arms industry. The resulting cost to the U.S. government (taxpayers) was greater than the income the U.S. supplier received from the sale of those arms in the first place. A really dumb trade-off.

The Pentagon and British politicians argue that arms exports create jobs in their countries. This hollow rationale seems immoral in justifying a few thousand jobs in the West at the expense of pouring more arms into the developing world that doesn't need them and cannot afford to buy them.

If we cannot accept such reasoning, it would not be surprising if a Columbian or Bolivian were to argue that exporting mind-altering drugs is justified and the production of cocaine creates jobs in their agricultural, industrial and commercial sectors.

Sales of arms and drugs export death and misery.

If we are frightened by the extent of drug trafficking originated from the South and directed to the North, we must also be scandalized by the scope and magnitude of indiscriminate arms sales from the North to the South.

Moreover, the idea of the arms trade as a money spinner is untrue. By contributing to the destabilization of developing countries through arms transfers, the arms exporters find themselves paying to pick up the pieces of conflicts they indirectly created (as the U.S. did in Somalia).

The problems facing the world today, and our apparent inability to solve them make for sobering reflection.

But the fact is that we do possess the ability to eradicate poverty, guarantee health care for all, and curtail the flow of arms. What we lack is only the will and the leadership (and the sense) to address these troubles that afflict our world.

Know what, folks? We've got a helluva lot of growing up yet to do.

September 8, 1997

There is an extremely crucial area of vital significance to our lives, our future, our pocketbooks and our taxes the media is not adequately informing us about.

This involves the extent to which our country is arming the world with the effect of inevitably endangering all of us in ways that were never intended.

For example, our share of the global arms trade that totals $32 billion jumped from 16 percent in 1988 to 50 percent between 1992 and 1994, and it's rising. A Pentagon forecast in 1995 indicated that the United States accounts for 63 percent of worldwide arms deals already signed for delivery between 1994 and 2000.

Dangerous to our best interests and security, U.S. arms dealers are selling $10 billion a year in lethal weapons to non-democratic governments that are mostly repressive dictatorships. These are governments that are abusing human rights of their own people and often engaging in aggression against neighboring states. Fueling this kind of insanity are arms from the five countries that dominate global arms sales—the United States, Britain, France, China and Russia.

Despite the global downturn in military production and defense budgets since the end of the Cold War, the Clinton Administration accelerated arms exports, to its shame and against our best interests, rather than embarking on a serious program of armament cuts and economic conversion. The administration is phasing out its conversion programs and boosting overseas arms sales that make even higher the profits of armament manufacturers. Such a direction makes shambles of the illusory peace dividend promised with the end of the Cold War.

Stupidly dangerous are the foreign policy risks of escalating arms exports because U.S. weaponry sold to the Middle East and other strife-torn regions fans the flames of war.

The 40 percent of major conventional weapons that went to nations at war between 1984 and 1994 was like pouring gasoline on the fire in Iraq, Somalia and Sudan. Even worse, the boomerang effect of the arms trade puts U.S. troops at risk everywhere.

The past five times U.S. troops were sent into conflict—Panama, Iraq, Somalia, Haiti and Bosnia—American forces were up against adversaries that previously had received U.S. weapons, military technology or training. This zeal for the buck from arms sales translates to Americans getting wounded and killed by "made-in-the-U.S.A." bullets and guns.

In the midst of all this utter lethal stupidity, innocent civilians were the major victims of war.

They accounted for half of all war deaths during the first half of the century, 64 percent in the 1960's and 74 percent in the 1980's. Civilian casualties already are higher in the 1990's.

Meanwhile, the poor at home and abroad are paying the price for escalating arms sales. Giving this a wrenching odor is the fact that the 1996 welfare reform law cut federal support for poor families about $7 billion annually over five years.

Wonder how much of the welfare subsidies we give the weapons makers was included in the $2.3 million that Lockheed Martin gave to our representative in last year's congressional campaigns to buy their support in perpetuating the gravy train? Lockheed Martin is "leader of the PAC" as the world's largest arms manufacturer. The PAC includes 25 weapons exporters who contributed $10.8 million during the past election campaign. The World Policy Institute said this is a 56 percent increase in political action committee soft money contributions over the previous peak of $6.9 million during the 1991-92 election cycle.

Those guys know how to play the game and there are enough money-hungry politicians in Congress to keep the gravy rolling to the boys in the arms business.

And the reality is that international arms sales drain scarce resources from developing countries and suck up money better spent on human needs and development programs rather than increasing the agony in volatile regions that should be weapon-free.

Why are we doing this to ourselves and to others who have suffered enough?

CHAPTER 23

The Power of Non-Violence

Always a challenge to a world awash in the insanity of violence and war is the option of non-violence, both philosophy and tactic, from "turn the other cheek" (don't we piously tout our identity as a "Christian nation"?) to Thoreau's "Civil Disobedience" to the "naked fakir," M. K. Gandhi's brilliant outmaneuver of the British Empire, to the great modern crusade and martyrdom of Martin Luther King, Jr. Simon commemorated the 25th anniversary of King's assassination with a tribute and this challenge in his column of April 13, 1993. Writing for September 7, 2002, he listed other historical successes of nonviolence as suggested alternatives to the policies of the Bush administration neocons.

April 13, 1993

It has been a quarter century since Martin Luther King was assassinated April 4, 1968. And it was 18 years after that our country marked the first national King holiday.

But in the intervening years since this charismatic and inspirational leader was killed, the need for his teachings and message of the power of love and creative use of non-violence to solve problems looms ever larger. And even a quick look around our nation and the world documents that King's example and message is sorely needed more than ever.

Yes, Martin Luther King was killed 25 years ago but... with his death a movement was born with its proof that if you touch people on common ground you can bring them together and let their goodness shine. All this spurred a meaningful evolution of the civil rights movement.

This great man, the youngest ever to win the Nobel Peace Prize, may not have erased racism, but oh how he changed things in his country. He wanted justice, peace and love, and he wanted them now and wouldn't settle for less.

King was truly a master strategist and he got things done. That was why so many wanted to stop him. He was too effective.

He opened doors, altered the complexion of our schools, changed government and even people's way of thinking. And undoubtedly he is responsible for the increased recruitment of blacks and minorities by universities and corporations partly due to their desire to respond to his death and example of his life.

It is also true that the tragedy turned many blacks toward elected office so that today they are congressmen, mayors, police chiefs and even a governor. Someday, because of King, the non-blacks of this nation will elect a black as president.

Perhaps as an even greater symbol and reality, because of King people no longer in our country need to go to the back of the bus. Nobody in America—the real America—should ever have to go to the back of the bus. King taught us that and in the doing demonstrated a greater understanding of what the real America is all about than all his superficial, hypocritical and biased detractors combined.

Who can forget the powerful truth of what King said: "Hate scars the soul and distorts the personality... Love is the only force capable of transforming an enemy into a friend." (What a challenge to our torn world and to the Christian church and its clergy to practice what it preaches.)

Or the powerful unalterable truth of "Injustice anywhere is a threat to justice everywhere... I can never be what I ought to be until you are what you ought to be. You can never be what you ought to be until I am what I ought to be."

Some have considered this legendary leader a sort of patsy or wimp for always turning the other cheek. But how many of his critics would have had the courage to knowingly and willingly because of principle, without flinching, face police truncheons, fire pressure hoses, cattle prods, tear gas, attack dogs and jail—all because of a deep belief in the American Constitution, its Bill of Rights and the principles of Christianity?

Yes, Christianity has not been tried and found wanting; rather it has been (and is) wanting and not really tried yet in our country and in the world. But King's life and example is inevitably moving us in that direction. Someday we shall overcome.

You know, isn't it ironic that in spite of the persistent attempts to smear him by a paranoid homosexual FBI director whose tactics and characteristics would have fit better in Nazi Germany than in a free democracy, King and his message and contributions loom ever larger in a nation and world that more than ever need his teachings—as the memory of J. Edgar Hoover sinks in ignominy.

September 7, 2002

The gung-ho extremists in the Bush administration, who dodged military service in Vietnam, and never smelled gun powder, but are hot for our troops invading Iraq (without them along, of course), sorely need lessons in reality, common sense and nonviolence before they drag our country down the road to disaster.

These hard-line zealots with blinders include Paul Wolfowitz, No. 2 in the Pentagon, Richard Perle at the National Security Council, and Otto Reich, whose hold on the Latin American desk is a recipe for disaster. The track record of this trio going back to the 1980's is shameful.

Along with the likes of Cheney and Rumsfeld, this group is far more reactionary, unilateral, ideological, belligerent and arrogantly opinionated than the experienced worldly realists like Brent Scowcroft (national security head for daddy Bush), Colin Powell and James Baker, the Bush I secretary of state, who has been trying to get through to the junior Bush before he booby traps himself.

The hard-line crowd are great at substituting rhetoric for facts and evidence. They and their dangerous hang-ups are also representative of what happens too often in history: old men sending young men to war and death.

The scary aspect to all this is why Bush II surrounded himself with such a collection of extremists so inimical to America's genuine best interests and its respect in the world community, where even our friends are signing off. Makes one question whether the junior George even understands the consequences of what his actions are producing.

Even though the following examples might be too basic and simple for zealous war hawks to understand, there's nothing theoretical about the many successes of nonviolent action, as contrasted to the multitude of failures of violence as proven through the course of history. If violence worked, then there would have been a wonderfully peaceful world for the past millenniums.

Among nonviolence's many successes were the downfall of communism in Poland and elsewhere, integration of lunch counters in the 1960's in the American South, the ending of Apartheid in South Africa, Gandhi's Salt March in India and withdrawal of the British after granting independence, and the successful Danish resistance to Nazi occupation in the 1940's.

Here are more examples of nonviolence working:

- A group of Argentine mothers, outraged by their government's silence about the disappearance of their husbands, sons and daughters, began marching in Buenos Aires' central plaza. They didn't stop until legitimacy of the country's military junta was undermined, leading to its downfall after the debacle of the Falklands War.

- When the doors of Birmingham's Sixteenth Street Baptist Church opened on May 2, 1963, 50 teenagers emerged. As waiting police packed them into jail wagons, a second line appeared, then a third and many more. Children as young as six stood fast until arrested. With the jails swamped, Police Commissioner Bull Connor ordered his police to disperse rather than arrest more demonstrators. With thousands more children there the next day, standing their ground in high-spirited nonviolent discipline, Connor's police erupted in frustration and hatred as police dogs tore into the marching lines and high-powered fire hoses knocked children along like tumbleweeds. News photographs attracted millions of distant eyes and Bull Connor's defenses were shattered, as segregation began crumbling.

- A nonviolent movement for change began in Nepal Feb. 18, 1990. For 30 years the corrupt and oppressive monarchy had banned opposition parties. With overwhelming public support, the movement for political freedom used sit-ins, strikes, all-women blockades and blackouts. This forced King Birenera to lift the ban on opposition parties and to hold the country's first multiparty election.

Again, nonviolence works. Violence not only doesn't, it makes things worse as history repeatedly shows.

PART VII

Moral and Judicious Use of the Environment

CHAPTER 24

Energy Matters

An interesting and instructive gauge of Simon's and the public's awareness of environmental issues emerges from a subjective contrast among the following three columns. In December, 1979, Simon is instructing, with no great sense of urgency, how to save energy by household conservation. By May 25, 2001, he is aggressively attacking the Bush II administration for its blatantly pro-corporate payoff, anti-conservation policies (along with his opening up a couple of other attack fronts at the same time). In April, 1996, he is sounding the alarm of global climate change and urgently denouncing the attempt by "the fossil fuel energy complex" to deny the impending crisis. Note Simon's careful argument from verifiable facts. Note, too, the prediction of general events and conditions subsequently specifically fulfilled in such as the devastation of New Orleans and the ravishing of coastal Bangladesh.

December 17, 1979

We are already in that time of year when our fuel bills start their relentless rise over the winter months ahead. So wouldn't it be good if we could at least lighten the blow by saving considerable money along the way? It can be done.

These realities are wrapped around the fact we can get far more than we thought from energy already being produced. Earlier this year the President's Council on Environmental Quality reported that total energy use in the United States need not increase greatly between now and the next 20 years until the end of this century. The Council made the flat statement that the U.S. economy can operate on 30 to 40 percent less energy.

This conclusion was substantiated by the venerable Harvard Business School that more recently released a remarkable report titled "Energy Future." It concluded that the U.S. economy can operate on 30 to 40 percent less energy and do it "with virtually no penalty for the way Americans live."

A surprising fact is that actions of individuals are as important as the policies of the federal government in producing real energy savings. Household energy savings alone can make a big difference in our total energy use and availability. Households alone use nearly one-fourth of all the energy consumed in this country.

But the larger message in the Harvard report is that conservation on any level is not a single isolated one-shot effort. It is a continuing one that requires a change in attitude more than in lifestyle. The real challenge of energy conservation may not be just to do it, but rather to believe that it can be done.

So here are some energy savers that you can use...

—The most energy-consuming appliance in your kitchen is the refrigerator. There are enormous variations among individual brands and models, and the least efficient use more than twice as much energy as the best. A manual-defrost refrigerator saves energy... if you defrost it once a month. Don't make your refrigerator work overtime by parking it next to a stove or a sunny window. And decide what you want before you open the door; each waft of outside air shows up on your bill. Try 38 or 40 degrees for the fresh food compartment and 5 degrees for the freezer... and you don't need the heating element that prevents outside sweating on in most climates.

—The best furnace-saving adjustment is the thermostat. A 10-degree nighttime setback can achieve 10-25 percent savings on heating bills while you sleep. And having your furnace serviced once a year can cut fuel use by 10 percent and pay for itself in a year. Oil furnaces, especially, waste a lot of costly fuel if not kept clean, and you can do part of the job yourself by putting in clean filters.

—If your hot water heater is warm to the touch, it needs insulation. A $23 fiberglass blanket will pay for itself, or you can buy foil-back insulation and tape it on your tank. (But don't let any of it slip down and cover the vents or you could have a fire.) Most thermostats are set for 140 degrees or higher. Turning yours down to 110-120 degrees will save $20 a year for an electric heater and about half that for gas. While a family of four uses about 65 gallons of hot water a day, they need that hot water only about four hours in 24. A timer will automatically turn the hot water on during the hours needed and save up to 35 percent on operating costs. Electrically heated hot water now costs in the $200 to $300 a year range. The annual bill for gas heating would be about $100.

—You can save five gallons of hot water every time you substitute a shower for a bath. It takes about 30 gallons of water to fill the average tub, but a shower with a flow of 4 gallons a minute uses only 30 gallons in five minutes. And a flow restrictor in the pipe at the showerhead, cutting it from 6 gallons per minute to 3, still gives a good spray and could save $40 a year on your electric bill. Surprisingly, water lost through steadily leaking hot water faucets can waste up to 27 gallons of oil or 3,484 cubic feet of natural gas each year on hot water down the drain.

—The average dishwasher uses 14 gallons of hot water per load, regardless of how full. So full loads reduce your hot water bill, and the "rinse hold" using up to 7 gallons is unnecessary if you've scraped your dishes before loading. Then another 10 percent of your dishwashing energy costs can be cut by letting your dishes air dry. If you don't have an automatic air-dry setting on your model, just turn the knob to "off" after the final rinse, and prop the door open a little for faster drying…and the humidity is good for your house.

—One brand of stove is about as good as another, though self-cleaning ovens tend to be well insulated. Avoid models with pilot lights if you choose a gas stove because they burn one-third of all gas in residential cooking and unnecessarily warm the kitchen in summer. Remember 20 percent of oven heat is lost every time you open the door, so keep peeking to the minimum.

—On your clothes washer that takes about 35 gallons of water for a full wash and rinse, changing the rinse water to cold, which does not affect results, will save a lot of hot water over the year. It costs you about 30 cents an hour to use your clothes dryer, so "solar" clothes line comes up a bargain! Beginning next month, the federal government will require washers and dryers, and some other major appliances, to bear energy-cost labels, so compare their energy efficiency before you buy.

—A couple other things… Fluorescent bulbs deliver 3 or 4 times more light per kilowatt-hour of electricity than incandescent bulbs, so enormous amounts of energy can be saved by switching from filament to fluorescent lights wherever practical. And remember that a charming wood-burning fireplace is a heat robber with over 13 percent of household heat going up the chimney if you leave your damper open when your fireplace is not in use. (But don't forget to open it when you light up!)

Conservation is not so much rejected as it is neglected. It's misleading to link it to austerity and sacrifice, and it has no heroes. The problem is simply awareness. Hope that helps.

May 25, 2001

Any way you cut it, the Bush people sure know how to shift gears and reverse directions slick as a whistle.

After insulting most everyone's intelligence by dismissing energy conservation as merely a "sign of personal virtue," rather than the sensible policy it is, CEO Cheney of USA, Inc., tried to scare us into junking environmental regulations so as to "better" meet a fabricated energy crisis that has suddenly emerged.

The Bushies apparently have decided the free market doesn't work after all for energy, so the government must provide an array of subsidies for energy producers. Even the conservatively libertarian Cato Institute calls the Cheney-Bush energy plan "a smorgasbord of subsidies and handouts for virtually every energy lobby in Washington." Yeah, the free enterprise system! It's "free" alright, courtesy us taxpayers. The non-naïve understand this is for the Big Money boys who bankrolled the Bush campaign and it's payback time, you know.

This contradictory pitch comes after months of reminding little energy consumers that the free market is sacrosanct and it would be awful, almost un-American, for the government to provide assistance. But now energy producers apparently need encouragement and help to do their regular job, so the government is providing it. No *mas* free market!

Topping CEO Cheney's list for the credit incentives is the one for those buying hybrid gas-electric cars. What makes this mock conservation goodie so funny is the fact that it was Al Gore's proposal during the campaign to give tax credits for purchasing hybrid cars. Even more ironical, it was George Bush's favorite gag line making fun of Gore's proposal that is now Cheney's lead "conservation" measure!

Showing through all this is the lust of Cheney and his collaborators for the big stuff where the refineries, pipelines, nuclear power plants, digging and drilling most anywhere. You see, there's not any big money in merely conserving energy. No pay-off or payback there. And all this despite the strong reality that conservation of energy is a lot cheaper than the stuff the Big Money are pushing—and that we'll be paying for.

Yet another Bush reversal: after backing out of the much needed Kyoto agreement to reduce grave global warming—and to the consternation of our allies, the Bush administration is now pulling the rug from under an agreement to enforce the treaty banning germ warfare. Ratified by 143 nations, the 1972 treaty prohibits development, production and possession of biological weapons. Six years of diplomatic negotiations have gone into the draft agreement to enforce the needed treaty. So again Bush administration actions are distressing our allies. Is it any wonder they voted us off the UN Human Rights Commission, and increasingly are complaining about America's arrogance and capricious unilateral actions—in a one world where cooperation is essential to progress and even survival?

The unusual haste and greasy math of the Bush tax cut is shaping up as yet another sleeper-hit on average Americans. No wonder the very undemocratic Senate Majority leader Trent Lott is making a mockery of Senate rules in trying to ram it through, while making sure no tax bill was available until the night before the Senate was to begin voting on amendments, so there would be no time for the bipartisan Joint Taxation Committee to draw up detailed cost estimates. Both Lott and the president know that the more this tax cut is examined, the more its support will erode. So our country is about to get hit with a tax cut that is extremely costly, so focused on wealthiest Americans, and so certain to drain vital resources for basic governmental services and for the already punctured safety net for needy Americans.

There are a lot more available examples to document dangerous actions of the Bush administration—after we get past George II making a major campaign promise to cut dangerous carbon dioxide emissions producing threatening global warming, and then reneging on his promise because he wanted to protect profits and pay back wealthy campaign contributors. These big boys expect a big return on their "investment," and if Bush kept his promise it would cost money to those who spent heavily to get the Bush presidency. Same for letting the mining interests dump more cancer-producing arsenic in our drinking water. Too bad the president seems unable to understand the real bottom line of, "How much will it cost not to do it right?"

There's the fluke of the Bush administration allowing the drug companies (among his biggest campaign contributors) to rip us off with the excuse they must make huge profits so as to finance research and development. So how come the drug companies spend twice as much on marketing as they do on research and development?

And how about that long-ago reality-spectacle of Ronald Reagan busting the air traffic controllers union and then getting an airport in Washington named after him? Or after railing against big government and even saying "it is the problem," now having the largest government building full of the most bureaucrats anywhere bearing his name! Funny, huh?

Just think how much better our country and the world would be if the Bush administration focused our material resources, talent and energy to meet real needs in the genuine interests of all people, not just wealthy campaign contributors.

April 5, 1996

If we go on pretending nothing is amiss with the world's weather and let ourselves be lulled by the chorus of the fossil-fuel energy complex that global warming is mere speculation or a doomsday fantasy, we could be heading for big trouble. It's not far-fetched to say this drift could become mayhem.

And if you don't think the energy big boys aren't spending big bucks to lull us into complacency so that wasteful industrial and polluting practices can continue unimpeded (with help of the GOP congressional majority), then why did the National Coal Association spend nearly a million dollars attempting to debunk global climactic change? During the past 18 months, the Global Climate Coalition (the oil industry's No 1 public relations outfit) spent more than a million dollars downplaying the threat of climate change.

Meanwhile, any way you cut it, a series of unusual weather-related events have occurred in our country and worldwide with increasing frequency. Unbiased experts with no ax to grind know these events have far-reaching implications for our planet and its inhabitants.

Who will deny that the record-breaking blizzards and deadly sub-zero temperatures ravishing the East and Midwest this winter were unusual? Seems that new record-setting weather extremes are becoming as commonplace as traffic accidents. Here are some:

- The 10 hottest years in recorded history occurred since 1980, and the British Meteorological office reports that 1995 was the warmest year since records began in 1856.

- Last summer in the Midwest, a heat wave followed a second "100-year-flood" in three years and caused more than 500 deaths.

- Northern California in the fall experienced the driest season in its recorded history.

- After five winters without a killing frost, New Orleans was infested with more cockroaches and termites than ever before.

- Over in London, the summer of 1995 was the driest since 1727 and hottest since 1659.

- In Spain, there have been four consecutive years of drought in a region where annual rainfall usually amounts to 8.4 inches.

All this was reported by Ross Gelbspan, a former co-recipient of the Pulitzer Prize for "public service reporting" who has written extensively about the environment in 30 years as an editor and reporter.

He warns that "the continuing emission of greenhouse gases would create protracted, crop-destroying droughts, a host of new and recurring diseases, hurricanes of extraordinary malevolence and rising sea levels that could inundate island nations and low-lying coastal rims on the continents."

In September, the Intergovernmental Panel on Climate Change (2,500 climate scientists) bluntly warned that we are entering a period of climate instability during which we can expect "widespread economic, environmental and social dislocation because of the continuing pollution of the limited space of the inner atmosphere."

Instead of knocking the environmentalists concerned about this (which is almost an art form in parts of the West), we would be smart to take the blinders off and realize all of us have a stake in what is happening to our environment, because it's where we live.

Everyone with heads fastened on can understand that government controls are necessary to protect our environment and Americans, before it is too late.

CHAPTER 25

Alternatives to Oil

In his word for September 17, 1979, writing in the wake of Three Mile Island, Simon addressed the problems of nuclear energy, not surprisingly, finding that option falling on the short side. Simon then favorably considered, for November 12, 1979, the feasibility of hydrogen as fuel for the future. And he most emphatically endorsed solar energy in his August 20, 1979 column.

September 17, 1979

Yes, this column had considerable to say when we were threatened by the near disaster at Three Mile Island when that nuclear reactor broke down, and it needed to be said.

But what has happened since then and its affect on all of us, both in the pocketbook and especially health-wise, warrants more comment. And when it boils down to your life and your money, it becomes rather meaningful.

The commercial nuclear power plant program planned in this country for the next quarter century represents a serious threat to your health and safety and to the health and safety of all Americans, and it is going to cost plenty.

Yes, despite the known hazards, despite the unresolved problems of safe disposal of lethal nuclear waste, and despite the growing danger and vulnerability of sabotage from terrorists who could gain an immense power to further their ends, despite all these realities, you are being asked to accept the nuclear program as necessary to solve our nation's energy problems.

No less an authority than the respected *Wall Street Journal* labeled these nuclear plans "atomic lemons," and said, "their unreliability is becoming one of their most dependable features." Still we are asked to accept the program as the mainstay of our nation's future electric power supply.

Reliable authorities have testified there is no practical solution for protecting our generation, much less our children's and grandchildren's, from the immense accumulation of lethal wastes that are inevitable in the nuclear power industry. Radioactive nuclear wastes are created when nuclear fuel is used up during the power plant operation. These wastes include strontium 90, cesium 137 and plutonium 239.

All are extremely toxic substances and it takes plutonium half a million years to lose its killing power. So remember that a typical nuclear power plant produces several hundred pounds of plutonium a year—and a particle of plutonium the size of a grain of pollen can cause lung cancer.

Yet we are being asked to accept nuclear power as safe, despite the continuing fact that there is NO method for long-term storage or disposal of these radioactive wastes that is workable. All proposed techniques for storing or getting rid of these wastes are merely in the research or development stage.

To make it even more ridiculous that we are being asked to accept nuclear power as the answer to the oil crisis, the U.S. Geological Survey discovered that there aren't enough known uranium reserves in the United States to fuel even the proposed nuclear power plants. There is no way a nuclear power plant will run without uranium, no matter how expensive that plant is.

Hannes Allfven, a Nobel Laureate, who is professor of physics at University of California at San Diego, recently said, "The technologists claim that if everything works according to their blueprints, atomic energy will be a safe and very attractive solution to the energy needs of the world. This may be correct. However, the issue is whether their blueprints will work in the real world and not only in a 'technological paradise.'"

Project this against the nuclear power plant track record of high-level radioactive waste leakage, automatic alarm systems not working, management failing to remove monitoring reports, inadequate preventative maintenance, and near-disasters all over the country. And the *Reader's Digest* reported that "The Nuclear Regulatory Commission has allowed serious compromises with safety to creep into the design, construction and operation of U.S. nuclear plants."

Enough said.

November 12, 1979

Politics, economics, a bearded Moslem holy man, and a crisis involving 60 Americans held hostage 5,000 miles away represent a mix that could push us along a road that would free us from the tyranny of oil and inflation. Far-fetched as it might seem in this instance, blessings can come in disguises.

Simply stated, it is the possibility of using hydrogen as the source of less expensive and more efficient fuel than short-supply and high-cost gasoline.

If the shoot-from-the-hip send-in-the-Marines crowd hollering for "leadership" has its way, we might need more gasoline and fuel oil than we've got because supplies from Iran could be shut off and we might need a lot more gasoline to run military vehicles, boats and aircraft proving we can't be pushed around. Meanwhile, under those circumstances, your car could be grounded.

Thus what is happening in Iran, along with escalating fuel costs and gas lines, could further ignite a revolution that has been simmering in garages and basement laboratories, but not much yet in big science and industry where it should be. This revolution is a search for new fuels.

There's an idea in the U.S. Patent Office that might do the job, reports the Washington *Spectator*. It is a process to separate hydrogen from water by electrolysis and feed it directly into an existing-type auto engine. The inventor is Archie Blue, a 75-year-old New Zealand auto mechanic. Using this system, Kenneth Green of Carson, Ia., is running a 1965 model Ford LTD on water and a little gasoline. And *Mother Earth News* reports a Virginia tinkerer who devised a water injection system for his 1978 Ford Fiesta "that gets higher mileage in normal around-town driving."

The significance of this is underlined by a Washington *Post* editorial: "Gasoline and diesel engines consumed just under 90 percent of all the oil produced in the United States last year. American cars consume one-ninth of all oil used in the world on any given day."

A key point is that hydrogen is something we already have in endless abundance. Tests document that it has an up to 50 percent better fuel efficiency than gasoline and is non-polluting. It burns faster and hotter than natural gas and has an energy release upon combustion of 15,300 watt-hours per pound as compared with 5,500 watt-hours per pound for gasoline. (Ever hear of the hydrogen bomb?!)

It also is significant that hydrogen as a source of thermal energy has a tremendous advantage over electricity: It can be stored for a later use but electricity must be used as it is generated.

A Denver *Post* article stresses that new directions for using hydrogen instead of gasoline are not pie-in-the-sky. It said, "The technology for producing hydrogen from water... has been well established for many years... nor is the technology for powering cars with hydrogen in its infancy..."

Ten nations are working on hydrogen research. Japan sees it as the ultimate fuel and plans a breeder reactor to draw hydrogen from water. Lockheed has applied for research grants for a hydrogen-powered plane, and General Electric has an advanced electrolysis technology program for large-scale commercial hydrogen generation. A study by the Institute of Gas Technology reports, "Of the choices of various chemical fuels available to us, hydrogen is the easiest to make and in many ways is the easiest to use."

A report, by Escher Technology Associates labeled "The Hydrogen Alternative," prepared under government sponsorship, states that "hydrogen produced from water by means of various non-fossil energy conversion processes based on nuclear, solar or geothermal energy sources, can be delivered to all the utilization sectors including transportation." The report proposes "a hydrogen railroad system development and demonstration project."

A Washington *Star* editorial titled "Has America Lost Its Genius" pinpoints a sore spot when it referred to a National Science Foundation study documenting "that in the post-World War II period, firms with fewer than 1,000 employees were responsible for half the most significant new industrial products and processes. Firms with 100 or fewer workers produced 24 times more major innovations per research and development dollar. Yet these firms received only 3.5 percent of federal research and development money." Draw your own conclusions.

Despite evidence that government and big industry shun the little guy and deny them recognition and funds, back-porch tinkering is in keeping with America's tradition of invention, and the backyard entrepreneur with a wealth of practical experience and ingenuity has succeeded where Big Technology has often failed.

It would be refreshing if the Big Boys could accomplish what John Lorenzen, a retired farmer in my native Iowa, has done as reported by the Associated Press. He makes 20 gallons of hydrogen every day with a simple machine fashioned out of scrap metal. This hydrogen fuel powers a conventional gas Delco-generator. Electricity produced by the hydrogen-powered generator powers lights, tools and heaters in Lorenzen's farm shop and machine shed.

And, yes, neither Thomas Edison nor Henry Ford had any scientific degrees or big-time research and technology behind them and look what they accomplished.

August 20, 1979

It seems to me it is long overdue for more people to be thinking and doing something about solar energy... so here goes a stab in that direction.

Experience, developments and our updated awareness during recent years strongly suggest that coal and nuclear power have no long-term futures. This leaves the sun as the only hope for solving rapidly increasing global energy needs. And you better believe it, especially if you've been contending with gasoline lines and worrying about an even bigger problem of heating and electrical bills this winter.

You see, the earth is fast running out of its precious reserves of "stored sunshine." That's what oil, coal and wood are, merely solar power captured in convenient packaging. Virtually all energy consumed by man has been fathered by the sun.

At our current pace of usage we will consume in the next 25 years (and that's just four years into the 21st century) energy in an amount equal to all the energy used by man in recorded history. This adds up to the fact that alternative sources of energy obviously must be found... and you don't have to be a genius to figure that one out. Savvy experts—those who are unbiased, agree that mankind must look to the sun to solve its energy needs.

Using solar energy can be as simple as drying clothes in the sun or as complex as orbiting solar satellites in outer space.

The simplest kind of solar, known as passive, involves merely building a structure so it can take maximum advantage of the sun's rays. An active system, involving rooftop solar collectors, can be attached to existing buildings to catch the sun during winter and to shield a house from the sun's baking rays during summer months. Pumps or fans can pull the heat from the collectors to a storage area, and then, like any other type of energy, solar can be used as needed—and it's possible to cool a house or office building by using solar energy.

These are the most basic methods for solar energy, and they are plans which are now economically feasible. There are more advanced ideas, and the No. 1 of these involves photovoltaic cells. These devices, originally developed for use on satellites, produce electricity when they are hit by the sun's rays.

Today the sun's roaring hydrogen-fueled furnace powers educational-television sets in Africa, offshore Coast Guard buoys and navigation lights on the Gulf of Mexico oil rigs. Even the crucial warning bell and lights of a Georgia railroad crossing rely on the sun to power them, and so do emergency call boxes on the beltways around our nation's capital. And nearly every spacecraft that has ever rocketed skyward has depended on purple-blue panels of solar cells.

Already more than 200 buildings throughout the U.S. are partially heated and cooled by the sun. Near Tucson, Ariz., one of the nation's sunniest areas, the Decade 80 Solar House uses water-filled solar collectors in its copper roof to provide all the test home's heat and hot water and 75 percent of its air conditioning.

Yes, there is little doubt that the sun is going to be a major source of energy for both home and industry. But the real dispute is HOW solar power will be implemented, WHICH method of solar power will be most widely used, and IF it can be made a reality without being dominated by the giant-rich oil and utility companies. These have been saying that only they can provide our energy and energy systems. If you believe that, then you could go down with the ship.

Like a cartoon series put it, with Big Oil speaking, "You want coal? We own the mines. You want oil and gas? We own the wells. You want nuclear energy? We own the uranium. You want solar power? We own the…er… ah… Solar power isn't feasible."

By really promoting solar we can conserve seriously dwindling oil and gas supplies, provide our country with a clean and realistic alternative to nuclear power, and help a wide range of alternative energy resources get off the ground.

Solar is the best energy source we have available. It's non-polluting. It's inexhaustible. It's terrorist-resistant. It's everywhere. And we need it.

What are we waiting for?

CHAPTER 26

Our Children, Our Future

Not surprisingly, environmental change has provided ample subject matter for Simon's columns through the years. Also not surprisingly, his concern frequently focused on children: thus he highlighted environmental health threats to children on November 3, 1997.

November 3, 1997

What are we doing to our children? What's happening that is putting them increasingly at risk?

In recent years, the scary increase in an array of childhood ailments should be setting off alarm signals. Childhood asthma jumped 73 percent in recent years, and it is now the No. 1 chronic disease in children, affecting about five million in the United States. Not only are more children getting asthma, but more are dying from it.

There also are alarming increases in learning disorders, behavioral disabilities, precocious puberty in girls, male genital birth defects and various cancers, particularly of the brain, and leukemia. The National Academy of Sciences calls these ominous trends. And the increase of childhood cancer and asthma is too rapid to be explained by genetics alone. While accidents still are the number one cause for childhood deaths, cancer rapidly is becoming a close second.

The reasons all this is happening became more understandable after recent scientific studies documented that children have a special sensitivity to environmental hazards. They are more vulnerable than adults and are at risk in ways health experts never before imagined.

For example, children are now exposed to more toxic chemicals than their parents were. Yet they take in more food, water and air pound-for-pound than adults, which gives them proportionately greater doses of contaminants. Little children also have higher exposure simply by living the life of a child. Crawling on hands and knees, they encounter pesticides, lead and other poisons lingering in dirt, carpets and house dust, which they swallow when sucking on a hand or thumb.

Contaminants passed from mother to baby before birth can alter a child's immune system, increasing the risk of cancer, infectious disease and other disorders. Exposure to agricultural pesticides and industrial chemicals can cause abnormalities in the reproductive system and increase the likelihood dust can disrupt brain development and result in attention and learning difficulties, and possibly future aggressive and antisocial behavior.

Laboratory tests by Greenpeace, the environmental organization, found that 25 of 131 products tested, from rain hats to doll strollers, contained lead levels close to or higher than the proposed health standard of 200 parts per million.

A study by a senior scientist at the Natural Resources Defense Council, titled "Children at Risk," identified the five worst environmental threats to children: lead, drinking water contamination, pesticides, air pollution and tobacco smoke. Studies prove these hazards are a greater threat to children than they are to adults.

"Lead is the worst, because it is toxic to the brain," said Dr. Phillip Landrigan, a pediatrician at Mount Sinai Medical Center and director of the National Academy of Sciences study. "It makes kids duller, distractible and prone to violence."

Landrigan also stressed that children today are exposed to thousands of chemicals synthesized since World War II that are largely untested, adding that fewer than half of the 75,000 synthetic chemicals now on the market have been tested for toxicity or their effects on children.

We know our children also are suffering damage from low-level exposure to industrial chemicals such as PCB's and some classes of pesticides. A study by the University of Minnesota Laboratory of Environmental Medicine and Pathology found higher rates of birth defects in children of farmers, also in children of non-farming families living in agricultural areas where fungicides and herbicides are used.

The study also documented a striking seasonal variation in birth defects. Those conceived in spring, when herbicide use is highest, ran the greatest risk.

Because of these threats to our children, the Environmental Protection Agency is being forced to consider tougher standards, to the consternation of corporations profiting from the status quo and their GOP defenders in Congress.

But it's urgent, because as with the doctor in the emergency room, the costs are tremendous if we fail to act.

We are overdue in realizing the significance of what Dr. Barbara Boardman, a mother, practicing pediatrician and key member of the National Academy of Science panel studying pesticides in children's diets, said: "If you alter brain development, you don't get a second shot at it."

CHAPTER 27

We Are What We Eat

While Simon gave space to the large issues such as global warming and climate change, he also researched and reported less sexy matters such as environmentally friendly and safe food; here he shared common ground with Wendell Berry: "…we need a science of agriculture that is authentically new—a science that feely and generously accepts the farm, the local ecosystem, and the local community as contexts, and then devotes itself to the relationship between farming and its ecological and cultural supports."[16] Writing for January 23, 1996, Simon addressed this issue. In a fascinating essay of February 25, 2001, Simon wrote of the return of the buffalo, its significance for Native Americans, for the Great Plains, and for our food supply.

January 23, 1996

A dangerous trend is happening around the world, and it involves the production of the food we eat. Traditionally, farming was a reciprocal process between people and the land. It was this close relationship that for generations preserved age-old practices keeping the land alive, the water clean and the people fed.

But there's now a shift that rapidly is making farming a process for generating profits and power. In the name of efficiency and increasing profits, multinational corporations consolidate to the point where a very few monopolize every aspect of food production—from patenting seeds to manufacturing agricultural chemicals, from growing the food, to processing, marketing and distributing it.

The outcome of this corporate agriculture (an insurance company is the biggest farmer in Nebraska) is the destruction of intact, sustainable, self-reliant communities and traditional cultures.

---

16. Wendell Berry, "Twelve Paragraphs on Biotechnology," in *Citizenship Papers*, Washington, D.C.: Shoemaker & Hoard, 2003, p. 56.

Globally, and in bigger agricultural states, people are less food self-reliant than ever as control over land and food systems is wrenched from families and communities and given over to multinational corporations and the global supermarket. This severing of traditional relationships between people and the land is a disaster for the communities and culture.

In 1950, 2,000 U.S. counties listed agriculture as their main source of income. Today only 19 counties make that claim.

Agri-business claims it is driven by the desire to benefit humanity and feed the "starving millions," but in practice worldwide it perpetuates crimes against people and the land in the name of profit. An example: Ciba-Gagy is the world's biggest agrochemical company with sales of almost $2.8 billion in 1994. The company admitted spraying the pesticide Calecron on unprotected Egyptian children to test its safety. As the rationale, the company wanted to know how much was retained in their urine.

Calecron is known to be linked with cancer, and a company spokesman admitted, "It was not correct for us to have done this."

This so-called green revolution of multinational, agri-corporations is accompanied by increased militarization and genocide as peasants, tenant farmers and indigenous people are forced off the land to clear the way for crops grown for export by these corporations, whose interests are protected by whatever means necessary, including military violence. Central America has been a prime example, where a class of landless peasants is being created, with squatter movements and guerrilla groups resulting.

In 1954, United Fruit Co. (now Chiquita) and the CIA combined to topple the democratically elected Guatemalan government of Jacobo Arbentz, which nationalized and redistributed 100,000 acres of fertile land being held idle by United Fruit to prevent competition. The result was 30 years of ruthless military dictatorship and the killing of thousands of innocent Guatemalans.

Then there's the land being poisoned by pesticides as farming shifted to corporations. Pesticides can cause cancer, birth defects, neurological damage and immune deficiencies.

In 1986, the Environmental Protection Agency rated pesticides as the greatest threat to our environment. In 1987, about 1.26 billion pounds of pesticides were used in the United States. By 1993, it was 2.23 billion pounds, with 80 percent used on corn, cotton, soybeans and wheat. Ironically, crop losses doubled as almost 500 major pest species developed genetic resistance to the pesticides. According to the National Academy of Sciences, 20 pest species are resistant to widely used pesticides. By 2000 (four short years away), the NAS estimates almost all major insect pests will show some form of genetic resistance to pesticides. It is later than you think.

All over our shrinking global village people are forgetting the wisdoms traditionally passed down through generations about soil, seeds, wildlife, the seasons and rhythms of nature and how to work with natural systems for mutual benefit. And too many of us are losers because of what is happening.

February 25, 2001

From a time and place when people were surrounded by wild animals, the world has since become a place where wild animals are surrounded by people. Yet despite this reality, an ironic reversal of history is happening right here in our country.

In the Great Plains that compromise 40 percent of the continental U.S., a regional reversal of our historic Manifest Destiny is occurring. And this significant change offers hope and promise of a better tomorrow.

The Great Plains now hold a small fraction of its former population. About one in four counties is in economic and demographic decline along with marked social distress. In the process, they have reverted to what is technically called "frontier status," which is fewer than two residents per square mile. The historian Frederick Jackson Turner declared the frontier closed in 1898, but subsequent events have shown he was premature because the frontier, as determined by population, is in permanent flux.

For example, in North Dakota, the frontier shrank to 21 percent in 1920, but over the past half century it has stretched again to cover three-fifths of the state. This is happening elsewhere in the Great Plains.

Adversities of this trend are underlined in the high delinquency rates for holders of Farm Home Administration loans, especially in the Dakotas and Nebraska, where production loan failures exceeded 40 percent. And in those states and others average farm income has plummeted. Adding troubles from drought, floods, wheat scab and bad years enables one to understand why more farmers are calling it quits.

It is an ironic reversal of history that, while farmers and other non-Indians are fleeing rural areas of Montana, both Dakotas, Nebraska and Oklahoma, all of which have suffered population losses since 1985, the Indian population in those states has doubled in the past two decades. Could it be called poetic justice that new demographics offer hope with return of the Indian and his cherished sacred buffalo?

To Native America and its First Americans, the buffalo is the elder brother, the teacher, and the First People on the Great Plains were the Buffalo People. Revered holy men of the Lakota Sioux say, "The buffalo gave their lives so that we might live: now it is our turn to speak for the buffalo, to stand for our relatives."

And they are doing that. A year ago this month, a half hundred Native People were on Tatanka Oyate Mani, the walk for the Buffalo Nation, a 507-mile trek from South Dakota's sacred Black Hills to the stone archway over Yellowstone's northern entrance. This reminded us that for thousands of years, Plains Indians built prosperous cultures on the buffalo's bounty: food, tools, clothing, utensils and shelter. It was the foundation of their lives and represented the whole universe.

Over those thousands of years, the Great Plains, the belly of the continent and largest single ecosystem in North America, was maintained by the buffalo. By their sheer numbers, weight and behavior they actually cultivated the prairie. Their thundering hooves in the earth as they moved by the millions resounded in the vast underground water systems, the famed Ogallala Aquifer, stimulating its health and seeding the prairie. The wanton destruction of the buffalo resulted in the geological and economic crisis now afflicting the region.

When 50 million buffalo roamed the prairie in the 19th century, there were more than 250 types of grasses, a profusion of prairie dogs, wolves, prairie turnips, mushrooms and a host of other species now either gone or endangered. Biological diversity plummeted with that massive shift that brought excessive cultivation and irrigation on land meant to be prairie grasses. Thus Great Plains topsoil is eroding and its ground water dwindling, as the prairies teem with pumps, irrigation systems, combines and toxic chemicals creating even more problems. With much of the natural ecosystem destroyed, what remains is in such precarious state that people who were part of it are being forced to leave.

After plummeting in numbers from 50-60 million to a remnant few hundred, with the marked reversal year being 1872-1873, this remarkable animal is coming back, with more than a growing 200,000 today. Nationally, 41 separate Indian tribes belong to the International Bison Cooperative, with its sole mission being buffalo restoration. On reservations from Taos Pueblo in northern New Mexico to Standing Rock in North Dakota, Native communities are welcoming back their relations. The Standing Rock system is restoration of small herds using the successful method of Arkansas-based Heifer Project that donates calves to families who then pass along one of their gift animal's female calves so others can breed herds of their own.

Dozens of western ranchers in the Great Plains have already converted their operation to buffalo, and the governor of North Dakota not long ago said the state would soon have more buffalo than cattle. There is economic sense for this, too, as many buffalo ranchers are selling bison on the hoof for double what they get for cattle. Health-conscious American consumers know that buffalo meat is much lower in fat and cholesterol, lower even than skinless chicken breasts, making it a highly marketable commodity.

There is also a growing movement for Buffalo Commons in much of the Great Plains that were meant for buffalo. Ted Turner has moved in this direction, removing miles of fencing on his ranch, allowing buffalo to roam naturally. This makes sense because the animals tend to keep moving as they graze so as to make lighter use of the landscape. This could be a key to restoring native prairie lands and not causing the erosion and over-grazing by cattle that tend to concentrate in areas of best forage.

Besides the better economic and environmental sense of buffalo (and eliminating costly farm subsidies that don't work), Duane Lammers, boss of the Triple 7 ranch in South Dakota, summed it up for many when he said, "What I like about buffalo, they're so damn little work," as he stressed they readily withstand winters that kill cattle.

Yes, the buffalo is back.

CHAPTER 28

The Struggle to Halt
Environmental Degradation

The sad saga of our world environment under threat is also a lamentable account of human greed and lust for power; it could, indeed, be viewed as a playing out of Karl Marx's worst nightmare. Writing for August 17, 2003, Simon sounded a grim warning of the EPA becoming another case of "the fox watching the hen house." His column for June 25, 1995, carried a strong warning about the Republican House's "Dirty Water" bill. Simon's informative column for January 3, 1997, detailed how an old 1872 mining act was enabling giant mining corporations to fleece American taxpayers and leave behind disastrous cleanup needs. Finally in a passionate alert of October 30, 1995, Simon related how Congress was threatening our country's natural heritage.

August 17, 2003

Most of you probably understand the meaning of the phrase, "foxes watching the chicken coop." On occasion, this column has called attention to realities of this as it applies to the Bush administration and people it now has running much of our government.

But it's time for some specifics to back up the thrust of this and its dire effect on our country and its citizens as national policy goes awry with seriously adverse effect.

As a 30-year cattle rancher operating with some federal government grazing permits administered by Bureau of Land Management in the Interior Department, it's logical using this government agency as an example because of my connection with it.

The Department of Interior is constitutionally charged with responsibility for protecting 507 million acres of lands that belong to all of us, the American people. It can be said it is our birthright that these lands be protected for us and for future generations.

Heading this vast agency as a member of President Bush's cabinet is a very powerful person named Gale Norton, who controls most of our public lands. Just as "by their deeds ye shall know them," so can you know much about Gale Norton's priorities by those she's hired to work for her. Bluntly, a list of key officials in Norton's Interior Department reads like a "Who's Who" of big-time special interest lobbyists, anti-conservationists, environmental polluters and bosses of the fossil fuel industry—all constitutionally obligated by oath to protect the 507 million acres of lands belonging to mostly average American people.

Norton's second-in-command is J. Stephen Griles, as deputy secretary. He is former vice president of United Mining Co., and was a big-money lobbyist for Occidental Petroleum, Shell Oil and National Mining Assoc. He worked for notorious James Watt when that inadvertent booster of conservation organization membership headed Reagan's Interior Department. During that time, Watt was probably the world's No. 1 example of a fox watching the chicken coop.

Associate deputy secretary and third in command under Norton (a new position in a growing bureaucracy), is James E. Carson, noted mostly for his giveaway of mining patents when he was another of James Watt's wrecking crew. Nominated for an Agriculture Department position under Bush I, the U.S. Senate refused to confirm him.

William G. Myers III controls all legal issues as Interior Department solicitor. Unusual even for a former lobbyist of the National Cattleman's Beef Association, Myers is a "kill all the varmints" advocate who favors buffalo slaughter and opposes the wolf reintroduction, regardless.

The special assistant for Alaska is Camden Toohey, who manages the 270 million acres of interior lands in our largest state. He's a former director of Arctic Power, the outfit that pushes aggressive oil drilling anywhere in Alaska, and especially in the Arctic Refuge that is an unequaled national treasure. (Any conflict of interest there?!)

Norton's assistant for Land & Mineral Management is Rebecca Watson, who oversees all mining, grazing and land management decisions. And this after being top lawyer for big oil, gas and timber corporations.

In charge of allocating water to balance needs of people and wildlife is a Bennett Raley, assistant secretary for Water and Science in Norton's Interior Department. But get this, he was lobbyist for National Water Resources Foundation and opposed our nation's much needed Clean Water Act. This guy was even against saving any water for endangered species as mandated by Congressional action and federal law.

Heading all these foxes watching the chicken coop is a lawyer who defended the lead paint industry and argued that Congress' Endangered Species Act is unconstitutional. Gale Norton also was lobbyist for big oil, gas, mining and timber corporations with Mountain States Legal Foundation as a protégé of the infamous James Watt; when he headed the Interior Department it was like having a mafia don being police chief.

It's bad enough when big money special interest lobbyists have great power outside the system, but having them on the government payroll creates a mammoth conflict of interest that is dangerous to the best of America. Instead of fulfilling their obligation to protect our country's natural resources and the environment, Norton and crew have been protecting profits of big corporations as they sell America "down the river."

In the doing, Norton is turning habitat for wildlife into a profit center for oil drillers, developers and big mining companies. And this same Norton even approved a cyanide leach gold mine (pollutes excessively) on Sacred Native American lands.

So is it surprising that long-term career people in the Interior Department, who really care about protecting our land and wildlife, are being "removed" as special interest political appointees take over?

Better get ready trying to explain to your kids and grandchildren why our nation's open green spaces, wilderness area, native wild animals, national parks and monuments are being destroyed—as our cherished American West becomes scarred and polluted... so that big money can make even more big bucks from the people's heritage.

June 25, 1995

If you aren't scared, then you ought to be, because your health and wellbeing are at stake.

Even after the Savings & Loan debacle that resulted from the Reagan administration getting government "off our backs," it is obvious that we're being hoodwinked again.

Under the guise of sweet talk about improving risk assessment, dropping unfunded mandates and getting government off people's backs, House Speaker Newt Gingrich and his right-wing cohorts mounted a sweeping assault on federal safeguards that protect our environment and thus our health and lives.

Heading for the trashcan are such historic and effective laws as the Safe Drinking Water Act, the Clear Air Act and the Clean Water Act, which for a quarter century have guaranteed our right to a safe and healthy environment.

To compound this tragedy-in-waiting, the Gingrich crowd has the polluters writing the federal rules that will further feather their nests, with the understanding that they will pass more money to right-wing congressmen.

Imagine having "representatives" of the people with vested interests write the laws that will affect them? This is worse than having the fox watch the chicken coop, as was the case with many Reagan appointees.

Examples of the good results of the Clean Water Act are endless— such as making the once-filthy and polluted Boston Harbor, Long Island Sound and the Potomac River again safe for fishing and swimming.

Recently the House approved H.R. 961, which we could aptly label a "dirty water bill," a wish-list-come-true for industry polluters who helped write it.

This bill would greatly increase water pollution, endanger your family's health and destroy America's life-saving wetlands that are the best water filters ever. And the giant, cash-rich polluter lobby is mounting a high-pressure campaign to ram this dirty water bill through the Senate, with the action in both houses driven by greed.

Here are some of the nightmares waiting to happen if this assault succeeds:

- More dioxin, lead and other chemicals pouring into our waters because of the Gingrich loopholes handed to giant manufacturing industries. This means you and I will get stuck downstream with rivers and lakes too dangerous for swimming and fishing.

- More sewage flowing into our rivers and oceans, because the GOP bill seriously would weaken sewage treatment requirements for coastal cities and small towns. This means that you and I will endure beach closings, algae blooms and contaminated seafood.

- More pesticides and fertilizers in our drinking water, because the Gingrich bill indefinitely postpones controls on the massive run-off of pollution from agriculture. This means that we will have increased risk of cancer, reproductive disorders and other illness.

- More destruction of wetlands and wildlife essential to a healthy and well-rounded environment, because the GOP legislation strips protection for almost 80 percent of America's remaining wetlands. Thus, big business will have free rein to destroy millions more acres of wildlife habitat as it makes big bucks turning it into developments with shopping malls, parking lots and congestion.

Dr. Phillip J. Landigan, a leading pediatric and environmental medicine expert, recently testified before Congress about proposed risk assessment changes.

He said that if Gingrich's proposed changes were in effect in 1977, we still would have dangerous levels of lead in our gasoline. As it is we have too much lead in our drinking water, and children with high levels of lead in their blood can experience learning disabilities, decreased growth, hyperactivity and brain damage.

Is this what some of you voted for in the last election?

January 3, 1997

Too many of us don't realize that we're ripped off by a looting of our nation's heritage and resources.

It is just as disgusting that those posing as our elected representatives are allowing this to happen and doing nothing about it.

The cause of this deplorable reality is a fossilized law known as the General Mining Act of 1872. A lot has changed in America during the nearly 125 years since that relic was passed for the purpose of helping the United States populate the West, when miners still went after minerals with picks and shovels.

Yet in spite of this, the fees for registering a mining claim remain only $2.50 to $5 per acre—and the miner can continue to own the land even if mining has stopped.

If a miner proves that a registered claim is capable of commercial production, then this ancient law requires that the federal government deed the land to the miner, even if the mine is a serious environmental hazard.

All this makes the minerals on public land about the only material in the world that can be bought for 1872 prices. And not a dime in royalties is paid to the public treasury for minerals belonging to all of us.

Like putting a lock on the barn door after the horse is stolen, the government cannot take action against a polluting mine until after the damage is done. Underlying the stupidity of this is the billions of dollars of cleanup costs that taxpayers must pay. Thus U.S. public lands owned by us can be ravaged, hazardous wastes created, streams polluted and national parks threatened—and Uncle Sam and we taxpayers will pay for the aftermath.

Here are just some of the endless examples of how we're being ripped off, and our representatives are letting it happen...

• The Canadian-owned Noranda mine paid the United States less than $25,000 in the 1980's for land containing its mine. That came to as little as $2.50 per acre. Now so as to supposedly "save" Yellowstone Park, the government is going to, in effect, buy back Noranda's land by handing over federal land with a market value 2,720 times greater. With 16,000 other mining claims in the Yellowstone ecosystem, similar deals to protect the land from destructive mining are a good way to bankrupt our country of its resources.

• Pollutants leading from Colorado's Summitville Mine—such as those causing tremendous degradation of western streams—poisoned 17 miles of the Alamosa River, a Rio Grande tributary. This requires a minimum $120 million cleanup, paid for by taxpayers, because the company that opened the mine is bankrupt.

• At least 80 percent of our country's 1.2 million mining claims, covering 20 million acres bought for peanuts, are inactive. But one deed holder who paid $170 for 60 acres near Phoenix turned the site into a resort golf course valued at $60 million.

• With an estimated 22.5 million ounces of reserves worth between $8 billion and $10 billion, the Canadian-based Goldstrike Mine on the Carlin Trend in Nevada paid the U.S. Treasury $9,765 for less than 2,000 acres a couple years ago.

Now this company's mines will be producing more gold per year than was mined during the peak year of the California gold rush. This makes the take from Cripple Creek, Sutter's Mill and the Klondike chicken feed.

Thus, this Canadian company's mine with the land it got for a song and its gold equal in weight to 366 Cadillac Eldorados, went from our national heritage for the price of a compact car—because of that archaic 1872 mining law our representatives haven't changed.

Mining companies always mount fierce campaigns to protect their profits when these are threatened. Much of the action is carried out by "Wise Use" groups that are heavily funded fronts for corporate interests. And thus, our representatives have been suckered into line.

If gold, silver and copper mines were required to pay the 12.5 percent royalty paid by companies for non-metal resources taken from public lands, $40 billion would be added to the public treasury. This would go a long way to wiping out the deficit and meeting our country's crucial needs.

October 30, 1995

As a very successful and famous movie star, Robert Redford is in a class by himself. He's a genuine outdoorsman and lived many of the leads he has played in box office hits.

He's blessed with a long and happy marriage, a rarity in Hollywood and so different from at least four Republican presidential contenders who couldn't make a go of their first marriages.

This gives extra meaning to a letter Redford wrote from Sundance, Utah. Here is a part of that compelling letter.

"One of the main reasons I live in Utah is the immense expanse of wilderness preserved here by our federal government—more than 10 million acres of national parks, forests and other public lands.

"These beautiful lands belong to all Americans. They have been handed down to us by past generations. Now we, in turn, are the guardians of this priceless heritage for our children and theirs to come.

"This is the original contract with America—to preserve a legacy of pristine wilderness that is unique, inspiring and accessible to each and every one of us.

"Incredibly, the new leadership in Congress is ready to break that long-standing contract. They want to begin selling off our natural heritage to private commercial interests in order to raise a few quick bucks—under the pretext of (supposed) deficit reduction.

"Our national parks would be closed down like military bases. Our national forests would be sold off and logged. Our wildlife refuges would be opened to destructive oil and gas development. Hundreds of millions of acres of scenic recreational lands would simply be given away.

"It is a sad day indeed when Congress is willing to deny future generations of Americans their rightful natural heritage—for the sake of a one-time budget savings. Surely there are better ways to balance the budget than looting our children's estate!"

Instead of gearing up a massive fire sale of priceless resources that rightfully belong to all of us, why doesn't Congress of supposed people's representatives do something meaningful about saving taxpayer money and deficit reduction by cutting the billions it doles out in corporate welfare?

Does the commercial exploitation this Congress is promoting for en-

richment of oil, timber, mining and big livestock corporations—exploitation
of public lands held in sacred trust for all future generations—represent a
quid quo pro for the big bucks these special interests shovel into the coffers
of those Congress members and the political party doing their bidding?

The devilish fact is that if this pending plunder and liquidation of our
country's natural heritage goes through, then those priceless assets belonging to all of us will be gone forever and Americans and their country will
be the poorer because of it. So are we willing to let signs be posted that
read "Closed to the public—reserved for commercial special interests"?
And how would President Lincoln react to this after he signed legislation
in 1864 to preserve Yosemite Valley "for all time"?

Another devilish fact is that the GOP-controlled Congress is rushing
many of these massive giveaways, that are stealing from our children, to
a vote—before Americans wake up to the fact our public estate is being
raided!

As just one example of the chicanery being foisted on us, Rep. James
Hansen (R-Utah) offered a bonus reform proposal that continues park
commissioners' monopolies with the annual rent paid to taxpayers staying
low—and that annual rent paid is less than three cents for every dollar
taken in. And Hansen's "reform" allows concessionaires to charge whatever
they want without fear of honest competition. Of course, it's a given that
the Gingriches will be well compensated for such services. Do you think
the special PAC money flowing into GOP coffers is philanthropy?

PART VIII

A Rancher and the Ranch

CHAPTER 29

The Sage Is Not Truly Purple

A part of the mystique and the seeming paradox of Gene Simon's life is the unusual blending of journalist and cattle rancher. And those who have had the privilege to know him would be hard pressed to determine which of the two roles he has loved most: this entire book should bear witness to the passion he feels for his country, his people, indeed, for the world—and for his journalist's responsibility as advocate and educator. In like manner, this section should convey some of the passion he carries daily into his life as a rancher. The stories and reflections convey the ambiance, without romanticizing, of ranch life in southwestern New Mexico. Simon's column for July 23, 1979, describes the day ending that old ranching standby, the roundup. Writing for July 21, 1980, Simon shatters, albeit a bit tongue-in-cheek, the myth of every cowboy a Dead-eye Dick. The confluence of an epic flood and Christmas provide a frame for the column of January 2, 1979. Some twenty-plus years later, January 5, 2002, Simon yet sounded as ranch-happy as he had in the beginning, despite his understanding, communicated June 29, 2002, of ranching's uncertain future, the fading purple on the sage.

July 23, 1979

Some days on a working cattle ranch can be filled with routine and monotony, but others can be real highs… like last Saturday on the Ponderosa in Southwest New Mexico.

To start, we'd been working for a month to round up cattle, bob their tails, and brand any calves, as part of a cattle count in connection with sale of the ranch. The goal was 600 head, cows, bulls or yearlings, an un-weaned calf and cow counting as a single unit.

We started the day with the count at 597, and were weeks ahead of schedule. The first 500 had come easier than that last 97, and the pickings were getting mighty slim. With good grass and water, those cattle were scattered all over a pasture about 30 sections in size. That's nearly 20,000 acres and most of it was canyons, mesas, ridges and benches with a lot of up and down all over.

Right off, even before the six of us split into teams of two, we ran into two cows with un-bobbed tails. When a corral is handy, you bunch them together, ease up behind with your knife at the ready, quickly wrap the fly swish end of the tail around your knife, and when the cow pulls away, the job is done. That's the way cattle are counted in a ranch transaction.

Out on the open range the job is more difficult. There one cowboy ropes the cow by the hind legs and, while his horse keeps the rope taut, the other cowboy slips up behind and does the job. That's the way my partner and I got two more that put us over the top with 601. And before the day was over our other teams had come up with five more. That literally made it "money in the bank."

We all shook hands on that, and to celebrate I'm taking the whole crew to a steak house in town next week. I've ordered six sirloins-for-two for the six of us. We're going to have some fun with two of the guys. One of them, who is a rabid Dallas Cowboys fan, has been harping about how the Pittsburgh Steelers won the Super Bowl. The other guy we call "Little John Wayne." I've arranged with the restaurant when the steaks are served to bring each of them a piece of meat about the size of half dollars. On the plate of the Cowboys fan I'll have a sign saying, "Dallas Cowboys Choice Steak." Then after we have our fun, we'll let 'em have those "Sirloins for Two."

But the big thrill of the afternoon was when we were spectators to a panorama of the wild. Our two dogs were running well ahead in the area we call "Big Timber." It's like a rolling grassland prairie with widely spaced huge Ponderosa pines, easily one of the prettiest sections of the ranch. As we paused to drink in all that beauty off to the left, we noticed two huge coyotes rapidly running on the diagonal to cut off our dogs. One was rangy and extremely light colored. The other was much darker and very chunky and powerful. He looked much like a wolf. The game warden said they could have been rare wolves that on occasion drift up into this country from Sonora, Mexico.

It is highly unusual for coyotes to chase dogs. Usually it's the other way around. The coyotes, or perhaps wolves, were concentrating so on the dogs that they didn't see us. As they were closing so rapidly on the dogs, I began worrying about my young dog, Tippy. So I made my move and headed to cut them off. The coyotes split when they saw me, and at that point the dogs turned and went after the smaller one. (They weren't so dumb!) The big one that looked like a wolf just backed off a ways and coolly appraised the situation. You had to admire his courage. Then he lifted his head, not 60 or so yards away, and let out the most eerie howl of frustration I've ever heard. It made your spine tingle. Heard at night, that would have done it!!

On the nine-mile ride back to the ranch from that 30-plus mile day we rode through Brannon Park, named after the old pioneer who home-steaded it back in the 1800's. True to its reputation, we encountered a big flock of turkeys and had fun galloping after them on horseback, and they scattered in every direction. And on top of the day, we almost ran into some cow elk and calves and later saw a small herd of deer up on a nearby ridge sharply outlined against a red-streaked western sky at sunset. With two golden eagles soaring overhead, that was the frosting on the cake for a truly memorable day.

Yes, the tangy mountain air with its pine scent, the blue sky, warm sun, eternal breeze and low humidity—and no gas problems with your horse—makes all this something to be cherished and deeply appreciated in your whole being. What a way to go!

July 21, 1980

Ever hear of a present-day Western ranch that had two dead-shot cowboys… one who shot his horse and another who shot himself?!

Well, I not only know about such a ranch, I happened to be operat-ing it and was there when both "incidents" occurred. They happened on Ponderosa Highlands Ranch 45 miles north of Silver City in southwestern New Mexico a couple of years ago. But they are still worth a column; it's not every day that you're in on a shoot-yourself and shoot-your-horse situ-ation.

Here's how it happened with the shoot-himself cowboy.

This dead-shot and I were working cattle on a mesa and stopped for a brief lunch break. After a sandwich as we were each tightening our cinches ready to ride out, I heard a shot and saw him bending over in what I first thought was mock agony. This fellow was quite a kidder and always pulling something. But this time it wasn't a joke.

Dead-shot foolishly had a cartridge under the hammer of his holster revolver and when his coffee thermos slipped out of his hands while at-tempting to put it in a saddle boot, it hit the revolver hammer and deto-nated the bullet. (No savvy cowboy has a bullet in either the to-be-fired or next cylinder of his 6-shooter. Either could be dangerous if he's thrown from a horse.)

The errant bullet entered the inside of the calf of his right leg and came out just above the ankle. A fortunately clean bandanna helped stop the flow of blood and I got him on his horse for the nearly five miles ride to headquarters through rough country. I rode closely on his right to catch him if he fell because he had a starboard list, and I kept talking the entire time to help keep him from fainting.

After finally making it back to the ranch and phoning hospital emergency, we made the 45-mile dash to Silver City. Then something else happened while waiting for a report after putting Dead-shot in hospital emergency. A county sheriff's car came screeching up with siren wailing and red lights flashing. A couple of deputies charged into the hospital with revolvers drawn. A few minutes later this perplexing thriller was repeated. Then the sheriff himself came barreling up in an unmarked car and also dashed into the hospital ready for action.

This was too much for an old newspaperman, so I went in, too; maybe there was a story to cover. The "story" was that the report of a cowboy shooting himself was garbled by an inexperienced switchboard operator, and the sheriff's office misunderstood it as a shoot-out at the hospital. And I'll bet I had to explain 10 times how my cowboy was shot.

Now for the cowboy-who-shot-his-horse… and this guy was a Texan.

The two of us were riding down a trail, me in the lead, and we peeled off at a "Y" to each look for cattle. A few minutes later I heard a shot… the second one I'd heard in a month where someone shot someone or something. This time it was a big dun horse named Buck, the one my Texas cowboy was riding.

Just a few minutes after my back got away from in front of him, this cowboy was checking his gun when it accidentally went off with the bullet going in and out of the left side of Buck's neck with about 15 inches between the holes. Nerve damage dropped Buck, but he was soon able to get back on his feet. And with feet in cowboy boots, that Texan walked with that horse the 8-plus miles back to ranch headquarters over a rocky trail. He won't forget that hike.

The "accident" happened on a Tuesday and the sequel is that Buck, who was the dumbest horse I've ever known and had nothing going for him but youth and size, was en route the next day to the Deming Livestock Auction. With dangerous mountain trails all over the ranch, it was too risky to let a horse with nerve damage carry anyone, even with similar assets and liabilities.

Me? I was beginning to wonder about ranching in general and cowboys in particular, and about what kind of an outfit I was running. Two can't-miss cowboys, one shoots himself and the other shoots his horse... both in one month! After those experiences I really began listening for shots. Curiosity was getting me.

January 2, 1979

Last week when this column was written a sequence of record-breaking cold and rain was beginning to add up to trouble here in southwest New Mexico. But when that story got out "under the wire," just before flooding cut us off, we didn't know how hairy things were to become. And we didn't know how unusually nice Christmas could be in the ranch country midst emergency conditions.

A combination of three things emphasized the devastating flooding of the Gila and Rio Mimbres rivers in this area of the Southwest, which apparently was well publicized on your TV set. First, the ground was saturated with Thanksgiving weekend rains, then there was heavy snow in the high country, and the ground was frozen by sub-zero temperatures. This trio of realities added up to heavy run-off and spelled disaster when the heaviest rains ever hit "arid" Arizona and New Mexico.

Rapidly rising streams and rivers knocked out bridges and utility lines, washed away sections of highways, turned fertile bottom-land orchards and hay fields into rocky gravel beds, and moved cabins and houses to unexpected locations. And some of those streams and rivers are now flowing substantial distances from their original courses.

Here at Ponderosa Highlands Ranch north of Silver City we were without electricity and phone for nearly four days (in an all-electric house), were cut off from the highway by a raging torrent in an usually dry stream bed until it subsided enough for crossing in a 4-wheel pickup.

It's amazing how one can make-do when it's necessary, and the excitement and unusualness even made it fun. One can't always eat by candlelight or get water from a stream to cook over an open fire. Besides, the water-curtailed ranch work schedule resulted in the woodpile being better stocked than ever before.

And what about Christmas midst the aftermath of such an experience and no trips to town?

Well, it's a lot simpler than the usual hectic rush most city people experience during the "holidays." And the resulting tranquility and slower pace makes it all seem much more like Christmas ought to be.

You cut your own piñon pine for a Christmas tree; you make wreaths out of red chilies from the Mesilla Valley near Las Cruces where they grow "the best chilies in the world;" you join Spanish-American Catholic friends for midnight mass at San Lorenzo Chapel where the priest from Spain doesn't pronounce his "j's" when we all sing "Joy to the World;" you gather mistletoe (It's pink here) and make an attractive decoration out of big round tumbleweed. Then at the Christmas tree decorating ceremony (a major event here) in the valley's only Protestant Church, Rio Mimbres Baptist, you write each child's name in icing on gingerbread men my wife made.

Another delightful custom in the Spanish speaking community is a real Santa Claus that goes from house to house after his arrival by boat on the Mimbres River. (That boat has to be very shallow-draft unless the river is flooding!)

Pot-luck meals are very popular in the close-knit community of this ranch country and everyone joined in a big feed and lots of talk and fellowship at the Round-Up Lodge where the Mimbres Valley Booster Club had its Christmas party. (Some people had to cross swollen streams by horseback to attend.) These infrequent get-togethers in scattered country are meaningful events for farm and ranch families and they make the most of them. It's a good catch-up time.

But tragedy also strikes at Christmastime and the whole area is shocked and grieves with the local postmistress and her family whose very young daughter-in-law was killed in a freak auto accident Christmas night. She leaves two little children, ages 9 months and 3 years. In the old-fashioned Christmas spirit, the entire community (that takes in about a 20-mile radius) turned out to help. The family's mobile home was cleaned, a lot of food was brought in, and a fund raised to pay for baby-sitters so the young father could continue working.

Yes, there are a lot of good people in this world and a lot of them have the Christmas spirit the whole year through. It's better that way, isn't it?

January 5, 2002

Here's something different to begin the new year. It was the first time in 29 years of cattle ranching (25 of them full time) I had this experience of being sandwiched between the old year ending and the new year coming, calf branding and trailing a herd to winter pasture.

Making it even more unusual was mothering a newborn calf New Year's Eve and then topping that with dressing out a home-grown turkey for a friend, just under the 2002 wire.

A high point of all this was getting back on a horse after a forced five-month layoff. This was mandated by back fractures when a fence stretcher slipped last summer and was later compounded around recovery time when "plumbing" problems cropped up requiring minor surgery.

Normally my ranch hand and I would handle all this, but knowing the old guy was still sort of half-mast, good friends volunteered and they sure made a difference. Never had such a plentiful on-the-ball crew: Jesse Baker and son Eric, Helen Hyatt and Jubal Williamson. And my can-do guy, Fermin Batista, was right in there front and center, doing his usual competent job. Couldn't miss with such a crew.

After branding eleven already big enough calves—earliest I've ever done this—we let them all rest while we "fortified" with my wife Libby's ample grub she always provides for cattle crews.

Then it was saddle up and move 'em out for the not-long three-mile trail to Table Top pasture. It was really living being back on a horse, but next morning my back knew something different had happened yesterday! But it was worth it, and the "plumbing" apparently wasn't scrambled.

During the night, a Brangus cow came back to the starting point and had a healthy bull calf. Later, a dozen other cows returned that had to be herded back to Table Top. While this was happening, that mama cow also headed back, leaving her calf. Never in nearly three decades of working with Brangus have I known one to leave her calf. Since we were running out of the daylight, the only option was to gather up that couple-of-days-old calf and take him home for the night. We found a calf bottle and nipple and good friend Linda Cox of El Rancho saved the day—or rather New Year's night—with a Ranchway milk-replacer. So that little fella got some needed nourishment before I remembered to dress out that turkey before it was new year.

A happy ending to all this is that it hit me (in bed) that the mama cow might come back to check out her calf. So shortly after daylight, the first day of 2002, we hauled him back and, sure enough, there was that worried mama cow. She knew it was her kid even while he was still in the trailer and she came running. So it was through a couple of gates and on to the corral.

Talk about a heart-warming reunion! And hopefully it will be a happy ever-after. Best part is I won't need to bottle feed that calf for a bunch of months like I've done before. Hope this experience is a good omen for the new year.

But here's one that sure is: On a typical bright, tangy crystal clear New Mexico morning seeing seven wild turkeys in our yard, four deer in the pasture across the river, six wild ducks in the pond, dozens of Gambel quail around the feed blocks on both sides of our house and all the bird feeders crowded, how does it get any better than that, along with riding out on a good horse? And being blessed is doing what you want to do, where you want to do it, and being able to do it—even crowding 86.

And come to think of it, being able to get reactionary right-wing extremists riled up once in awhile with a newspaper column! Sure do hope '02 will be a real good year for all of you—all *buenos, no mala,* and *nada* you can't handle.

June 29, 2002

A recent week on Idaho ranches opened the window to more understanding of the harsh political and economic realities facing the ranching industry today. Collectively, these realities are clashing with the romantic myth of the cowboy, and sentimental values won't resolve the severe challenges facing ranching.

The realization is unavoidable that ranching's future is uncertain as the risks grow and the returns fall. And what's happening in Idaho is essentially mirrored all over the West, and especially here in New Mexico. The problems are basically the same, with differences mostly being those of timing and degree.

Ranching today accounts for about one-tenth of 1 percent of all jobs in the West, as researched by University of Montana economist Thomas Power. Rather than rural economies relying on ranching, as many once did, now it is ranching that has become a relatively small part of an increasingly high-tech and service-oriented economy, not only in Idaho but in virtually all Western and cattle-producing states. This switch is somewhat comparable to people long ago being surrounded by animals. Now it is the animals that are surrounded by people.

Big corporations dominate the beef market, and in the bigger-is-better livestock industry, small ranching operations are getting outmuscled. Larger feedlots can supply beef to market more quickly and at a higher profit. It's not in the cards for smaller ranchers to out-maneuver and out-market the bigger operations. The challenges become even greater because of increasing regulations to protect water and endangered species. Along the way, ranchettes and subdividing could become the gravestone for the family ranch. It is in this arena that ranchers themselves are increasingly in conflict. Some are licking their chops to make a killing subdividing, while others want to keep things the same.

So it's not just the conservationists and environmentalists who are at

odds with the cowboys. Stronger adversaries of the West's ranching industry are market forces and dietary habits, as Americans eat less beef.

Reflecting trends all over the West, since 1970, Idaho's beef operations
have dropped from 11,500 to 7,600 in 2001. And Americans eating less
beef pay nearly a third less for the meat—after inflation is factored in, than
they did 20 years ago.

What makes this difficult to understand is the trend of cattle prices.
In 1950, calf prices jumped to $26.40 per hundred pounds. In 1975, when
cattle numbers peaked in Idaho at 2.1 million head, the price was $28
per hundred weight. In 1988, calf prices had risen to $88.50 per hundred
pounds. This year, calf prices in Idaho ranged from $80 to $95 per hundred
weight, and they've been higher at Deming Livestock Market. On May 29,
I got $108 per hundred for a 335-pound steer calf.

As ranching has become a smaller part of an increasingly high-tech
and service-oriented economy, ranchers like farmers are losing political
clout to urban businesses and nationally to environmental groups because
they have the numbers—and even politicians can count. So it is not surprising that many ranchers are feeling isolated.

A fourth-generation woman rancher in Jordan Valley, Ore., where we
also visited ranches on a *Western Livestock Journal*-sponsored trip, said it this
way: "You've got Republicans on one side protecting a corporate America
that's destroying competition, and on the other side, Democrats are supporting the Green movement that wants to regulate us off the land."

There are inaccuracies in the Democrat part of this quote, and it should
be noted that Democratic support of the Green movement is sketchy, as
some few remaining moderate Republicans are environmental supporters.
Perhaps this underlines the wisdom of the observation that the person
who said there are two sides to every question grossly oversimplified it.

There's irony in all this, too, because many ranchers are Republicans,
despite the party's Big Money-Big Business oriented policies working to
the detriment of the little operator. Documentation of this reality is ample.

There's also another irony. More ranchers need to comprehend the
truth and wisdom of what a great Republican president once said: "The
underlying principle of conservation (and environmental policies) has been
described as the application of common sense to common problems for the
common good." Theodore Roosevelt said that and his wisdom implies that
any good rancher is also an environmentalist, or ought to be. Without the
land and environment around him healthy, the rancher is out of business.

Architect John Marvel is ranching's harshest critic, especially in Idaho.

He's made a second career shooting holes in the cowboy myth that he says obscures the true legacy of the West, its geography. "It will continue to exist with all its stupendous scenery and mighty vistas whether there are cattle and sheep using those lands," Marvel says.

He wants the federal government to pay ranchers for their allotments (which do produce only a small percentage of beef eaten in the United States) because cattle grazing has caused widespread erosion, spread alien plants like cheat-grass throughout the range, and threatens endangered fish and wildlife.

Marvel also says the imagery associated with cowboys was created by literary figures from the East. *Don't Fence Me In* was written by Cole Porter of Indiana, and Zane Grey was an Eastern dentist.

Doesn't all this suggest there's a lot more to many things than meets the eye?

CHAPTER 30

A New Mexican Bestiary

Ogallala Sioux holy man Black Elk, telling his story, noted, "It is the story of all life that is holy and it is good to tell, and of us two-leggeds sharing it with the four-leggeds and the wings of the air and all green things..."[17] So have felt countless visitors to "Gene and Elisabeth's" Rancho del Rio, absorbing the contentment of lives well lived in harmony with "the four-leggeds, the wings of the air and all green things." And it is most of all such as these following "down-home" columns which most save intellectually-insightful Simon the journalist from being just another capital city pundit. Could any Washington or Santa Fe correspondent, sipping the White House or Round House bubbly, have written as Simon did on June 12, 1995? In like vein, a column of September 14, 2003, finds Simon musing across the boundaries between his journalism and ranching passions, on Israel's loss of the high moral ground, new convictions from the Corporate Fraud Task Force, and "hanky-panky stuff between wild and domestic turkeys" along the Rio Mimbres. The column of August 28, 1978, tells a tall tale of bear killing. November 13, 1978 records the acquisition of a cow dog, one of the most important animals on a functioning ranch. Finally follows one of the best loved columns of all Simon's career, an account written in the early 1980's, the death of Ole Dan; because for those of us who have loved and lost horses, the column is genuinely timeless, the looseness of its dating is perhaps appropriate.

June 12, 1995

After raising almost every kind of poultry and animal since I was a kid, there are still surprises that crop up. And it's full of reminders of what we can learn from the animal world.

It's calving time again, and again I'm in awe of how those mama cows can communicate with their calves, who obviously understand so well. Just

---

17. As quoted in Wendell Berry, "Think Little," in *A Continuous Harmony*, New York: Harcourt Brace Jovanovich, Inc., 1970, p. 85.

another example: Little calves always tag along with their mama, and yet there are times when they stay where mama puts them in a sheltered place when she goes off for water or food. But you usually know where that calf is, because the cow frequently looks in that direction to make sure all is well with her calf. And if the mama knows the river is too high for the calf to cross, it quickly understands and doesn't fret about staying with another cow. How can that happen without good communication between cow and calf, and the baby sitter, too?

My admiration grows for Buff Orington bantams as mothers; these little hens will mother just about anything. The smallest broad-breasted white turkey chicks I could get at the feed store were almost two weeks old, which normally makes a transfer to foster parent risky. But I gambled with a dozen and after dark slipped a couple under the longest setting bantam, so her shock wouldn't be too great.

After another hour, I transferred her to the special coup with all of them under her. The next morning, it was like old home week with those not-so-little turkeys gathering around when she clucked over special food, like old, cut-up hard-boiled eggs that are excellent for young chicks.

Another bantam hen recently hatched seven little African guineas that are obviously doing fine with their foster mother. And yet another is successfully mothering a peacock chick that fell out of the hay mow nest and was unable to keep up with the others because of some injury. But that mama bantam is going to bring it along.

Those bantams have guts, too. While one was scratching around in the corral with her chicks, a cow started nosing around. With loud cackling and wings flaying, that little two-to-three-pound bantam hen drove off that half-ton of beef with no hesitation.

You know what just hit me, especially after reading again about the virtual epidemic of child-abuse across our country, with parents sometimes brutally beating their kids? There isn't any of this in the animal world that I've ever observed. Seems the so-called animals treat their young a whale of a lot better than do many of the human animals. What does this tell us?

Don't think there's any animal much smarter than a smart horse. I've got some that can open gate bolts and latches, and they've got fantastic memories as to where the good grub is or where a gate is open. But even more impressive is how well they get along together. My best cow horse is *numero uno* of the four, and all he has to do to get into another's stall is merely touch his rump. But he never does it in a nasty way and the others never resent it. They just back out and enter another place, calm as can be. I know some human animals that wouldn't handle it that well. And I know danged well that my horse wouldn't be gullible and dumb enough to get taken in by the likes of Rush Limbaugh with his piles of inaccuracies and bum dope.

September 14, 2003

The growing number of topics for columns is really not surprising considering proliferation of significant happenings most everywhere. These are increasingly crowding-the-gate as each week's deadline approaches.

There's the riveting account of a visit to Israel by an American Quaker Jew born in Palestine! While Stanley Zarowin's report was objective and balanced, he did cite his expectation that people of a nation who endured the Holocaust and gained their own homeland "would respond less brutally to the Palestinians' quest."

Then there's the growing perception a lot of organized crime is embedded in capitalism! How else can you read the Associated Press report about the Corporate Fraud Task Force obtaining more than 250 fraud convictions? These included at least 25 former CEO's, as 354 more people are charged with corporate crime in the suites, and the government obtains $85 million in fines, forfeitures and restitution.

Even more "grabbing" is the string of documentation that the recent massive blackout in the northeast can be "traced to a dim bulb in the White House," as America's heartland journal *The Progressive Populist*, headlined it. The administration's deregulation phobia is sending us into the dark ages as Big Money utilities reap more billions in profits. Remember Ronnie Reagan's deregulation that brought on the massive scandalous S&L rip-off costing taxpayers untold billions?

And that can't-see-the-woods-for-the-trees editorial in the Carlsbad *Current-Argus* (9-5) captioned "Democrats need to come to senses." In effect, it urged them to be Republican-lite, and predicted Bush's re-election. (I'm saving that one!) The Carlsbad paper seems unaware that more than two-thirds of eligible voters didn't vote in 2000 and 2002. And the basis for Bush's selection was less than half of scarcely one-third of voters, with the Republican congressional "landslide" in 2002 being a hair over half of a third. Any Democratic candidate who can activate the silent majority of voters will bring home the bacon, and Howard Dean is well on the way to doing that. Simple arithmetic says anyone who gets the majority of two-thirds-plus of former nonvoters will top less than half the other scarcely one-third.

So with these teasers behind us, here's this week's column about a big problem. Everybody has them. Problems are everywhere though it was Mark Twain who said: "Most of the troubles in my life I have never had."

Here's the growing problem at this *rancho* on the *rio* (where the *agua* has mostly went) that I'm thinking is a rarity elsewhere. It involves turkeys, six dozen counting both domestic and wild.

Occasionally we see a few wild turkeys here on the Mimbres River though such sightings are unusual. Two years ago a mama wild turkey began hanging around, becoming a little tamer though maintaining her wariness. Then it disappeared for a few weeks but returned with a friend. This was springtime and both soon disappeared. Thinking maybe the coyotes or bobcats got them, we forgot about it until mid-summer when those two turkeys were spotted with five half-grown chicks, one showing its daddy was my Red Bourbon gobbler. All have survived to be adult turkeys, which indicates they ain't dumb.

This preceded the explosion. After bobcats fattened last winter on 10-11 turkeys and 3 peacocks, my remaining 4 hens and 1 gobbler went into high gear. The result: a bumper crop of at least three dozen assorted-size young turkeys. But almost half of them are bronze, which says that hanky-panky stuff between wild and domestic turkeys works both ways. Meanwhile, four wild hens scattered and produced 27 chicks at latest count.

What's making the problem acute is these four flocks of wild turkeys are becoming tamer and now come in every evening to feed with the home flock, though we often try to scare them off, as I don't want the mixing.

There are already enough problems with broken cottonwood limbs as the home flock is getting heavier. Now those young wild turkeys are acting like they own the place, and I'm too "chicken" not to feed them at least a little. Fortunately they still roost high in cottonwoods along the river, and I'm trying to keep them in their natural surroundings.

As it is, the three adult wild gobblers often hang around most of the day, which sometimes requires "running them off." But it's getting to the stage where they thumb their noses when this happens, or at least yawn!

The big downside of the turkey volume here is they ain't doing my wife's cherished herbs and flowers any good—which reality doesn't make for a happy home!

Regardless, how many of you need to chase wild turkeys from your place a couple times a day? Never thought that would happen here.

August 28, 1978

We didn't get that mountain lion reported in this column last week, but since then we did get a huge cattle-killing bear! And this one was caught in the act of eating fresh-killed Ponderosa Highlands Ranch beef here in southwest New Mexico.

But the bad part is I wasn't in on this one. It was my luck to be on the hunt that came out zero. Anyway, here's how it happened.

Ranch foreman Charles McCargish had found a big steer calf killed and partially eaten by a bear in rough country about five miles north of ranch headquarters. All the signs told this veteran cowman and experienced outdoorsman it was the same stock killer that has been feeding on ranch beef for years. In fact, a while back McCargish had hit the bear with a 45 slug that didn't even phase the giant.

So the next day before daybreak three mounted men and nine dogs headed for the kill site. Besides foreman McCargish, there was his son, Mike, a 17-year-old cowboy who can ride with the best of them, and Owen Fowler, a middle-aged high school biology teacher whose hobby is hunting killer bears and mountain lions—on weekends and whenever he can get a day off. Owen, who has some of the best lion and bear dogs around, is the Daniel Boone of the Gila high country, which he knows like the palm of his hand.

In nothing flat, the dogs (4 veterans and 5 young ones who had the experience of at least one kill) hit the bear's trail and within a quarter mile came on another freshly killed calf. The hounds' baying on a hot scent had scared the bear off this kill, but he had left his name card by again eating parts of it. He was lighting out fast, though obviously gorged from his interrupted feast. Another trademark of this bear is going after "wet" cows and their milk bags. These are the ones that have just calved.

A bear like this one, even with a full stomach, can outrun a fast horse downhill and that's what this old cow killer was doing as he tore up and down ridges, moved out on a mesa and then circled back right past his kill of the day before, scarcely a quarter mile from the second one.

By this time the dogs had run him fast about a mile and a half and were getting bushed, but their savvy showed in the way they took turns taking short rests while the others kept on the trail. And the horses were getting winded, too, but Mike was out in front about a quarter mile by the combination of a good horse and being higher than the other riders, and he was catching up with that bear.

This old veteran killer, who was smart enough to survive a decade of hunting seasons by never treeing, finally had to do that as there were no other options left. Exertion had caused a couple inches of back-fat or tallow to melt, his stomach was still gorged and too full to have run it off, and he was winded and frothing at the mouth. So he finally made it about 20 feet up to the first limb of a big Ponderosa pine.

Thus less than an hour after the dogs hit the scent and found the second calf-kill en route to the one of the day before, Mike McCargish got his first bear ever, with one 30-30 shot in the side of its head... from as near as his horse would let him get to that dread bear smell, which was too close at the tree's base.

The cinnamon colored bear was dead when he hit the ground, with five busted ribs and a stomach that split on impact because of its being stuffed with beef. In nearly a quarter century of bear hunting, Owen Fowler had never known this to happen.

Dressed out at the kill site, the big bear measured nearly seven feet in length and weighed over 400 pounds. An experienced pack mule had to be hobbled to get the bear loaded, after he first stampeded and dumped the bear. The horses wouldn't even go near that dead bear.

So, at 17, Mike McCargish has made some history in this Gila high country. His father thinks its just part of the job and his mother, Joan, takes it all in stride in her calm way. But there's someone else who thinks it's terrific. This is Debbie Allsup, of Silver City, a 15-year-old high school sophomore who has been team-roping with Mike in rodeos. She's sort of his girl, too; he's just recently discovered 'em!

And the moral of the bear story: often you can get into trouble more easily than you can get out of it.

We'll try to get some pictures for you.

November 13, 1978

This report has just now been double-checked for accuracy. Here's the setting...

It is 8 o'clock on a Sunday morning (11-5)! You're in southwestern New Mexico at 6,200 feet elevation. The thermometer on the shaded west side of the house reads 28 degrees, and it frosted last night. There's a light breeze from the southeast.

And what are you doing? You're in your bedroom slippers and pajama bottoms—sweeping a concrete apron in front of your garage on the east side of a ranch house. While your breath can still show steam in the brisk morning air, the sun is pleasantly warm and you're comfortable. In fact, while you lean against the back of your car, it's downright warmish and your skin is almost hot from these unfiltered rays of the morning sun. And the back of the car you are leaning against is already like a pleasant radiator for just-right heat.

The air and view around you is clear as a bell. That's one of the many assets of this southwestern part of our country. Because of clarity of the broad vistas at most times, mountain ranges, rim rock and mesas that are actually many miles distant seem almost nearby. There's no pollution or prevailing humidity to obscure the view.

And while you're exulting in all this, who is intently watching you? It's a dog, and herein is another story.

If you've never had a dog that was not much of anything to begin with and then seen him develop, there's a gratifying experience ahead of you. Its satisfactions are tremendous.

A bluff and hearty rancher up the Mimbres Valley named Will Graham, a veteran of this cow country, gave me a 6-month-old male dog that is an Australian shepherd and ¼ Australian blue heeler. His name is Tippy, after the Mexican custom of giving animals names that reflect their appearance. And Tippy fits with white tips to his tail, feet and on his forehead.

For the entire six months of his life Tippy had been penned in a chicken coop, which severely limited his learning and experiences. Rancher Graham didn't have time to work with him but the dog was potentially too good to dispose of. So I finally got another dog, after a couple of years recess from having dogs all my life.

It was difficult to even get a collar on Tippy and he had to literally be dragged from his pen. He was terrified tied in the back of a pick-up on the 3-mile ride back to our ranch. But he was already demonstrating an inner common sense.

For the first few days, Tippy showed neither affection nor any playfulness, but he never growled or snapped, just watched. However, patience and praise for any progress soon paid off. Patting and rubbing his ears and head after gently pulling him toward you with the chain soon had him coming to you freely.

On the third day he was closely heeling on walks, but still with the chain. Then on the fourth day, on an impulse, I took the chain off during a long walk. Since then, Tippy needs no chain, and from that time he began to show playfulness and affection. But he is still wary of others and will not permit anyone else to pet him. This and other evidence indicates Tippy will probably be a one-man dog, which has both advantages and disadvantages.

One of the latter is what happens when I go away. I don't have an answer for that one yet.

Anyway, with the good progress Tippy has made in his new world, the next logical step was to take him along when I work cattle by horseback. Tippy took to this like a duck to water and thoroughly enjoys it all with an eagerness that is contagious. All this is very gratifying and it adds up to the tremendous satisfaction of the companionship of man, dog and horse. This means a lot here in the ranch lands of the Gila high country.

I sure like my new dog.

Early 1980's

Ole Dan died Oct. 20. It was about noon when the vet put him to sleep.

And that evening we buried him... in the cottonwood grove by the river where he liked to loaf in the shade on hot days as he swished his tail at flies.

Dan was 27, which would have made him over a hundred if he were a human. But he was almost human, this wise sorrel horse that was the best cow pony I ever had. And if he were a human, you would have called him a class guy who never lost his cool or dignity, a solid citizen you could depend on. He was a real competitor, too, who just couldn't stand letting another horse get ahead of him in a run.

Dan and I had been together for 17 years and we've ridden a lot of miles and a lot of trails together in all kinds of country and kinds of weather.

I got Dan at the X Lazy V Cattle Company in Congress Junction, Ariz., back in 1973. We were there buying cattle for the Ponderosa Highlands Ranch near Lake Roberts, then owned by News Printing Company of Tarentum, Penn.

They loaned me Dan when we were working cattle on that range and I took a shine to that horse from day one. He had it, all the way. He was special. And all you had to do to make this horse look proud was put a saddle on him ready to mount up. He liked that, and he was always ready to go and give you his best.

A horse like that would make any cowboy look good. When a calf would break out while you were trailing a herd, Dan knew exactly what to do and he did it quick and he did it right. And he watched out for you, too. If a muddy boot slipped out of the stirrup while you were mounting up, Dan would wait until you got set before moving out.

But as happens to all of us, old age caught up with Dan along with all the complications that can go with that. But even in his later years he was still taking little kids for careful rides, like the 42 in one day from Central Elementary school the past early summer.

A few days ago Dan showed up with a bad gash in his hip, but he never flinched when this was treated. That's just the way Dan was. Then when he didn't come in on Oct. 19, I knew something was wrong. So I found Dan lying on his side by the river, and he couldn't get up. He could barely raise his head, but we got it up enough so he could drink from a bucket, as he was very thirsty. But I knew his time had come, and so did the other horses standing around watching. You knew they were concerned and wanted to help their friend because horses can build deep friendships among themselves. And Rusty, my Australian shepherd, understood, too, because he kept licking my hand. Guess he was trying to comfort me.

Anyway, Dan loved apples, so while waiting for the vet to arrive, I fed him three apples, and he ate them all, lying there flat on his side. I think that last food made him feel a little better. And then I covered his head with a light tarp to keep the sun off. If horses have their heads in the shade, then it seems they think they're all in the shade. And that sun was mighty warm on a sparkly day here in Southwest New Mexico.

A good neighbor, the nearest one, three miles away, offered to shoot Dan for me to put him out of his misery. But I wasn't going to let Dan go that way, even though that's the usual in such situations in ranch country. And when an animal dies around here, you simply snake a loop around a leg and pull it out to a likely spot where soon the coyotes, buzzards and ravens do the clean-up in what could be called the continuing cycle of life where some must die so others can live.

But I wasn't about to let this special horse take that route. So another good neighbor came over about sunset with a backhoe and front-end loader and dug a 6-foot grave for Dan. We buried him there in his favorite grove by the river at sunset with the backdrop of a beautiful rose-tinted western sky that is the time when Dan and I liked best to ride together.

And you know, I thought I was sort of a tough old cowboy, but I'm not. I learned I couldn't handle this one. I was even too chicken to be around when the vet did his job and my neighbor did the grave work. I couldn't take it.

I know this will probably come across like maudlin sentimentality but once in a while when I'm feeling "that way" I'm going down to Dan's grave by the river, probably at sunset, and just sit there a little and think about the trails Dan and I have ridden and all the things we've done together over the long years.

I love that horse, and I know he liked me, too.

So long, Dan. If there's a horse heaven, that's where you are now.

Afterword

The single column of September 9, 1996, which closes the volume, was penned during an election campaign. Perhaps it is relevant to a current election campaign. Certainly it tells us plenty about Gene Simon.

September 9, 1996

Tuning in on all of the Republican and Democratic conventions, reading the platforms of both parties and thinking a lot about our options in the coming presidential election has me reflecting back on the 47 years I was a registered Pennsylvania Republican.

This political affiliation continued after I moved to New Mexico until the Reagan years when the sleaze of that administration, its wildly irrational armament spending and the piled-high red ink of its deficits compelled me to change my registration to Democrat—which I never before thought possible. An independent affiliation was preferred but perhaps this would be a wasted vote under our present system.

I know now more than ever that as a matter of principle and ethics, I cannot support the Republican Party or its candidates in the coming national election. And I've never before voted a straight ticket.

Here are some of the reasons:

Being old enough to remember some major political battles—Franklin Roosevelt's to launch Social Security, Harry Truman's for affordable housing, John Kennedy's for civil rights, Lyndon Johnson's for Medicare, Jimmy Carter's to preserve the environment, Bill Clinton's to secure family leave legislation, it struck me that every of one these worthy causes benefiting all Americans was achieved against fierce Republican opposition.

The Newt Gingriches and Bob Doles refer to the "good old days" of national trust and tranquility, when before FDR able-bodied men unable to find work stood in bread lines because there was no unemployment insurance (also opposed by the GOP), when banks weren't a safe haven for savings, when the poverty rate for senior citizens was three times higher than the general population, and when teen-age girls were butchered in back-alley abortions because of no acceptable alternative to unwanted pregnancy.

It was Republican administrations that presided over a redistribution of income and wealth from a majority of working people to a shrinking share of the electorate at the top of the economic pyramid. And this upward shift of wealth has been aggravated by Republican-style tax cuts for corporations, deregulation (that brought on the S&L debacle) and shrinking domestic government.

In a Dole presidency we'd get another round of supply-side economics that will inevitably make it all worse. Yes, the facts shout loud and clear that the Republican Party is inherently incapable of dealing with a dangerous-rising income inequality because its core constituency is reaping the benefits. And the blatant way the GOP congressional majority has been bought by the special interests substantiates this.

Then there's the dismal thought of a future Supreme Court appointed by Dole with extremists in the Christian Coalition calling the shots, the almost as bad thought of the far-out gun lobby being back in the saddle again, and the harsh reality of the tax cuts Dole's offering me at the expense of the poor who need Medicaid and food stamps.

Sure it's 1996, but maybe this election is about who cared about the poor and elderly back in 1936, and working families in 1966, and who will be responsible for saving or savaging our entitlements before 2006.

Yes, maybe the coming election is about the difference between compassion and mean-spiritedness, between the politics of conscience and the politics of the special interests. Think about it.

Gene Simon

Born in Iowa, Gene Simon was for twenty-eight years publisher and CEO of four western Pennsylvania newspapers and a printing company. At age sixty-two he began a second career cattle ranching in southwestern New Mexico, a career now in its thirty-fourth year. Reluctant to give up journalism, he had a weekly column which ran for twenty-seven years, mostly under the title of "Think about It," published in eleven newspapers in three states. Gene and his wife Elisabeth live on and work their Rancho del Rio on the Mimbres River.

Larry Godfrey

Born and raised in the Bighorn country of northern Wyoming, Larry Godfrey has spent his life teaching writing and literature to both university and high school youth around the world, from Hyderabad, India, to Muscoda, Wisconsin. Author of a novel, Dancing with Gods, and a herd of short stories and poems, Godfrey and his artist wife Elvira live in the high desert country of New Mexico.

Printed in the United States
202887BV00003B/1-114/P